# STAR JOURNEY HOME

## CONNECT WITH YOUR HOME PLANET AND OVERSOUL

### GREG MARTINS
NASA AEROSPACE ENGINEER, RETIRED

Star Journey Home
Connect with your Home Planet and Oversoul

Copyright © 2025 Greg Martins

All rights reserved. No part of this publication may be reproduced, distributed, or transmitted in any form or by any means, including photocopying, recording, or other electronic or mechanical methods, without the prior written permission of the publisher, except in the case of brief quotations embodied in critical reviews and certain other noncommercial uses permitted by copyright law. For permission requests, write to the author at the address below.

ISBN: 979-8-9926015-2-7 (E-book)
ISBN: 979-8-9926015-1-0 (Paperback)
ISBN: 979-8-9926015-0-3 (Hardcover)

Library of Congress Control Number: 2025906985

Cover design by Cherie Fox at www.cheriefox.com

Printed in the United States of America

Greg Martins
242 S. Washington Blvd #324
Sarasota, FL 34236

For more information on this book, the author, and book-related programs and events, please contact me at StarJourneyHome@GregMartins.com, or visit my website: www.GregMartins.com

# TABLE OF CONTENTS

Acknowledgments . . . . . . . . . . . . . . . . . . . . . . . . . . . . . . . . . . . . . . v
Introduction . . . . . . . . . . . . . . . . . . . . . . . . . . . . . . . . . . . . . . . . . . vii
Chapter 1    Dream Job . . . . . . . . . . . . . . . . . . . . . . . . . . . . . . . 1
Chapter 2    Strong Callings . . . . . . . . . . . . . . . . . . . . . . . . . . . . 6
Chapter 3    Developing Intuition . . . . . . . . . . . . . . . . . . . . . . . 17
Chapter 4    Extraterrestrials, Dreams, and Meditation . . . . . . . . 33
Chapter 5    Changes Afoot . . . . . . . . . . . . . . . . . . . . . . . . . . . . . 46
Chapter 6    Beatrice . . . . . . . . . . . . . . . . . . . . . . . . . . . . . . . . . . 52
Chapter 7    Interning at NASA . . . . . . . . . . . . . . . . . . . . . . . . . 64
Chapter 8    Remote Viewing and Astral Exploration . . . . . . . . . 76
Chapter 9    Vision Quest . . . . . . . . . . . . . . . . . . . . . . . . . . . . . . 89
Chapter 10   Akashic Records . . . . . . . . . . . . . . . . . . . . . . . . . . 108
Chapter 11   NASA Space Shuttle Payload . . . . . . . . . . . . . . . . 126
Chapter 12   The Oversoul . . . . . . . . . . . . . . . . . . . . . . . . . . . . 136
Chapter 13   Alpha Centauri . . . . . . . . . . . . . . . . . . . . . . . . . . 150
Chapter 14   The Pleiades . . . . . . . . . . . . . . . . . . . . . . . . . . . . 167
Chapter 15   NASA's Lunar Reconnaissance Orbiter . . . . . . . . . 180
Chapter 16   NASA's LRO HGAS in the Making . . . . . . . . . . . 192
Chapter 17   Healing and Past Lives . . . . . . . . . . . . . . . . . . . . . 212
Chapter 18   Home Star Systems & Home Planets . . . . . . . . . . 223
Chapter 19   When Loved Ones Pass Away . . . . . . . . . . . . . . . 239
Conclusion . . . . . . . . . . . . . . . . . . . . . . . . . . . . . . . . . . . . . . . . 255
Appendix: Home Star Systems & Home Planets . . . . . . . . . . . . 261
About the Author . . . . . . . . . . . . . . . . . . . . . . . . . . . . . . . . . . 287

# ACKNOWLEDGMENTS

*An immense thank you to Bruce Hurd as my book editor, writing coach, and guide for taking this book through to publishing. Your integrity and friendship have made writing this book an absolute pleasure.*

*To Dad for your endless encouragement, guidance, and support of my dream to work for NASA.*

*To Mom for your love and encouragement in my exploration of metaphysics.*

*To Leah Stansell for your loving friendship and invaluable mentorship in my development as an intuitive and reader of the Akashic Records.*

*To Mary Elizabeth Thunder for your kindness and generous support of my spiritual growth and walk on the Native American path.*

# INTRODUCTION

Being drawn to the stars as a child, I regularly pondered all things space-related. I often wondered why I was so called to the night sky. Throughout this book, I share the paths my calling has taken and how extraterrestrials (ETs) subtly, and sometimes not so subtly, connected with me as I developed spiritually, metaphysically, and scientifically. For those unfamiliar with the term, metaphysics can be described as the branch of philosophy that studies the nature of reality and consciousness.

Feeling extraordinarily comfortable connecting with ETs and other worlds, I suspected years ago that I must have worked with ETs before this life. My belief in reincarnation opened the door to this possibility. My mentors and spiritual advisors also felt I was no stranger to the realm of ETs. Through my experience and research, I have come to the clear understanding that the Universe is teeming with intelligent extraterrestrials from many worlds, and a large percentage of Earth's population has connections with them.

Do you feel your home planet may be somewhere other than Earth? If you feel connected to the stars in the night sky, you are among many sensing a deeper aspect of our true nature. My experience tells me that most people living on Earth have their home elsewhere in the Universe. For those of us in that category, we were born here, but our souls call a different planet home. Even if Earth truly is your home planet, you most likely have connections to other worlds, too.

Connecting with my home planet has been one of the great highlights of my life, offering empowering reassurance whenever I focus my attention homeward. Alongside that journey, I discovered and

# INTRODUCTION

experienced my Oversoul — a higher aspect of my soul connected not only to me, but also to my home world. I find these concepts profound and I'm excited to share them with you.

After benefiting from connecting with my home planet and Oversoul for about two years, I yearned to expand my activity with the extraterrestrial realm in some way. It was in 1993 that I ambitiously asked my mentor, Leah, if I could learn to use the Akashic Records (ARs) to help people seeking information about their ET connections and to find the home planets and Oversouls for people, as she did. The ARs are energy records of every person, place and event that has ever existed. Leah and her spirit guides not only gave me the thumbs-up to do this work, but also provided me with a connection to a spirit guide who works with the ARs. He would help me access information from them. Decades later, after retrieving AR information for many clients about their home star systems, home planets, Oversouls and more, I felt driven to share what I'd found, and this book was born.

My access to the ARs is not unique to the world — Edgar Cayce, one of America's most gifted psychics, brought global awareness to the existence of the ARs by performing over 14,000 AR readings for clients from all over the world in the first half of the 20th century. While in a trance-like state, Cayce provided undeniable insight into, and remedies for, thousands of clients' health-related inquiries. Cayce also addressed past lives, ancient mysteries and much more.

My ability to confidently retrieve information from the ARs came from years of practice and intuitive development. Like most of us, I wasn't born with obvious psychic abilities. I've included stories in this book that reveal how I explored and developed skills like meditation, working with the human energy field, remote viewing, telepathy, dreamwork, and Out-of-Body Experiences (OBEs).

Encouragingly, everyone can develop the intuitive ability to determine their home star system, home planet and Oversoul on their own. Your soul angel and spirit guides are available to help you access that wisdom and guide you in this exciting journey.

On the more down-to-earth side of things, my passion for astronautics, and aptitude for math and science, led me to set my sights on working for NASA. The extraordinary story of how I was hired as a college-level intern by NASA's Goddard Space Flight Center in Maryland kicks off this book. That opportunity launched my rewarding career developing spacecraft mechanical systems as an aerospace engineer. To give you a glimpse behind the scenes at NASA, I've included firsthand experiences from working on high-profile spacecraft projects during the Space Shuttle era and beyond.

The Akashic Record readings I've performed have not been limited to finding information related to people's home worlds. I've helped clients seeking clarity about both physical and non-physical ET encounters. This book includes examples of those readings, as well as another favorite of mine: using the ARs to explore clients' past lives and the roots of their emotional and physical challenges in this life. I also explain how, together, we used that information to promote healing through energy work, forgiveness, and reclaiming personal power.

Lakota Native American spirituality and ceremony have also shaped my relationship with star people. These sacred traditions have kept me grounded and healthy — and, in several instances, opened the door to personal, conscious ET encounters. During three Vision Quest ceremonies, I experienced fully conscious OBEs initiated by ETs. Although the beings didn't allow me to remember any face-to-face interactions with them that may have occurred, I share these stories here not only because they're fascinating, but because they highlight the real presence of extraterrestrials close to our solar system.

In the book, I refer to over two dozen star systems and planets I've found in the Akashic Records as clients' homes. Maybe your home is among them. I also include details from AR readings that offer insight into what life is like in these extraordinary places. Many of the readings and experiences I've included in this book are supported by corroborating stories from others, adding weight to these remarkable claims.

The final chapter, "When Loved Ones Pass Away," shares some of my personal experiences with life beyond the veil. These encounters gave me a deep sense of peace as I dealt with the loss of loved ones. It is my hope that this chapter will bring peace to those struggling with the passing of someone dear.

Above all else, I want to present a convincing case for your consideration that we are far more than what is typically presented here

## INTRODUCTION

on Earth. We are eternal beings connected to each other and to life throughout the Universe in the most personal and profound ways. Within us are incredible abilities that can expand our understanding of who we truly are. This understanding of the true nature of life, based on a profound universal love, is deeply comforting on so many levels. I invite you to read each chapter with an open heart to help you on your journey to deeper understanding, healing, and enlightenment.

I respectfully offer this book for your consideration. I wish you the very best as you travel on your personal path, wherever it may lead.

# 1

## DREAM JOB

"Is this Greg Martins?"

It was 1982 and I was a senior at Embry-Riddle Aeronautical University in Daytona Beach, Florida. Normally I wasn't home in the middle of the day, but my upset stomach had dictated a time-out, so I had recently laid down. Unexpectedly, the phone next to the bed rang, and I answered it. I didn't recognize the man's voice on the other end of the line, but his subtle upbeat tone had me interested. My ears perked up. Little did I realize that what was to follow would change me forever, in so many different ways. I would later recall it as the most pivotal moment in my life.

"Yes, this is Greg."

"Hi, Greg. My name is Stew Meyers. I'm the Mechanical Engineering Branch Head at NASA Goddard Space Flight Center's Special Payloads Division...."

My heart started racing.

*This is it!* I thought. *My opportunity to get into NASA!*

This was what I had been dreaming of since I was a child. I held my breath and tried to focus my thoughts as I heard him continue ....

To set the stage, one fine fall day in Daytona Beach during my senior year, I envisioned taking a nice bike ride through the suburban streets to unwind from my busy schedule as a full-time aeronautical engineering student. I was in my final year at Embry-Riddle, and I cherished my dream of working for the National Aeronautics and

Space Administration (NASA). From an early age, NASA space flight captured my imagination and deep interest.

Designing and building spacecraft to explore planets and stars sounded as natural and right for me as playing my guitar to relax. NASA's new Space Shuttle program was coming on-line as well, opening a world of opportunity for aspiring young engineers like me.

NASA Goddard Space Flight Center in Maryland attracted me the most out of the ten main NASA centers. Actively involved in spacecraft development, NASA Goddard was a short trip to my hometown in Massachusetts and provided the familiar setting of rolling hills and changing seasons. I had recently written a school paper about Robert Goddard, the founder of modern rocketry, enhancing my fondness for the facility.

I had applied for internship positions at a number of NASA facilities over the last several semesters. I had a strong belief that if I could get my foot in the door as a NASA intern, I would be golden! Embry-Riddle offered the Cooperative Education (Co-op) program to students interested in interning, and NASA participated nationwide.

I had the additional advantage of attending Embry-Riddle, a very highly regarded aviation-focused school. I later learned that many of NASA's senior engineers knew of Embry-Riddle's excellent reputation for its Aeronautical Engineering program. I sent out my usual flurry of internship applications at the beginning of that fall semester, knowing it may well be my last opportunity to apply for an internship. I was scared to think about how difficult it could be to get into NASA after graduation, when hundreds of other star-gazing engineers would likely be applying there.

Even at this relatively young age of 21, my spiritual awareness was helping manifest my dreams. For years, I believed we could attract what we desired by imagining a strong connection with it. I sometimes visualized the words "NASA Goddard Space Flight Center" in huge letters ablaze in fire while I told the Universe all the reasons why my working there would be a perfect co-creation for everyone involved.

An avid bike rider, that afternoon when I got the fateful phone call I was dressed in my favorite frayed denim shorts with a worn-thin T-shirt dangling from my belt loop. I was all set to grab my ten-speed and head out the door when I noticed an upset feeling cropping up in my stomach. Disappointed, I waited a few minutes to see if I should hold off on the bike ride. The lousy feeling deepened, so I reluctantly surrendered to lying down to rest a while. I settled into a centered meditative state to help calm my stomach.

In a couple of minutes, the phone broke the peaceful silence. In the era before cell phones and answering machines, we always picked up the phone. That was when Stew Meyers introduced himself to me. I couldn't believe it! I sat up, wide eyed, as he reported he'd recently hired a fellow Embry-Riddle student as a Co-op intern, and he wanted another. Encouragingly, he declared he was an aviation enthusiast and that he knew Embry-Riddle put out skilled engineers.

This sounded great so far! He asked me if I'd be interested in a Co-op position in the spring helping him with a Sounding Rocket nose-cone ejection test. My jaw was on the floor.

"Yes!" I declared. This was exactly what I had been visualizing. My heart was pounding as I realized I was suddenly in the middle of an impromptu job interview. My mind raced as I quickly came up with a strong rationale why I would be perfect for the position. I was excited, yet I realized that I needed to be convincing. I felt I had to land this job.

I began selling myself by describing the limited knowledge I just happened to have about NASA's unsung Sounding Rocket program. Sounding Rockets "sound the atmosphere" and the lower outer space regions around Earth. They carry scientific instruments into those regions for about twenty minutes of data-collection focused on atmospherics, radiation from space, magnetics, and more.

In just a few moments, Stew was clearly satisfied with our conversation and offered me the job! I accepted on the spot and waited to hang up the phone before completely jumping out of my skin with excitement. I knew at that moment my dream was upon me! I was going to work at NASA Goddard! Surprised that my stomach felt completely normal, I went out for a celebratory bike ride. I felt like I was riding on air as I kept rerunning in my mind what had just happened. Throughout it all, I couldn't stop smiling. I don't think the smile left my face for weeks.

# DREAM JOB

Even then, I knew my getting this job was a "God-job." God-job is a term I've come to use when I clearly see the influence of the Universe orchestrating the circumstances of my life. Who, or what, caused my stomach to suddenly feel upset, keeping me home for NASA's call? I'm sure that Stew had a list of highly qualified and motivated students who he could have reached out to if I hadn't been home to answer the phone and sell myself as the best candidate.

This "support from the Universe" also seems to have stretched back to my paper route as a teenager. While collecting the weekly newspaper fee at a particular man's door, he brought up his interest in Sounding Rockets. I had never shared my personal interests or goals with him, so I chalked this up to a pleasant coincidence, and listened intently.

I hadn't heard of Sounding Rockets before that. In hindsight, I see how that seemingly inconsequential experience turned out to be pivotal in my being hired as a NASA intern, which led to a wonderfully rewarding and exciting 35-year career as a NASA Aerospace Engineer at Goddard Space Flight Center.

My deeply fulfilling NASA career and my lifelong personal journey of exploration and discovery into the nature of reality and consciousness are inextricably intertwined. Throughout this book, I will share the highlights of my NASA career in a way that blends cohesively with this deeper inner journey of my life.

I am honored and blessed to have had such an exciting, productive career. I worked with many extraordinary, dedicated, caring people, and I want to share this phase of my life for two primary reasons. One is to give a glimpse into the exciting world of NASA. How does NASA do it? I'm happy to share my perspective as a new hire and throughout my life as a senior lead-engineer developing payloads for launch in Space Shuttles and expendable rockets.

Secondly, I want to show how this phase of my life was fundamental to the development of my character and professional perspective. My outlook and training have driven how I approach the metaphysical world of subtle details and challenges.

As many readers know, metaphysics is concerned with the fundamental nature of reality. As a team leader at NASA, I developed many skills needed to meet project requirements, schedules, budgets, and overall mission success. A willingness to learn, dedication to scientific understanding, consistency, faith, humility, courage, and following my gut instincts are all elements I embraced in my career. I find these same characteristics indispensable in navigating my work with the other-worldly topics of this book.

As a young teen, I spent many nights staring up at the night sky on the small porch attached to the side of the house. With the porch light out, our quiet suburban neighborhood afforded me dark skies with a tremendous view of the stars. *There's got to be intelligent life out there,* my mind insisted. I came to realize it was my intuition calling me home. I felt a familiarity with the stars.

An Unidentified Flying Object (UFO) could have descended and landed in my yard, and I would have smiled with acknowledgment. It wasn't until many years later that I understood just how deep my connection to "life out there" really is.

One evening in my mid-twenties I quietly asked the Universe if my consistent desire to explore our connections with the stars was important for me to pay attention to, or was it just a mild obsession that carried no connection to my soul's path. Within a three-month period, three older adults who didn't know each other and with whom I was only slightly acquainted, if at all, each shared an unsolicited affirming answer to this question. One of them even said I was like an "ambassador between worlds." With that, I thanked the Universe for guidance and knew then that following my heartfelt passion for the stars was truly a calling.

# 2
## STRONG CALLINGS

*What is this?!*

  I sat dumbfounded, staring wide-eyed as from the downstairs bathroom window I watched a large unidentifiable craft fly slowly out of view over my house. It was a clear night in 1974, and I was a 13-year-old at home in Holliston, Massachusetts. I was sitting on the toilet, of all places! What a place to get visited by a UFO! The bathroom window and shade were both up, allowing a gentle breeze to enter through the screen.

  When I noticed the nearly silent craft moving over the house, I presumed half of it had already passed overhead, given its arrangement of lights. Traveling north over the back yard, the craft was around 20 feet wide and had several large different-colored steady lights vaguely forming a semicircle. I couldn't make out the craft's outline, given the darkness. I stared at it with wonder and calm curiosity. My mind wrestled with what I was seeing, trying to make sense of what was hovering over my house.

  *It's very odd! It's moving too slowly to be an airplane, and there isn't an airport nearby. A helicopter is out, since I don't hear any rotor blades. This has a quiet, low-pitched droning hum, too.*

  As the UFO disappeared from sight over the house, I turned my gaze back to the bathroom, deep in thought about the experience. I didn't consider running outside to see it, probably because I was on the john. Still, so many questions ran through my head.

*Why is this craft flying over my house?*
I had no answer to this for almost half a century.
*Do I have any missing time due to this craft? Probably not since no one is banging on the door telling me I've been in here too long!*

Even today, I still have questions about this profound experience. How do we validate the existence of extraterrestrials (ETs) without requiring a face-to-face encounter with them? Hundreds of Americans have reported having face-to-face encounters with alien beings and shared their stories with the public. Eyewitness testimony, physical exams of unusual skin marks, radiation effects, and what appear to be implants from the encounters provide significant validation. Even more impressive, the presence of UFO landing tracks and other related environmental impacts provide even the hardened skeptic with compelling evidence.

As I have expanded my knowledge of metaphysics and researched countless UFO-related reports, I am convinced that ETs exist. Even more remarkably, I have confirmed my beliefs by connecting with them intuitively and by indirectly connecting with them during out-of-body experiences (OBEs). I'll share examples of my OBEs in future chapters.

At the time of my UFO experience as a 13-year-old, I had been solidly focused on NASA as my career choice for quite a while. My job at this point was to enjoy life and continue doing well in school. Mom and Dad provided well for me and my five siblings in our quiet middle-class neighborhood. Feeling secure, I eagerly explored many interests: UFOs, extraterrestrials, science, NASA, metaphysics, karate, guitar playing, and more. Thank God for my centeredness and inner sense of security at that time. Because I was steady and calm for a young teenage boy, I could emotionally manage the occasional bullying from overbearing classmates and perpetual cluelessness about how to handle my romantic interests in girls.

My five siblings and I all seemed to have different interests, and my parents did their best to encourage us along our way. To their credit, they let us follow our own paths without interference, except when school, household chores or other family needs arose. My oldest sibling, AnneMarie, had the frequent duty of helping take care of the kids, which often prevented her from having the freedoms we younger siblings later enjoyed. As the fourth-born child, I grew up in a less strict environment than those before me since my parents had become more relaxed in the art of raising children.

My Dad was raised in Fall River, Massachusetts with four siblings, among a mostly Portuguese population. Motivated to create a promising future, Dad was drawn to the Navy to serve his country, see the world, and attend a four-year college after service at no cost under the GI Bill. Shortly after enlisting in 1950 at the early age of 17 for a 39-month service commitment, Dad was trained as a radar operator and served on the *USS Estes* amphibious command ship in the Pacific. The *USS Estes* was a Navy flagship outfitted with advanced communications equipment and war rooms. This ship and its extensive control center were used considerably over the next two years during the Korean War. After the war, a rather historic test took place, and many sailors and high-ranking observers watched from the *Estes* and accompanying fleet.

"I was astonished when the light of the blast hit me!" My dad exclaimed.

I listened intently.

"Even though I was crouched down, facing <u>away</u> from the blast zone, hands covering my closed eyes, the blast was so bright, the bones in my hands revealed themselves to me as if I were seeing an X-ray image of them!"

It was the fall of 1952, and Dad had the unique experience of witnessing the first hydrogen bomb detonation test. The bomb was secured on a platform on one of the islands in the Eniwetok Atoll, which is part of the Marshall Islands in the Pacific. Many sailors on the command ship, including my dad, experienced the explosion from the deck at a distance of 32 miles. Before the blast, they were told to crouch down facing away from the bomb test site. Following the blinding flash of light, the sailors were told they could stand and face the blast.

"The deafening noise and wind hit me next!" Dad recalled in a weighted voice, shaking his head in awe.

"It was a ferocious explosion," he recounted. "Five-hundred times stronger than the atomic bomb dropped on Hiroshima, Japan in 1945. We all watched in awe with blind faith that what we were witnessing wouldn't destroy us all in the days to come. A huge mushroom cloud rose slowly and ominously in the distance. We later learned that the island had been completely annihilated, and a deep underwater crater had unexpectedly been created in its place."

I sat quietly, muscles tensed, taking in his fascinating recollection of the event.

Dad, now 92, appears to have been spared any possible radiation effects from the nuclear explosion, but he was later given a disability rating for his resulting hearing impairment. I once jokingly told him that the radiation was the reason all his kids are short. He assured me I was short because he was short!

Three days after Dad's exciting term of enlistment in the Navy was complete, he entered the Bradford Durfee Technical Institute, now the College of Technology, in Fall River, Massachusetts. He earned a Bachelor of Science degree in Textile Manufacturing four years later, in 1957. Dad's interest in textile manufacturing was sparked by the beautiful weave patterns he observed in Japanese clothing while on liberty in the Navy.

In addition to developing an interest in Japanese textiles while on liberty, Dad also enjoyed singing with the local bands in night clubs. The bands typically played American music, and when he told them he could sing, he was often invited to sing with them for an hour or more.

# STRONG CALLINGS

*Dad singing at a night club in Japan while on liberty during his Navy years*

"My shipmates loved to go with me on liberty," my dad recounted with a chuckle, "because when I sang, our table got free drinks."

Mom and Dad met while my mom, Agnes, attended Saint Anne's School of Nursing in the same town where Dad went to college. There she earned her nursing degree. Mom was raised in a strongly Catholic family in nearby Dartmouth, Massachusetts. In 1955, Mom and Dad were married by Mom's brother Joe, a Catholic priest.

In a couple of years, Dad began his five-year position in textile manufacturing quality control at Celanese Corporation in Cumberland, Maryland. Living in Cumberland, he and Mom were busy raising my three older siblings and me. My sister AnneMarie and my two older brothers Michael and John were a happy handful – healthy and full of energy.

Cumberland is a beautiful Appalachian Mountain town in the panhandle of Maryland. I don't have memories of living there, but Dad said he was sweating bullets when my mom was days away from giving birth to me – I came into the world between two snowstorms in February, 1961.

When I was two years old, we moved to a newly forming middle-class neighborhood in Holliston, Massachusetts, southwest of Boston. This is where my siblings and I grew up. I vividly recall bouncing up and down on the front bench seat of my dad's car as we drove up Gorwin Drive to see how our new house was progressing. I remember the homes as empty wooden frames on large dirt lots. Seat belts and toddler car seats were not required at that time, so standing up in the front seat to enhance my view was fair game.

My mom enjoyed being a maternity nurse at Framingham Union hospital when she felt secure enough leaving my older siblings in charge at home to keep things running smoothly while she was out. Dad chose to settle the family in Holliston after accepting a job offer to become the assistant to the corporate director from the long-established textile manufacturer Ludlow Corporation in Needham, Massachusetts.

Five years later in 1967, Dad ventured into a new field of work with the Polaroid Corporation in Waltham, Massachusetts. Dad became a well-respected quality control engineer in Polaroid's ground-breaking film-developing department. For those who may not be aware, Polaroid corporation invented the SX-70 "instant camera" which used self-developing film, allowing the user to see the picture develop in-hand shortly after taking the picture. Dad maintained a hard-work ethic that served him well throughout his professional life.

Dad's retirement luncheon at Polaroid, which I attended at age 27, left no doubt in my mind how well-respected he was for his dedication, insight, and integrity. I was so proud to be his son, watching him from one of the many large reception tables. Seated at the front of the room after our meal, Dad was the center of honor, praise, well-wishing, and a stream of good-natured jokes that left my cheeks sore from laughing.

At age six, my innate interests were strongly coming through from somewhere deep within me. This first became apparent from the television shows I regularly watched. Fast becoming a sci-fi, techy, space geek, my favorite cartoon characters were Marvin the Martian from Looney Tunes, and Mr. Wizard in Tooter Turtle. My favorite prime-time shows were Time Tunnel, Lost in Space with the Jupiter 2 spacecraft, Star Trek, Black Sheep Squadron about a famous WWII fighter aircraft squadron, and The Six Million Dollar Man featuring a NASA test pilot enhanced with superhuman abilities after a crash. I resonated with the shows' themes of bold exploration, advanced technology, flying fast sleek aircraft, venturing into space and being part of a successful team. I enthusiastically wanted to be a part of their world.

*Some of my favorite TV shows growing up.*
*(Images courtesy of IMDb, The Movie Database (TMDB), and DuckDuckGo)*

"Houston, Tranquility Base here. The *Eagle* has landed!" These words will echo through my mind, and the minds of many space enthusiasts, forever. The entire world watched the TV broadcast of this event with amazement and global comradery as Neil Armstrong took the first step onto the moon for humanity.

Huddled around the TV set, my parents, siblings, and I watched quietly as Walter Cronkite, a seasoned news anchor, reported the exciting details of the nail-biting Apollo 11 lunar landing. Cronkite then aired the live video feed from the surface of the moon as Armstrong stepped down the ladder of the lunar lander and onto the surface of the moon. Cronkite was visibly moved by this historic event, and I was so marveled by it that I decided I needed to be part of the space program when I grew up. I was eight years old. I imagine this exciting feeling ran through half the kids in America. My dream was born on that day.

*Maybe I can become an astronaut some day!*

Why do so many kids want to be astronauts? Pioneering the vast unknowns of space in a huge rocket, where courage, skill, and the world's support are yours were the fantasies of many kids. I, and doubtless many others, intuitively felt that space travel could one day introduce us to beings from another world. Little did I know my connection with the stars and fascination with otherworldly beings would one day bring me into their realm in a unique way.

"What are you doing?!"

My younger brother asked with a perplexed look, staring at me lying on the hardwood floor as he put a small pile of folded laundry on my bed. As he turned to walk out, I calmly replied.

"I'm meditating."

He simply chuckled. He was dumbfounded, and unexcitedly walked out of the room, re-closing the door behind him. I was around sixteen years old, and Matt was eleven. I was learning to meditate while lying down. I discovered I couldn't stay focused while attempting to meditate lying in bed because my arms would touch my sides, distracting me. I soon trained myself to meditate with my arms touching me, and happily used my bed from then on to meditate before falling asleep. My brother Matt often jokingly referred to me as "Guru" after that. The name still sticks today.

My mother introduced me to metaphysics around this time. She handed me a small paperback, called *The Seth Material*, by Jane Roberts. Jane was a relatively new, but popular trance-channel who channeled a being named Seth. As a "trance channel," Jane experienced Seth speaking directly through her. Her voice pattern, inflection, and general manner of speech differed significantly from her non-channeling state. According to Jane, Seth described himself as an "energy personality essence no longer focused in physical matter," and was independent of Jane's subconscious.

Mom had several of Jane Roberts' books, and I enjoyed hearing her enthusiastically share what she'd been discovering as she read each one. Seth matter-of-factly reported on the nature of reality and consciousness. I vividly recall sitting on the living room couch with my jaw open as I read *The Seth Material* in amazement. I felt like I had struck literary gold. I eagerly drank it up, thrilled to see that our existence included so much more than what our general day-to-day life presented. The book's topics include reincarnation, the space between physical lives, health and healing, dreams and out-of-body experiences, the true nature of time, the nature of physical reality, the multi-dimensional self, and more.

*The Seth Material by Jane Roberts*

A highlight in my budding metaphysical life, and my mom's as well, was the weekly intuitive development class my mom hosted at our house when I was a teenager. Her friend and metaphysical teacher, Ann, needed a new location to continue offering these weekly classes and Mom excitedly persuaded my dad to let her hold the classes at our house. My father has always been a skeptic of "psychic phenomenon," but he agreed. He only attended the first couple of classes since he didn't feel compelled to spend the time and energy to explore them further.

We always had five to ten attendees, and I was grateful to be one of them. Ann had us practicing psychometry, seeing auras around each other, meditating, intuitively connecting with our spirit guides, and more. Psychometry is the divining of information about people or events associated with an object solely by touching or being near the object. Ann was a natural at these activities, and Mom and I always looked forward to the classes.

"Look at that!" I exclaimed in amazement, pointing toward the hall on the opposite side of the room during breaktime.

I watched the clearly defined astral body of a cat prance down the hall and up the staircase! I was sitting on the living room floor next to the fireplace facing the hall twenty feet away. Our calico cat, Sufi, was curled up on the floor nearby, asleep.

The astral body is a subtle energy body that is essential for the existence and function of the physical body, and through which consciousness can function separately from the physical body.

*This is likely Sufi roaming the house while out-of-body!* I concluded.

I had been learning about astral projection, and this galvanized the concept in my mind. The astral cat was transparent, with the size, shape, and definition of a glass version of Sufi. This see-through, colorless cat moved exactly as a cat would, bouncing lightly as it trotted along, tail flickering about. My intuitive senses were waking up, and I loved it.

Over the decades, I've discovered the makeup and some of the capabilities of my intuitive senses. For example, clairvoyance is one of the main intuitive senses human beings possess, and my experience of seeing the astral body of the cat illustrates this sense.

Another common example of an intuitive sense is our gut feeling. This is clairsentience, i.e. clear feeling. Clairsentience is the ability to perceive, or sense, information through emotions or physical sensations about a situation or person without logical reasoning. It is a natural instinct. Clairsentience allows us to feel subtle energies from people, unseen beings, places, and objects.

Claircognizance, i.e. clear-knowing, on the other hand, is the ability to know something without any physical or emotional sensation. It is insight that arrives without any reasoning or prior knowledge.

In the next chapter I will define our other main intuitive senses and how I awakened them by working with my subtle human energy field. Through these senses I have discovered the ever-present existence of other dimensions and levels of consciousness. This fascinating exploration has led me to a clear and repeatable ability to intuitively connect with beings beyond our physical realm, including ETs.

# 3
# DEVELOPING INTUITION

**W**hoa! *What are those arcs of white light coming out of her joints?* I gasped in amazement. It was clear that none of my classmates were seeing this, since I was the only one with my eyes riveted on the teacher standing in front of the room. My classmates were finishing up their brief hellos with each other, and my high school Science Fiction teacher was beginning to speak to the class.

I was excited to see the arcs weren't vanishing, so I could take in as much as I could of this spectacle. This was like nothing I had ever seen.

Long ghostly arcs of white light jutted out and upward like soft, curved swords, in single symmetrical pairs from each of her ankles, knees, hips, wrists, elbows, shoulders, and even her neck. I was fascinated. The arcs were typically about 20 inches long and held a steady appearance as she slowly moved about, gestured, and spoke. She had a relaxed, yet engaging teaching style, and it was clear she liked this subject as much as we did.

My mind wrestled with what I was seeing, and I struggled to focus on her presentation. Sitting in my usual seat a few rows back on the far right, the room lighting was typical, and I didn't need to spend time wondering if this etheric display might be due to my physiological state. I wasn't on any medication, and I was mentally and physically clear and rested. My vision was also excellent without glasses.

The arcs lasted for most of the class. They faded away at some point, and I never saw them on her again, or on anyone else since.

Then 18 years old, I had recently spent the good part of a year exploring meditation techniques and becoming acquainted with my energy field. I could only surmise at the time that my intuitive sense of clairvoyance must have opened and tuned in to a specific aspect of her energy. I was very intrigued, and I heartily hoped for more experiences like this.

In this chapter I share how developing productive meditation techniques and gaining a greater understanding of the human energy field and our body's seven main chakras (our energy centers) led directly to the development of my intuitive skills. This development has been key to my many exciting metaphysical experiences throughout my life, like the arc story above.

About a year before that arc experience, and inspired by my earlier metaphysical experiences, I continued my deep dive into these areas of exploration to aid in my lofty goal of having an Out-of-Body Experience (OBE), also known as an astral projection. I came across the subject of OBEs after reading briefly about it and was instantly captivated with the concept. This far-out fantasy was a great motivator.

*How exciting! I should be able to do this.*

I eagerly hoped that simply relaxing through meditation and having the intention to be out of body might just be enough to do it!

I was very encouraged by having clearly seen Sufi, our house cat, having an OBE. My interest was further piqued by reading *Journeys Out of the Body* by Robert Monroe. This was his first of three books on the subject in which he shared many of his personal, captivating OBEs. Corroboration was demonstrated for many of Monroe's experiences because he was able to verify what he saw during his OBEs with the people he saw in them.

I often daydreamed about flying to other countries in my astral body, or simply appearing there with the speed of thought. I excitedly dared to pick the Moon as a future out-of-body destination!

Despite my enthusiasm, I had some doubts. I realized I didn't know that much about meditation, the human energy field, nor the astral body. My research indicated that OBEs used a person's subtle astral energy body. Thinking of meditation as simply "focused attention with a quiet mind," I began exploring with determination and boundless curiosity.

As time went on, I enjoyed moderate success in feeling the energy of the trees when I walked along quiet wooded paths. I could feel their life force energy enough to validate its existence. I also quickly became adept at deeply relaxing my body while lying in bed. I discovered meditation was keenly influential for my spiritual growth, and I knew I would enjoy these activities for the rest of my life.

*The peace and relaxation that permeates my body during these meditations is priceless*, I thought with gratifying assurance.

I knew that I wanted to explore this far beyond what I had done. I decided to seek out someone who could be my informal teacher. I wanted my guide to be a wise and experienced teacher who could help steer me as I pushed my own personal boundaries.

*I'd love to talk to someone who knows about astral projection, too — a person who's done it, since I have no experience with it. Surely there must be someone in town I can reach out to.*

My mind cast a wide net, as I considered everyone I could think of who might be a suitable candidate.

It was then that one man came to mind – Alan. He was dating my friend, Linda, and I sometimes saw him exercising, or meditating right out in the open at Goodwill Park downtown, a common social destination for many of us high schoolers. The fact that he was so open about his spiritual practices was a huge point in his favor. I'd never met Alan, but he seemed like the kind of guy who just might have *some* experience with astral projection.

Linda spoke highly of him, and she was very happy in their relationship. She thought Alan would be willing to talk with me, since he indeed had some experience with my interests. Alan was just a couple of years older than Linda and me. He was a long-haired, nature-loving guy in top athletic shape, often wearing nothing but baggy, colorful yoga pants. Displaying deep, soulful eyes, Alan was calm and centered. As I would discover once I became friends with him, he also was a serious explorer of philosophy and higher consciousness. He appeared to have a satisfyingly simple, healthy lifestyle, which I admired.

I visited Alan many times in his downtown attic apartment. We often walked the back roads of his neighborhood, talking about philosophy and metaphysics. Alan told me that before I attempted astral projection, I should learn more about the human energy field. This was because once I left my body, I would be in my "energy body," and I needed to understand what that would entail. I told him that it made sense, and to my delight he offered me some meditation techniques to explore. This was just what I needed! He suggested I focus on breathing energy in and out of my body because that's a fast and effective way to feel the energy in and around us.

"I've been interested in sensing my energy field more clearly, so this is perfect," I told him.

The next night, I was armed with a plan. I laid down and calmed my excitement as I launched into my recently developed basic relaxation routine. Soon I took my first experimental breath, focusing specifically on breathing energy in from my left side. Promisingly, I felt a distinct inward flow of energy during my inhale.

*Wow, this really is happening.*

I mentally celebrated at the top of my breath, attempting to remain calm. I exhaled out the same side, feeling the energy move out as naturally and peacefully as an ocean tide. This was an eye-opening experience. I felt the same consistent effect breathing energy through all six sides of my body that night – my left, right, front, back, head and feet. To my surprise, I noticed I was much more relaxed after doing this simple exercise just a couple of times.

The following night, I excitedly expanded my energy-breathing exploration with an idea I came up with during school that day.

*What if I breathe in the energy from the <u>walls</u> in my bedroom?*

*Everything is made of energy, so perhaps I can <u>feel</u> the walls this way. This would significantly enhance my intuitive sense of feeling (clairsentience)!*

Feeling like a kid in a candy store, I repeated what I had done the night before, and then took it further by sending a small amount of my energy out the left side of my body to my bedroom wall eight feet away. When I sensed this energy reach the wall, I felt what seemed to be the size and shape of the wall. I then breathed in what felt like the energy of the wall using the energy channel I had made. I exhaled the energy-laden breath through the other side of my body. I was now aware of the wall's inanimate, light density. I found this exceedingly intriguing and encouraging. I repeated this process with the other five surfaces in the room. Having done this, I lay there on my bed feeling the walls of my room in amazement.

*Who the heck else would be doing this?!* I chuckled, thinking of my brother Matt discovering me meditating on the hardwood floor not long ago.

I was peaceful and relaxed but couldn't help having a slight grin on my face. Then I loosened all my muscles, allowing them to relax.

As an aside, I now realize that I was able to easily feel the room's energy because clairsentience is my strongest intuitive sense. We all have natural intuitive strengths and weaknesses.

On other nights, I applied this energy-breathing technique to the boundaries of the house, and then went further, extending out to locations far beyond the house and yard until I eventually included the furthest reaches of the Universe in my practice. This journey of expansion took 60 to 90 minutes to complete.

On nights when I made it to breathing energy from out in the Universe without falling asleep, I lay there and enjoyed the incredible feeling in my body. My emotions and mind had calmed to a murmur and my energy felt light and serene. I also sensed an energetic connection some deep distance into the Universe that filled my entire body. After many nights applying this practice, my body became so used to energy flowing through it that at the end of the process I typically felt energy flow on its own accord unimpeded into my feet, up through my body, and out my head. I was so deeply relaxed that I felt only the shell outline of my physical body. I could not feel the rest of me.

Just as amazing to me was that I could vaguely sense the egg-shaped volume of my energy field, which I noticed extended several feet from my body. This was all very profound to me. I never thought I could achieve such a marvelous state of mental, physical, and emotional grace. In this state of bliss, I allowed my consciousness to drift off to sleep. These were enthralling experiences, which I looked forward to on those nights I was able to engage in deep meditation. The mornings after these meditations left me feeling peaceful, centered, and refreshed on all levels.

I kept Alan appraised of my discoveries and progress during the months I practiced my meditation technique. I enjoyed sharing my experiences with him, since we both felt spiritually uplifted recounting the benefits. I also appreciated his follow-on suggestions. He didn't outwardly encourage me to focus on astral projection, but he did encourage me to further explore and nurture my own spirituality.

Over the months of enjoying my energy-breathing routine, I developed, and regularly performed, two other practices while relaxed in bed that I felt might lead to an astral projection. One was to mentally imagine rolling out of my body and walking through the house, keenly observing what I saw, and then checking my accuracy the next day. This was interesting and fun because I sometimes saw unexpected items in rooms that proved correct. I had read that mental projection exercises like this can lead to spontaneous astral projections.

My other practice was imagining myself free flying as I drifted off to sleep. Since flying dreams are said to be unconscious astral projections, it seemed reasonable that I might realize I'm dreaming while free-flying and thus manifest a conscious astral projection. I loved the progress I made with these techniques. Still, I was disappointed that I didn't have my first fully conscious, out-of-body experience until age 22, five years after I began seriously meditating.

Since my first OBE in 1983, I have experienced over a dozen fully conscious OBEs, which have opened me to a world of discovery about my higher-consciousness, my subconscious mind, and our multi-dimensional reality.

During my college years, I became aware of an energy body I had. In my relaxed states, I sometimes felt an energy version of my arm or leg floating loosely just beyond my physical body. I was astonished that my sense of feeling occurred solely in the energy version when it moved and wasn't present in my physical version. The energy version felt identical in size and shape to its physical counterpart, except it was light as a feather and unaffected by gravity, as if floating in the air.

I noticed that I could move these energy versions of my legs and arms simply with my intention. If I willed them to move in a particular direction, they would move accordingly, and repeatably. I had lots of fun with this. It was exciting to explore this new version of my body, which I presumed was my astral body. I wondered if I could loosen my entire energy body within my physical body, and then just will myself completely out of my physical body.

One night when I was in my mid-fifties, I was lying in my bed in the quiet river-front neighborhood of Herald Harbor in Crownsville, Maryland, and I did just that! Awakening from a dream, with my astral body floating loosely within my physical body, I decided to have some fun with it. I imagined rolling out the right side of my body. To my utter delight, I felt myself rolling out just as I was imagining it. I felt as if I had physically rolled out of bed, except I was light as a feather, and felt no pressure from the mattress. Excited, but keeping calm, I then imagined being in a standing position. Instantly I was standing on the floor in my astral body, facing the far closet.

*Free at last!*

I was thrilled, but I kept my excitement to a mild level to prevent myself from being pulled back into my physical body. Over the years prior to this, I used my will to initiate three other OBEs. I'd had other OBEs, but they occurred unexpectedly. I am sharing this OBE with you because I find it particularly fascinating.

While standing in my astral body by the bed, I moved my astral fingers using my intention, marveling at how they moved exactly as my physical fingers would.

*To the living room!* I ordered. I felt like a captain leading a scouting mission.

My astral body responded on command by floating at a walking pace through the open bedroom doorway and down the hall. No need for legs — this body moved on command simply by using my power of thought! The house was dark, save for the faint glow of light from the streetlight in front. I stopped in my living room to briefly look around. Everything appeared as it normally did.

I turned my attention to going through the wall to the endless outdoors. Fixated with anticipation, I confidently initiated the move.

*Outside*, I commanded.

Instantly I floated slowly toward the wall.

*No need for using the door*, I chuckled.

Through the wall I went. I'm always captivated by the feeling of going through physical matter. The wall felt like a five-inch-thick feeble energy panel — a sentinel in the physical world, but a mere well-formed vapor-like barrier in the astral world.

*Oh my God!* I marveled. I was astounded by what I saw.

Outside, the sun was shining, and my tree-and-bush-laden landscape was ablaze in rich, vibrant radiating colors. Energy was coursing through every part of every plant and tree, flickering off leaf tips like tongues of fire. I was awed by the brilliant, beautiful display. I had discovered a whole new world!

*I wonder if insects or animals see it this way.*

I hoped so, for their sake.

I stood watching in amazement at this spectacle of life that I could never have imagined.

Then I was suddenly surprised to see Mom standing in the driveway ten feet away.

*Hi Mom!* I exuberantly called out from my mind.

Mom had died years prior, but there she was — looking straight into my eyes with a calm, serene smile. Her body appeared solid and as real as anyone's.

*That's odd.*

*She isn't reacting.*

*Is she really there?*

*Is she a figment of my subconscious?*

*Uh oh, I'm fading away!* I disappointedly realized.

I knew what it felt like when an OBE was ending. I knew my excitement might have been the trigger. My consciousness faded from the driveway. Without delay I found myself facing the ceiling, hovering over my body. I allowed the familiar ending to OBEs to naturally take its course. I automatically floated gently down into my physical body. I allowed myself to ground well into my body before moving and then quietly celebrated the experience while lying comfortably on my back.

A multitude of metaphysical phenomena were at work in this OBE. First, it was very apparent my consciousness was fully active and mobile <u>outside</u> my physical body. This by itself demonstrated to me that we are multi-dimensional beings. I seemed to be my normal self in all ways except I was out-of-body. I could feel material and see more clearly than ever. I don't recall if I heard anything.

Second, I believe I observed a blending of two dimensions. The subtle energy layer(s) of the plants and trees overlapped their physical layer, just as my energy body vehicle is one component of my form. Usually when I experience an OBE into nature, I don't see the radiant energy layers I witnessed there.

Third, I traveled into the daytime, which demonstrated my consciousness went to a different time, given my OBE occurred at night.

Fourth, an aspect of my deceased mother may have actually been with me. I believe she is currently alive and well without her physical body, living in another plane of existence. My OBEs tell me that we do indeed have an energy double in which we can travel, so perhaps an aspect of her was paying me a visit.

Since my mom did not respond to me, it is possible she was a manifestation of my subconscious mind. If this were the case, it would demonstrate the concept that our mind does indeed influence our reality — at least on the astral level.

By sensitizing myself to my energy field during my bedtime energy-breathing practices as a teenager, my early efforts to feel the energy concentrations at my seven main chakra centers was made easier. As many of you might know, our chakras are energy centers that are the interface between our physical body and our more subtle energy bodies, constantly running energy back and forth between them.

As I learned about my chakras during my high-school years, I knew I had a deep connection with my heart chakra without having to do anything. The love I felt inside was the radiance from that chakra located in the center of my chest.

My solar-plexus chakra was also easy to feel. This chakra is located at, or slightly below, the base of the sternum. Our "gut feeling" comes mainly from there, and partly from the chakra in the abdomen. I put my attention on the area surrounding my solar-plexus chakra to see if I could feel an energy concentration. Encouragingly, I could. My chakra felt like a ball of energy.

I then chose to explore my third-eye chakra located between the eyebrows because clairvoyance, i.e. clear sight, is possible when this chakra is active. Clairvoyance includes seeing things that are not visible to the ordinary eye, such as auras, spirits, non-physical realms, and physical locations beyond our sight. The latter is referred to as "remote viewing." From my perspective, my third-eye chakra seemed inactive, so I needed to wake it up.

*I hope this works*, I muttered to myself as I got ready to head out to my school bus stop.

*What the heck, it seems like a reasonable approach, but I do feel silly!*

Dampening my forefinger with my tongue, I touched my third-eye area which made me acutely aware of that spot. At least once a day for seven days I trusted this routine would likely bear fruit. On the seventh day it did, and I reveled in feeling a noticeable new pressure sensation at my third eye! I was excited. Celebrating the success of this little experiment, I continued damping my third-eye chakra a little each day, and the pressure sensation increased gradually. Given that one of the intuitive gifts the third-eye chakra offers us is clairvoyance, this effort likely contributed to my being able to unexpectedly see the flaming energy from the non-physical world during the OBE I just described.

Our intuitive senses are associated with our chakras in complex ways that I understand only partially. The other four of the seven main chakras are the root chakra, which is slightly forward of the tailbone; the sacral chakra located a couple of inches below the navel; the crown chakra at the top of the head; and the throat chakra. For completeness, the known intuitive senses that humans possess are as follows:

Claircognizance is intuitive knowing, while clairsentience is our intuitive sense of feeling. Clairvoyance relates to seeing, and clairaudience relates to hearing. Clairtangency, also known as psychometry, describes sensing something intuitively from an object simply by touching it, while clairempathy describes feeling another person's emotions. A less familiar intuitive sense is clairgustance, which is about tasting. Clairalience involves intuitive smelling.

As an example of clairalience, have you ever smelled the tobacco or perfume of a past loved one so obviously that you wondered if the smoke or perfume was actually in the room?

While weaving through the packed high school hallways between classes in my senior year, I often wondered what some people were like as they passed by, and what it might be like if we met. I was interested only in girls when it came to romantic thoughts or adolescent cravings, but there was one guy that I had a gut feeling about.

*I should meet that guy.*
*There's something about him — something familiar.*
*He seems pretty laid back and approachable.*
*I don't know what this is about, but I should make the effort to meet him soon.*

I had no idea who he was, but these thoughts occurred frequently.

While enjoying a night out with my friends Bob and Cathy at a drive-in movie, I was handed a clear opportunity to meet this seemingly familiar mystery man. During intermission, I noticed he was sitting in the driver's seat of a car diagonally across the dirt intersection from our car. His date was sitting in the front seat with him.

*It's now or never,* I muttered to myself.

I excused myself from the car and strolled slowly across the empty intersection, avoiding staring at his car as I approached.

*This is important,* I told myself, so I was willing to brave through it, hoping it wouldn't become an uncomfortable situation.

When I got to his door, our eyes met with mutual cordial smiles. He appeared as relaxed as anyone could be, and my shoulders naturally dropped as I became less tense. He and his date looked at me expectantly.

"I've seen you around and something inside me said I should meet you," I said with honest, unexpectant eyes.

"I'm Greg," I said, as I gave myself a mental attaboy for finally meeting him.

He responded with a genuine smile and appreciative handshake. He introduced himself as John and then introduced his girlfriend, Liz. He broke the ice further by asking me the standard question,

"How are you doing?"

"Good." I smiled appreciatively.

Our conversation evolved from there.

When I told him I had been playing guitar for a few years, he got excited and said he had been too. A little discussion about our guitars revealed we had nearly the exact same uncommon Yamaha model guitar. We were both amazed by this and found that we also liked playing songs by many of the same contemporary pop rock groups. We excitedly exchanged phone numbers, anticipating having some fun jam sessions soon.

## DEVELOPING INTUITION

Feeling mutually grateful that we'd met, we parted for the night. As fate would have it, our budding friendship led to becoming best friends. I also felt at home with John's parents and siblings, and I was often invited over to share the holidays with them. Playing guitar together and astronomy are two major interests John and I share. We often made music at Goodwill Park and at parties as people listened and sang along. John and I keep in touch to this day.

Feeling the unexplainable connection with John in the hallways, given I had no idea who he was, was a very rewarding demonstration of clairsentience and claircognizance. I was glad I was developing my intuition!

*John (on right) and me in 1981 (Photo credit: Cheryl Brassard)*

In the next chapter I will share how my conscious connection with ETs began to develop. One way we connected was through the dream state, and another was during meditation.

Sleep is a vital human function that allows us to heal and revitalize our mind and body. Sleep also allows us to dream. I have learned that dreams offer a gateway to other dimensions and levels of consciousness, as well as being a way for our subconscious mind to express itself.

With practice, I found that during meditation I could sense and communicate with other beings — ETs included. While this may sound extreme or unheard of, none of this is ground-breaking. For millennia, countless others have developed the skill to intuitively communicate with non-physical beings, and even ETs, across the miles. I am simply one of many learning to hone this ability. As with developing any new skill in my life, this took practice, patience, and humility. In this case it also took a large dose of consistently clearing my body's energy channels and learning to discern what I was truly experiencing in this new realm.

My lifelong passionate interest in chakras and the human energy field has rewarded me with extraordinary experiences and deep understanding.

For those who would like additional, slightly more academic discussion about the chakras and the human energy field, I've provided more of what I've learned and experienced below. Although this information is very helpful, it isn't essential for understanding future chapters.

As I've found, the seven main energy chakras in our bodies offer a gateway to other dimensions and levels of consciousness, just as our energy bodies do. Later in the book I will share some personal experiences that demonstrate this more deeply than I could have imagined.

As a teen I enjoyed routinely trying to feel my chakras and see what intuitive gifts they might reveal over time. Perhaps my less familiar chakras would perk up by giving them some attention, just as I found my dreams at night became more vivid and meaningful when I started paying attention to them.

At that time, I didn't consider myself particularly intuitive. I also knew from experience that I needed to work on developing my intuitive skills or they would remain minimal. Even now, with my wealth of experience, I am clear that if I don't practice and maintain my intuitive capability, I am limited to what I can experience in our multi-dimensional universe.

Reading *Meditation, Gateway to Enlightenment* by Elsie Sechrist, and other material, I realized that the seven main energy chakras create an interface with the physical body through the seven endocrine glands. The glands and chakras stimulate each other in accordance with our thinking, emotions, and energy level.

The human energy field is made up of an electromagnetic field, a life-force energy, and likely fine matter. Mainstream science says that every atom in our body is made up simply of "energy" at its most basic level. The magnetic field in and around our bodies exists because our bodies are electrochemical. This field is shaped like a bar magnet's magnetic attraction field and is illustrated below. It has also been shown that each of our organs has its own unique magnetic field resonance.

The medical industry has documented a correlation between the use of magnetic fields and healing. A 2022 paper in the National Library of Medicine describes this healing relationship like this: "Recently, magnetic fields have been extensively used in various bioengineering and biomedical applications, both for diagnosis and therapy." (https://www.ncbi.nlm.nih.gov/pmc/articles/PMC9318684/)

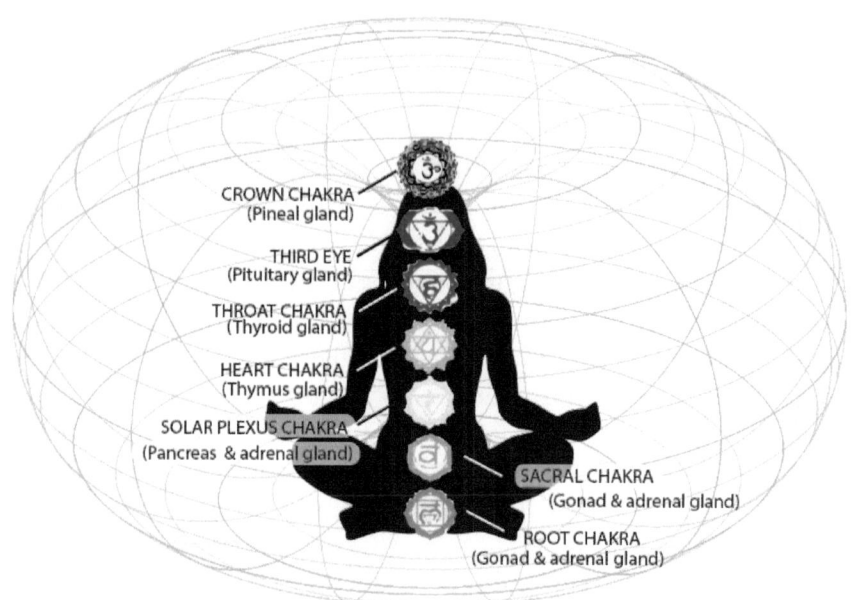

*Human magnetic field, chakras and associated endocrine glands (Source: Media1.iterated-reality.com/2015/02/chakras.jpg)*

Energy moves with intention, but we can also move energy with our hands, as Reiki masters, energy healers, and I can attest. A fun exercise for learning to feel energy, without using the breathing technique, is to compress energy between your hands. This can create a very noticeable pressure on the palms of the hands as the gap between them decreases. Some people who try this report feeling tingling or heat, and others feel a literal pressure. To increase your success in this exercise, energize yourself a bit so you feel lively, like you would feel when your favorite sports team scores a goal, for example. Then take your attention <u>away</u> from your palms as you push them together. This helps prevent the mind from influencing the energy.

I have experienced many energetic and intuitive gifts from opening my chakra centers on a regular basis. Let me elaborate on this and then I will share a method I use for opening and clearing the chakras.

Each chakra is open to some extent — some more open than others. Consider whether your sense of love for yourself and others is at a fulfilling level, or has an emotionally painful experience caused you to close your heart chakra for emotional protection? If you feel love, your heart chakra is open.

Opening a chakra enhances its energy flow, which helps clear out stuck energy and emotions held in that area. This in turn promotes rejuvenation, healing, and enlivening of the physical body and subtle energy bodies. By opening chakras, we feel better and intuitively sense better on all levels. We feel unconditional love when we open our heart chakra, and our gut-feeling and inner compass are enhanced when we open our solar-plexus chakra. When I clear my root chakra, near the base of my spine, I feel divine energy race up the center of my body, stimulating the four chakras above it, and I also feel divine energy run downward from the root chakra into the Earth, which helps me feel more grounded.

One of my favorite chakras to stimulate is my third-eye chakra. This is not because of the amazing clairvoyant sight I've experienced many times at that spot, but for two other reasons. One is the feel-good hormonal secretion that bathes and nourishes my body, often accompanied by blissful feelings at that chakra and at some of the chakras below it. The other is the feeling of divine connection to an expansive, elevated realm beyond me. Three times in the past I have felt what I refer to as "divine faith" through my third-eye chakra. At those times, I experienced a divine knowing that all is well at a higher level of consciousness and being. Intuitively, I deeply knew this. Now I understand why some call the third-eye chakra "the seat of the Christ consciousness." The word Christ comes from "Christos," a Greek word meaning "Anointed One."

One method I use to more fully open a chakra, or energy center, is to imagine a ball of divine white light at the chakra. If we relax our mind when we do this, our energy field will relax and impurities in the chakra will tend to pop out. The divine white light does the work due to its high vibration. The clearer the chakra, the brighter and more functional it will be, and the easier it will be to experience.

# 4

# EXTRATERRESTRIALS, DREAMS, AND MEDITATION

*Whoa, this is mind-blowing!*

Here I was, suddenly aware of myself sitting comfortably in the passenger's seat of a car with three humanoid beings from another world! My first reactions were awe, gratitude, and curiosity. As we drove along the quiet, suburban street I stared in amazement at the driver. Covered in hair, he loosely resembled Chewbacca from the Star Wars movies. Those who have seen the films know Chewbacca is a walking, full-body dust mop.

The driver's hair was much shorter and straighter than Chewbacca's, however. In addition, his lips were thinner, and his nose was much smaller in profile than Chewbacca's. I don't recall seeing any clothing on him. An elderly couple of similar form sat quietly in the back seat, looking straight ahead as if I weren't there. They wore a small amount of clothing and sat closely together. The weather was pleasant, and the driver seemed to be in no hurry. He didn't react to my presence, either.

Boldly, I reached slowly toward the driver's arm to feel his thick, straight hair.

*Wow, the hair feels so real!* I thought, as I dared to slowly trace my fingers down his arm.

*It's so smooth. I'm so glad he's not objecting to being touched!*

The hair was brown with shades of blonde, red and black. In the next instant, we were all in the living room of a quiet, sunlit home. My friend and mentor in real life, Leah, was there too. The walls of the room were all white, without decorations. I don't recall seeing any furniture. Leah went off with the middle-aged driver while I stood with the elderly couple. We didn't speak, which felt awkward, but I could sense they were comfortable with the moment.

I was not aware I was dreaming. When I awoke, I was elated by the experience.

Our dreams are usually related to recent experiences and subjects we've been focusing on. I can confidently say that neither of these situations would have caused this dream. I hadn't recently watched any sci-fi movies or read any sci-fi books, and my mind hadn't been focused on ETs. I had this dream in my late-40s, and although I knew these types of ET beings were significant in my life for years before the dream, I had not thought about them for a very long time. It was very apparent to me I had connected with them while sleeping, and my dreaming mind reflected this.

The sleeping dreams I've had over the years in which I connect with actual ETs are a significant part of my spiritual journey, and I will share about it in this chapter. I was amazed by, and grateful for, each dream because they demonstrated that my interests in ETs were heard and acknowledged. In each case, they were connecting with me when least expected.

I will also share a meditation from my early 20's in which I believe an ET came into my consciousness and spoke to me. I was not thinking about ETs during the meditation, which I believe eliminates the possibility that wishful thinking manifested the event.

The experiences I'm sharing span several decades and illustrate that communication with other beings is possible through the dream world and meditation.

I started consciously working with sleeping dreams in my junior year of high school, scheming that if could get my body to fly in my dreams, the experience might turn into a fully conscious astral projection.

When I first started paying attention to my dreams, they were black and white, and mostly nonsensical. However, the more I paid attention to my dreams, the more meaningful and colorful they became.

I began keeping a dream journal to document my progress. The journal was a simple 6"x8" spiralbound notebook with thin, strong cardboard covers.

While downtown one day, I sought out an artist friend of mine and enthusiastically told him about the journal, asking if he would consider drawing a wizard on the front cover. This was a special book, and I wanted it to represent the budding, mystical side of my life. He smiled and happily agreed. When we got back together days later, I trustingly handed him my journal, hoping I would like his wizard rendition. He quickly and confidently began scribbling an image with his pencil.

I smiled as a masterful wizard's face and beard with iconic pointed hat began taking shape. In a few moments he put his pencil back in his top pocket. I was thrilled with the pencil sketch, and I grew even more excited when he pulled out a few colored pencils. In seconds he brought the wizard alive with color and depth. A simple, yet perfect wizard now stood vigil over my dream journal. I looked forward to the dreams that would soon fill the pages.

*My first dream journal*

The first dream I recorded was of dozens of different colorful, mostly military, aircraft flying slowly overhead. They were excitingly low, nose-to-tail and wingtip-to-wingtip under a calm, sunny sky. This dream came as no surprise to me, since I loved airplanes. A huge flying wing aircraft was the crowning end piece of the dazzling armada. I was going to college the next year to start classes in aeronautical engineering, so this dream made me feel at home with my plans.

I often had my eyes on military aircraft publications in my junior year, and to my delight, I had several dreams in which I found myself in the pilot's seat of jet aircraft. In real life I didn't know how to fly, and my dreaming mind reflected this whenever I lost confidence in the cockpit. I banked a Harrier jet into the trees in one dream while performing a vertical takeoff in a moonlit field. In a later dream, I was a confident test pilot flying several military jets in succession. A man standing by the runway in a lab coat, holding a clipboard, recorded my findings after each flight.

Becoming a U.S. Air Force test pilot was part of my intended career path. By taking this on, I could fulfill my desire to fly amazing aircraft and gain the experience needed for acceptance into NASA's astronaut program. At that time, most of NASA's astronauts had taken this path. They were the best of the best in their field, however, and I realized gaining entry into Air Force pilot training and, later, test-pilot school would be steep challenges. I felt I had the potential to succeed, though, and I had optimistically planned out a viable, but by no means guaranteed, career path.

First, I planned to enroll in the Aeronautical Engineering curriculum and the Air Force Reserve Officers Training Corps (AFROTC) at the finest aviation college in the country, Embry-Riddle Aeronautical University in Daytona Beach, Florida. I knew I would need to earn a coveted pilot training slot during ROTC. Upon graduating with a Bachelor of Science degree, I would be commissioned into the Air Force as a second lieutenant and begin pilot training. After graduating from pilot training, I would eventually attempt to enter test-pilot school and serve as a test pilot. My next step would be to apply to NASA's astronaut-training program. While I was very aware that the challenges would be extremely rigorous and the competition very stiff, I also knew that without a plan, it was certain my dreams would never come true, so I forged ahead.

I was completely at home with technical challenges, math, science, studying, physical fitness, and being part of a team as well, so I felt confident enough to embark on this path. I hadn't, however, been compelled to learn the basics of flying during high school, mostly due to the prohibitively high cost of flight lessons. I also didn't feel drawn to learning about cockpit flight instrumentation and controls during high school, nor was I particularly drawn to being a military officer. Instead, I was clearly more interested in NASA, UFOs, metaphysics, and the concept of star beings. I was doing well in school, taking advanced placement classes when I could, and I also had guitar-playing, a paper route, and a productive commitment to learning karate adding to my life. I was happy as I finished high school and headed to college.

Over the decades, my experience has taught me that dreams are not only a place for our subconscious to work out emotional and mental waking-state challenges, but they also offer a gateway to other dimensions and levels of consciousness. To my delight, I've had many dreams that included what appear to be genuine connections with higher levels of consciousness, UFOs, and ETs. I came to these conclusions by considering the dream contexts, the experiences I had during the days following the dreams, and in some cases the corroboration I was able to uncover by talking with people later.

In the previous chapter I shared my close-up sighting of an actual UFO outside my bathroom window. I had a dream 10 years later that was eerily related. In the dream, I was in the same bathroom witnessing a large UFO hovering outside the window. I called excitedly to my sister Sue to come and see it. Next, I unexpectedly floated through the window with ease, feeling the semi-solid makeup of the window and wall as I passed through it. I continued floating automatically toward the UFO. I felt calm and curious. Then, still unaware I was dreaming, I found myself flying slowly away in the UFO, looking back at the house.

Later that same night, I dreamt I was an astronaut looking down on the magnificent blue Earth from about 150 miles up in orbit. I was with two other astronauts, and we all wore Apollo-era spacesuits which were the norm during my 1974 UFO sighting from the bathroom. I don't recall whether or not we were standing on a platform in orbit, but it appeared we were not in a craft. While contentedly observing the Earth, we discussed how we felt about the experience.

I was highly intrigued by the UFO portion of the dream for two reasons. First, my subconscious mind might have been telling me I was in touch with beings from my UFO sighting 10 years earlier. Secondly, even if that were not the case, I feel that I had an OBE into an actual ET craft in the dream. Feeling the bathroom window and wall pass through me as I floated out to the UFO told me this was an OBE, as opposed to being only a dream in my head.

Looking back at Earth in that dream also hints that my consciousness was space-traveling. I felt as though I were floating above the bright, realistic-looking Earth below me. It was unlikely that my subconscious mind created this scenario because it appeared and felt so real.

Even as I began exploring these important metaphysical aspects, my focus was also on other, more down-to-earth portions of my life. Specifically, I enrolled in my first semester of classes at Embry-Riddle one balmy day in the fall of 1979. In the late afternoon, I stopped to sit on the steps of the university center to take in the view of the small academic buildings and campus flight line – the university was built adjacent to Daytona Beach Regional Airport with access to the runways. Single engine Cessnas and similar aircraft sat quietly waiting to train students. I reflected on how blessed I was to have accomplished so much since arriving in Daytona a couple of weeks earlier. I wondered what my life might look like some day, hoping my future would be bright.

I enrolled in AFROTC in my first semester, along with taking a full load of five academic classes. My technical classes were Calculus 1 and Chemistry 1 – both very demanding. Eager to begin classes, who would have guessed that Hurricane David would come through and disappointingly delay the start of the semester by two days?! David was a Category 2 hurricane at that point, and I remember seeing a small tree or two fly by my front window as I confidently sat in the house I was renting, waiting it out. Since I grew up in New England, this was my first hurricane, but I felt safe in the cinder-block home.

At the end of the semester, I received an A on my AFROTC course, and A's in my technical classes, giving me a 3.67 Grade Point Average

(GPA). I was off to a great start! I was surprised, though, to find I wasn't as enthusiastic about AFROTC as I thought I would be. The experience was okay, but it didn't excite me – not a good sign. Now, in mid-December, I was finally going home after four long months of classes and finals. Excited to be back in Massachusetts with family and friends, Christmas break was fun at home, at high-school parties, and when playing guitar with my buddy, John!

Dreams continued to play a big part in my life, with the next four dreams occurring in my 20's.

*Door, Damn it!*

I commanded the presence of a door in a sleeping dream, pointing at the location for the door to be. Instantly a vault-like steel door appeared in the wall, providing an opening to the outside where a sun-lit, wooded path awaited me.

Aware I was dreaming, I no longer allowed myself to be at the mercy of the challenging dream scenario. I was in a windowless, doorless, small two-room building with a thief I had just easily thwarted, and now I wanted out. This is an example of a lucid dream, which is a dream wherein the dreamer is aware they are dreaming and can then affect the outcome.

Since dream characters and settings usually represent aspects of ourselves, I later reasoned that the thief represented a stressful situation I was facing in my waking life and the lack of walls and windows represented a closed-in feeling. Claiming my power in the dream world resulted in the dream becoming safe and accommodating, as represented by the stout doorway and nature path I eagerly stepped on to.

In the next dream, my consciousness accessed the future!

*Déjà vu! This is just like what happened in my dream!*

Sleeping on my sister Sue's couch in San Rafael, California during a Christmas visit, I dreamed that Sue's roommate, Brian, and a friend of his walked in from a late night out. In the dream I noticed the details of their clothing and their calm demeanor as they walked in and headed toward the hall. What felt like just a few minutes later, I awoke when Brian and his friend entered the home, exactly as I had dreamed, clothing designs included.

I readily conceded that time is a strange thing as they walked by, realizing my dream-state consciousness had just skipped over the boundary of time.

The next two dreams illustrated to me that I can receive messages from other beings while asleep.

*ETs are really giving me messages. These dreams are only two months apart, and have the same message*, I thought as I recorded the second dream in my dream journal.

In the first dream, I was doing carpentry work in a small sunlit loft, and I became aware of an unseen man telling me he was extraterrestrial and that he would be around and return when he needed to. I realized he had been speaking for some time, but I was unaware of him. Once I comprehended his message, he stopped repeating it.

The dream setting for my second dream was my bedroom in the house where I grew up. Over the years I've come to realize that a dream occurring in my childhood house is connected to my higher consciousness and I should pay particular attention to what is happening in the dream. In this dream I was listening to music from a rock group that was popular when I lived there. In between songs an unseen man began talking assertively about the extraterrestrial presence on Earth and their future visits, but I didn't recall the specifics of his brief statements on the topic.

Thinking about these two dreams when recording them, I realized that these were true ET messages. I hadn't been thinking about ETs visiting Earth at that time, so the dreams weren't reflecting any of my waking experiences. Also, it didn't seem likely that the ETs symbolically represented a part of my consciousness. Given this, it's unlikely that my mind made up the dreams.

The next dream is unlike any of the previous examples, for several reasons. First, I communicated with other beings in this dream. Second, my body carried a vibration sensation from the dream world into my waking state. Third, I discovered the day following the dream that a friend unknowingly had a hand in the manifestation of the dream experience.

In the dream, I'm walking along a lonely moonlit road. Endless fields of tall grass and crops line the road, giving me the feeling of being cut off from the rest of the world. Out of the dark I see a mechanical being floating slowly toward me! I run in panic. The being has a wide dome-shaped head, a cone-shaped torso, two arms and no legs. After a brief sprint down the road, I assume I evaded it.

When I look back, I realize it's coming for me again! My heart is pounding.

I dive into the tall grass. Face up, I'm hoping the mechanical mystery man won't see me. As luck would have it, Mr. Robot floats over to me and stops.

I'm shocked, but less panicked, given it's not harming me. My breathing calms a bit.

"Come with me," he says telepathically in a male voice.

I feel I haven't much choice. But my curiosity is now gaining ground. As I get up and walk along the road with Mr. Robot, I feel a bit like I'm being kidnapped. My apprehension grows when I see a semi-transparent alien-looking man slowly floating in our direction – another slightly overwhelming experience, but I remain calm. I figure this guy is running the show, given his more humanoid make-up, and we stop when he reaches us.

"You know I love you," I telepathically utter to the man. I wanted to see if his response would be benevolent.

"We love you too," the etheric being kindly replies, hearing him only in my head.

"You do know what love is?" I ask to make certain.

"Yes," he replies.

I walk along with them, now feeling Safe. Soon I find myself in a room with a large dentist-like chair and many bright white lights. There are ceramic lumps on the chair. I am asked to lie on the chair. I comply, and feel the chair begin to vibrate as energy rushes into my lower back.

I woke up suddenly, my back still vibrating. I lay there confounded by what just took place.

The following day I shared this fantastical dream with my friend and mentor, Leah, who has considerable abilities to communicate with spirit guides and ETs.

"You were in a healing dimension," she matter-of-factly replied.

I listened intently.

"I asked my spirit helpers to give you a healing, since you told me about your cold, but I'm really surprised the healing happened this way!"

"I did feel somewhat better after the dream," I confirmed.

Thinking long and deeply about this dream over the weeks that followed, I decided that this was, indeed, much more than a dream. I came to a number of conclusions:

The beings and my subconscious mind created the dreamscape for this interaction, using my memories to make up some of what I saw and experienced — perhaps the chair or the fields, for example. The beings were ETs or spirits. If they were spirits, they may or may not have ever had a physical body. It's possible that my mind, or their purposeful intention, influenced their appearance so I would be comfortable with their images. The beings were using their multi-dimensionality since they clearly did not unlock the deadbolt on my front door and cart me off as I slept. They either moved my physical body through a wall or window in some dematerialized form, or more likely, I was having an OBE.

The fact that my back was vibrating significantly when I awoke told me this was likely not just a dream. While emotional hangovers from dreams are somewhat common, physically vibrating is not. Finally, Leah had submitted a request to her spirit guides and helpers for my healing a day or two before the dream. That implied a distinct cause-and-effect element for my experience. I also know that healing and clearing performed on our energy bodies will help heal the physical body. This apparently was what I was undergoing during this experience, because I did feel somewhat better after the dream.

In another slightly different but affirming ET dream later in life, at age 39, I experienced a woman from a UFO, and then several days later I had a strong energetic reconnection with her while I was awake.

In the dream, I am outside in the yard where I grew up in Massachusetts. The sun is shining, and the weather is warm and comfortable. I look up and see a silver disk-shaped UFO, approximately 25 feet in diameter. It has a domed top and is moving slowly over the treetops on the west side of the lawn. Heading in my direction, the UFO stops just past the trees, about 50 feet away.

In the next instant, a woman is standing next to me. She is wearing typical street clothes, appears to be about thirty-five years old, and is mostly silent. I don't recall what she said.

When I awoke from the dream, I realized the craft looked very similar to some I had seen in photos and videos in the past.

As I shared the dream a few days later with a friend during dinner, I surprisingly felt a strong spontaneous energy reconnection to the craft and the woman. I felt her energy and the energy of her craft enter my energy field on my left side. I had experienced several non-physical visits from beings claiming to be from the Pleiades star cluster throughout the years prior to this dream, and I recognized the familiar Pleiadian feel to her energy. This was a clear indication to me that the dream experience involved an energetic connection with an actual Pleiadian.

The Pleiades is an open star cluster of hot, young blue-white stars. The Seven Sisters, as they are also referred to, are easily visible in the fall and winter skies of the northern hemisphere. Located about 440 light years from Earth, the stars in the Pleiades are inhospitable to humanoid life because of the high radiation levels emitted by the stars. Despite this, there are some possible explanations for the Pleiadians' origin that I will describe later.

Because of these wonderful, diverse experiences I've had, I'm fascinated with how truly multi-dimensional we are. While dreaming I appear to be accessing my subconscious mind, my higher consciousness, other beings and dimensions, and occasionally even future time periods.

I am not alone in this awareness. The shamans of the world have been teaching us about the nature of our existence for centuries. A shaman is a spiritual mediator and experiences a close relationship with the larger spiritual universe, endowing him or her with powers to divine or heal. Shamans feel that people can explore other realms during sleep because their energy body and consciousness can journey without bounds. They also feel that we can time-travel while sleeping.

Shamanism was prevalent in many indigenous cultures around the world for millennia before modern times. From the Americas to Central Asia and Africa, shamans played a crucial role in the spiritual and cultural life of their communities, using their knowledge and abilities to heal and guide their people. Today shamans are found in many countries, living as an integral part within the dominant cultures.

Dreams, consciousness travelling, and OBEs aren't the only modalities in which I have experienced ETs. I have frequently engaged with ETs while meditating. During an evening meditation in my 20s, a being came into my energy field, sharing that he was from another planet. A very old, dark-skinned, wrinkled man's face appeared in clear detail in my mind about 15 minutes into my meditation. His face looked as though it was only 18 inches away, and he was looking directly at me. His facial features reminded me of Native Americans. I was relaxed and sitting peacefully in my well-lit room with my eyes open the entire time. I prefer to do my meditations with my eyes open for alertness.

"We have the Sacred Pipe in our world," he said telepathically.

I was amazed to hear him say that. Having been involved in Lakota Sioux Native American spiritual traditions since the mid-1980s, I was familiar with the significance of the Sacred Pipe, which is central to their spirituality. The Sacred Pipe is a prayer tool, and when used with reverence in conjunction with prayer and Lakota ceremonial songs, the Pipe connects strongly to the Divine. It can be used for healing, obtaining guidance, protection, and more. In my experience, Pipe ceremonies strongly center me in higher levels of consciousness and the God-essence within me.

"I am from the star system of 'Odella' in the Pleiades," he added, his face unmoving.

I was amazed by what I was experiencing. I was in a humble, quiet state of mind when he appeared, so I was sure I wasn't making this up.

"We have strife on our world too," he added, comparing his world to ours.

The man's old face faded away shortly after, and I sat in gratitude wondering why I was honored with such a visit. His energy was clean, heart-centered, and in harmony with the high-energy vibration I enjoyed in my meditation.

He reminded me of something an acquaintance of mine often told his audiences. Grandpa Wallace Black Elk, a well-respected Lakota (Sioux) Native American shaman, described himself as being a 19th generation Lakota – ten on Pleiades and nine on Earth. The Lakota tell sacred stories related to their origination from the Pleiades Star cluster. My meditation experience confirmed the validity of this oral tradition.

As I've described in this chapter, I have found that dreams and meditative states are common avenues through which ETs can connect with us. I have also had deeper experiences in which I intuitively connected with ETs and UFOs. Many of the experiences were corroborated by other people; I will explore these in later chapters.

Along the way, I discovered that my dreams became much more vivid and meaningful specifically because I paid attention to them and learned how to interpret their possible meanings. I am not alone in this view, as there are many books explaining how to remember and interpret dreams and even how to work with them in real time while lucid dreaming. A book I found particularly useful was *The Dream Game* by Ann Faraday.

The first step in helping your dreams become more vivid and meaningful is to tell your mind that you would like this. Because our minds respond to our requests, stating "I will remember my dreams in the morning" several times a day will also bear fruit over time.

# 5

## CHANGES AFOOT

I phoned Dad during a break on campus, slowly pacing back and forth in a quiet, open, sunny area away from other students. Taking a deep breath, I surrendered to the moment as I waited for him to pick up. He answered with his usual upbeat attitude and motivated tone.

"Hi, Greg! How you doing?!"

"Well Dad, I'm confused about some things," I said, letting out the breath I was holding, looking down at the ground as I paced slowly forward.

"Oh, what's that?" he asked in a tentative tone. A pregnant silence followed.

*Here we go.* I mustered up my courage.

"Dad, I just don't feel comfortable continuing my pursuit of pilot training," I revealed. "I can't really see myself becoming an astronaut, either, given this."

I continued sharing without pausing. I wanted to express all that had happened and everything I had thought about, as unsettling as they sounded. My dad had no idea I was considering such radical changes.

"Should I even stay in aeronautical engineering, given I'm not headed for test-pilot school? Maybe I should do something like gardening instead. I think I would like that. I don't know what the right path is for me anymore."

What led up to this began a couple of months earlier. It was early in my second semester at Embry-Riddle, and I was scheduled to take the

Air Force Officers Qualifying Test (AFOQT), a required written exam I needed to pass to be formally accepted into the Air Force ROTC officer commissioning program. I hoped to score high enough to qualify for the Air Force pilot-training slot I'd dreamed of. Scoring well on the qualifying exam would also help me compete for an AFROTC college scholarship to cover my tuition while I attended college and completed officer training.

I chose to take the exam as a college freshman for this financial consideration. I also opted to take the aircraft navigator test to see how I would score. I hadn't considered the idea of being a navigator prior to taking the test, but I felt I shouldn't rule out the option. I was excited with the prospect of pilot training. I knew the initial training would be in the T-37 jet trainer, in which the instructor sits next to the student pilot. Pilot training would begin shortly after I graduated with a B.S. degree and was commissioned as a second lieutenant at the same time.

The AFOQT is a challenging standardized test, similar to the SAT and ACT college entrance exams, with additional questions geared toward aviation and flight instruments. I was barely 19 years old and didn't know much about flying or navigation, because I had never studied these. In hindsight, I realize it would have helped if I had focused on them before the test. Unfortunately, no one in my ROTC group, including the officers in the detachment leadership, ever brought up the idea of preparing for the unique topics on the test.

The result was that I didn't do well on the pilot or navigator portions of the test. I scored high enough on the navigator section that I was offered a navigator slot; however, I was ranked at number 145 on the list. This meant there were 144 other cadets who would be offered college scholarships and navigator training before I would be. I was very discouraged. Not only was my getting chosen unlikely, I didn't really want to be a navigator. I was told I could retake the test later, but now I had a concrete feel for the stiff competition I faced.

I shared my disappointment and revelations with my parents over the phone. Hearing my disheartened tone, they chose their words carefully, offering me the supportive encouragement my parents were always good at providing. I felt blessed to have them as parents, and I let them know I loved them and appreciated their support.

# CHANGES AFOOT

Uncertain about my future in the Air Force, I continued with my second semester of ROTC. I had volunteered for a leadership role as a cadet, sometimes leading our group of about a dozen cadets through formation drills during field training. I enjoyed this, but at that point I wasn't actually excited about being in ROTC.

I also began dealing with a conflict in my heart about being a fighter pilot. I wanted to be an Air Force pilot as a lead-in to astronaut training, but I struggled with the idea of flying a killing machine. While I wholeheartedly agreed with the necessity for military deterrence and offensive engagement when warranted, I also realized I was more wired for exploring the quieter realms of higher consciousness. Perhaps most importantly, I saw that I was much more interested in being a civilian than leading a military life.

*Maybe I can become an astronaut as a civilian with advanced degrees? That doesn't feel good, though. I'm not feeling a pull inside me to get more than a bachelor's degree.*

I was at a crossroad. Do I stay in the aeronautical engineering program? Do I even stay in college, for that matter? After all, it appeared I wouldn't be headed down the path of becoming a test pilot, or an astronaut.

After sitting on these thoughts and feelings for a day or two, I decided to phone my dad to reveal my quandary, seeking his gentle guidance. I knew this would be a sensitive topic for him, given he was very proud of me, and he highly valued college education. I was feeling the emptiness of an undefined future. The usual conviction and security I felt for years was now thin ground on which for me to walk. What kept me afloat was my deeper sense of self. As I took stock of what I had to offer I knew I would succeed in something. I knew I was smart, open-minded, and happy to explore new options. I also realized I worked well with people, and I had parents who were supportive and encouraging.

When I finished sharing my dialogue with Dad – during the conversation I described at the beginning of the chapter – he audibly struggled to find words. I didn't like shattering the world he had envisioned for me and supported for so long. I appreciated the bond we had developed around my career path. I was the only child of six who followed his suggestions of getting a technical college degree, so I knew I was a bright light in his life. I could tell he was sweating bullets. I was in a place of humble surrender, open to whatever thoughts he may offer.

Dad calmly encouraged me to continue engineering school, giving me good reasons why I should stay the course for now. His coaching made sense. He reminded me how much I enjoyed engineering school. It was true that I loved math, science, and technical thinking, so I was happy as an engineering student. It was then I decided I would drop out of ROTC but continue with my engineering classes as I aimed for a bachelor's degree.

"I would be very happy being in the space program working on spacecraft systems," I told Dad.

"Another mountain peak to shoot for," I said with a tentative voice.

I shared that getting into NASA would likely be as competitive as being selected for an Air Force pilot slot. I reassured myself, and my dad as well, when I also admitted I would enjoy working for an aerospace company doing spacecraft or aircraft engineering if I didn't get into NASA.

Dad was happy to hear me say that. And I was glad to be on the other side of the emotional stress I was experiencing. We talked about the college tuition I would now need to cover for the next three years. Dad agreed to continue sending me money each month to cover my typically modest shortfall. I would continue applying for grants and tuition loans through the generous financial aid office on campus.

I continued my class work, uninterrupted, but I did withdraw from AFROTC soon after my talk with Dad. While I understood what I was doing was a major change in my plans, the overwhelming emotion I felt was relief. It was clear to me that I was making the right choice and that my future was bright and promising. When I told the ROTC department that I was going to withdraw from the program, I don't recall trying to justify my decision. If I did talk with them, the conversation was likely brief.

Thank you, Dad, for your invaluable wisdom, encouragement, and reassurance through this trying semester of my freshman year. Your ever-present support, along with Mom's, enabled me to stay on track toward a bright, exciting future. My new goal allowed me to continue reaching for the stars, and in some ways, this was an even more direct path. I would focus on a NASA career much sooner now, and that was exciting. I also would learn I would have much more opportunity to pursue my metaphysical interests in ETs, UFOs and more, since the highly demanding life of a military pilot was now off the table. To my delight, as the Universe would have it, the stars would be reaching back.

With a bold new vision for my life, my second semester was coming to a close. I was truly enjoying my technical classes, which included Aircraft Drafting, Calculus II and Chemistry II. My spirits rose, and I maintained my GPA at 3.6.

Embry-Riddle is the dream university of many young aviation-minded men and women. To understand this deep connection, I'd like to share a brief history of its development and contribution to aviation, since I find it exciting and inspiring.

Beginning as a spirited vision in 1925, T. Higbee Embry and John Paul Riddle formed a company at Lunken Field in Cincinnati, Ohio, with Embry as president and Riddle as general manager. The company became known as "Cincinnati's first aviation corporation to amount to anything." The Embry-Riddle Flying School began teaching future pilots how to fly that next spring.

*Founders of Embry-Riddle flying school in 1926*
*(https://erau.edu/about/brief-history)*

In 1939, Riddle began training college students to fly at the University of Miami, increasing his fleet to 15 aircraft. When the U.S. was thrust into World War II, Embry-Riddle's four training facilities welcomed airmen from the Army Air Corps and the United Kingdom's Royal Air Force for flight training, aircraft mechanic training, aviation instrumentation building, and more. Thousands of pilots got their initial flight training through Embry-Riddle as they prepared for deployment to all the different overseas theaters of war.

In 1965, Embry-Riddle moved their world-recognized operation to Daytona Beach, Florida. With twenty aircraft, the Institute's humble ground facilities at Daytona's airport began with vacant World War II era barracks, classrooms, old Army and Navy offices, and whatever they moved up with from Miami. It was a place to start! A few years later, Embry-Riddle Aeronautical University was born with full accreditation. It stood as the worldwide leader in aviation education, and this tradition continues today. This was an incredible accomplishment by a team of dedicated visionaries, and I'm proud to be counted among the graduates of this wonderful school!

# 6

## BEATRICE

"Get in the house now!" my girlfriend's mother bluntly said to her when she got out of the car I had just put into park. My girlfriend, Bea, knew we were in trouble and quickly complied, her mother following her back into the house. I was at home on Christmas Break from college in my sophomore year, and we had just returned to Bea's house from a rare night out together. Bea was still a junior in high school, and we had developed a deep, loving relationship during the summer that had continued as a long-distance relationship throughout the fall. That night, I drove us in my mom's car to a bowling alley in a neighboring town. Instead of going into the bowling alley, Bea hesitantly agreed to my suggestion to simply stay in the car, as we talked and held hands in the parking lot.

Bea's parents called the bowling alley for some reason and were not happy to find we weren't there. I can imagine what might have been going through their minds. I believe they trusted me, but now that trust was broken. Back at Bea's house, her dad asked me to come in the house and explain what we did that night.

I worsened the situation by lying to him. I told him that we were in the bowling alley but didn't hear the intercom page for Bea. Bea's dad listened to my explanation and was not happy with it. He and I had enjoyed a cordial relationship before this, and now I had unwittingly damaged it. He opened the door for me to go, and I left wondering if he bought my story.

"You should have been honest with my dad," Bea said to me on the phone the next day.

"I knew we were in trouble when I saw them outside waiting for us," she said in a sullen voice.

"My dad didn't like that you lied to him. I'm grounded."

"Oh no! I can't imagine not seeing you this last week that I'm back!" I gasped.

"You should have told him the truth, and we would have been all right."

"Oh, man, I really screwed up!"

"My dad was really surprised you would lie to him, and he doesn't like you now."

I had made a huge mistake. I was not a liar at heart, but I didn't want to admit I had broken my word to her dad, thinking he would buy my story. Bad idea. A couple of days later, at my request, her dad agreed to allow me to come over to apologize for lying about taking his only daughter to the bowling alley. I went to the house, and while standing in the same spot where I had lied to him just inside the door, I gave him a heartfelt, authentic apology with tears in my eyes. I would respect him on every level after that.

Bea and I were allowed to continue spending time together for the remaining handful of days I was home for winter break. Neither of us considered asking her parents about our future together, given my overstep.

I first met Bea when I went home for the summer of 1980 between my freshman and sophomore year at college. I had enjoyed my first year at Embry-Riddle, and I felt my life was on the right track, especially after deciding against becoming an Air Force pilot. During the summer I was happily living at home, working, socializing, and relaxing. In these months, I and many high schoolers I knew, frequented Goodwill Park in downtown Holliston. This is where I met my meditation mentor Alan a couple of years before. As it would turn out, I was about to meet a very special lady there as well. As the summer began, I hadn't started working, so I had free time on my hands and enjoyed going to the park.

Goodwill Park sat behind the Mobil gas station downtown. The park was several acres in size with tennis courts and restrooms separating the baseball field from the half-acre popular gathering area that loosely doubled as a playground. Small groups of teens, many of whom I knew, routinely gathered in that half acre to sit in the grass and talk, throw frisbees, or watch friends play tennis. I typically found friends to sit with and I sometimes brought my guitar. My best friend John and I often played guitars in the park alone or with our friends listening in. Beyond the baseball field were cliffs that were easily climbable for anyone wanting to go thirty feet up to the many acres of frequented forest at the top.

One warm, sunny day I noticed a particularly attractive woman at the park. I had never seen her before. She and the guy sitting with her were about my age, and she didn't appear particularly responsive to his interest in her. From my vantage point 40 feet away, I saw she was nicely dressed and very pretty. She was wearing blue jeans and a blue denim vest over a white blouse. I was especially impressed with her slender figure and long, flowing Farah Fawcett-style, wavy brown hair. Farah Fawcett was a glamorous TV icon in the 1970s.

A few days later I noticed her at the park again when I walked in. She was standing with the same guy about 40 feet into the park. I was very interested in meeting her, but I didn't want to be obvious or intrusive about it. I walked over and joined a small group of friends sitting a fair distance from them on the sparsely populated lawn. I asked my friends if they knew who she was, but they returned empty answers. They didn't know anything about her. I found myself both discouraged and hopeful at the same time.

*That's probably her boyfriend. But she doesn't appear to be interested in him.*

A gentle, subtle intuitive sense told me it was important to meet her. I decided I would soon take the bold step of introducing myself to her when the time was right. I was shy about introducing myself to women. At the same time, I was drawn to her because she was mysterious and mostly alone, in addition to being beautiful. That "aloneness" was what I needed to have the courage to approach a woman I didn't know. It was difficult enough for me to meet someone like her, and I didn't want to have to intrude into a group of strangers to do it. All the while, I sensed there was something deeper about my attraction to her.

I left the park that day hoping the time would soon come when I could approach her. Being surprised at my strong infatuation with her, I was nearly jumping out of my skin in anticipation of meeting her as soon as possible. I didn't want her to get away.

The fateful and endearing day came very soon. I was sitting on a stone wall in the park with my friend Kevin, 30 feet from the park entrance. The wall stretched from the street to the tennis courts and acted as a natural boundary for the grassy playground area. My spirits peaked when my mystery girl walked through the park entrance, appearing to be alone, walking a bicycle at her side. Kevin and I watched her in silence as she walked through the park and sat down cross-legged about 40 feet away, laying the bike in the grass by her side.

"Do you know who she is, Kevin?"

"No, but I'd like to," he said.

*Who wouldn't*, I thought, but refrained from saying so.

"Something inside has been pushing me to meet her every time I see her," I said.

"I'm going to go introduce myself," I told him as I stood up.

*Now is my chance, and I'm not going to let it pass.*

My excitement was stronger than the nervous feeling in my gut.

"Really?" Kevin said with a surprised, attaboy tone.

Without hesitation I casually walked toward her. She saw me coming and appeared comfortable. This was a bold step for me. Although I felt nervous, I was confident I was doing the right thing. I was finally going to meet her.

I introduced myself and she said her name was Bea. She was beautiful. With a smile and a few welcoming words, she invited me to sit down. Her pleasant, relaxed nature put me more at ease. Still, we both were a little nervous. It appeared we each wanted to make a good impression. She was comfortable making eye contact with me and asking questions about my life. I was equally interested in her.

Bea was 17 and still in high school. I learned she had a brother George in my grade. I casually knew George and we both appreciated this quickly discovered mutual connection. George had graduated in my high school class the year before. He was a fun guy, and well-liked at school. Bea lived with her adoptive parents less than a mile up the street from the park. Both Bea and George had been adopted together at a young age. Bea said her parents were nice people, but felt they were a bit over-protective.

The more Bea and I talked, the more obvious it was we enjoyed each other's company very much. Bea found my college life and NASA-aspirations admirable, and more importantly she didn't show any concern that I would be away for the fall semester. I was also very happy to hear that she was in the process of moving on from the rocky relationship she had been having with the guy I had seen her with.

Bea and I were quickly bonding, excited by our mutual interests and attraction to each other. Bea enjoyed learning chords on the guitar, working with the elderly, and to my surprise, stargazing. She also shared that she sometimes could intuitively predict outcomes of events as they unfolded. I didn't need to ask what she predicted about our budding relationship, since I felt it would likely continue well. I admired Bea's maturity, her sense of self care, her beauty, her interest in metaphysics and the stars, and her genuinely loving attitude. We had plenty to talk about.

After our enchanted hour together, Bea reluctantly said she had to go home. We made plans to meet again at the park the next day. I walked her to the park entrance, and we hugged goodbye. Watching her ride away, I was on cloud nine.

Bea and I met each day and quickly fell in love. We marveled at how comfortable, natural, and deep our relationship felt. I liked her parents, and they welcomed me into their home. As the summer went on, our love for each other deepened. We typically spent our time in the Holliston area, occasionally venturing out into neighboring towns in my mom's car.

*Bea with me at my home in Massachusetts, Summer 1980*

One day Bea rode her ten-speed bike over to the wood shop to see me where I had been working for my older brother's friend, Doug. I did less than acceptable work that day. Doug was gone for half the day and left me instructions to drill half-inch holes into some custom trim moulding he'd made. Being fixated on Bea, many of the holes I drilled ended up with chipped edges, as Doug would point out in front of us upon his return.

"I can't use these!" he said with near disgust.

"I have to remake nearly all of these," tossing a bad specimen onto the table.

It's a good thing Doug was easy-going, and he liked my work prior to this. I tried to explain my substandard work, half-heartedly, by blaming the drilling results on the knotted wood. Thankfully, Doug's disposition quickly shifted, given he was obviously enamored with Bea's presence. He wasn't used to having a beautiful woman in his wood shop. It was clear all was forgiven when Doug half-jokingly said,

"No working while Bea is here!"

We agreed with a smile and a sigh of relief. Doug smiled at Bea and me and asked us about our new relationship.

Doug was a great guy to work for. He produced high-quality furniture, and I mainly performed the surface finishing work – sanding, staining, and applying the clear coats to the finished product. He was fun to work with, too. He had a zany sense of humor like me, and he paid well. The shop was in the basement of the old four-story Goodwill Shoe Factory where they manufactured leather shoes and boots in the first half of the 1900's. We occasionally found the relics of the shoe-making craft in nooks and crannies around the shop. The ceilings were low, and I had the fortune of being short enough at 5'4" to walk under the beefy wooden ceiling beams without ducking down. Doug was slightly taller and not as fortunate.

Doug was Italian with thick, black, tightly curled hair. We wore thin lab coats in the shop to keep our clothes clean. One day as I watched Doug getting covered in sawdust while using the table saw, I couldn't help chuckling over his appearance. He looked like a mad scientist, with his lab coat, round eye goggles and curly, somewhat disheveled hair covered in sawdust. That was a good summer job, and one I often returned to while in town during college breaks.

Leaving Bea for my sophomore year of college was heart-wrenching. During our last week together that summer, my stomach was in knots over our impending separation. Bea was still in high school and felt her parents would not allow her to move to Florida with me. Part of me understood that she wouldn't be able to move away from her parents until she turned 18 and graduated from high school. Still, there was another part of me that knew deep in my heart that leaving for such a long time and being so far away would be an unbearable strain on our relationship, one that I cherished deeply.

Bea was my true love that summer and we kept in touch often while I was away at school in the fall. I enrolled in only four classes that semester instead of the usual five or six, since I knew I needed some time to emotionally recenter myself while missing Bea.

When Christmas break came around, I was happy with my grades and was excited to go home, relax, and see Bea, my family and my friends. I was also looking forward to the crisp winter air and New England environment. Holliston, Massachusetts, and its surrounding area is beautiful, with hills, lush trees, lots of granite, and old vintage homes. I missed that familiarity since Daytona Beach has a completely different environment.

My whole family got together at the house in Holliston over the holidays. We always had a good time together and that Christmas was wonderful. For Christmas eve, Mom and Dad would typically prepare a buffet of miniature sandwiches from Russell's Supermarket downtown, along with homemade items. My sister AnneMarie brought her boyfriend, Mark, who my dad didn't like. I had Bea with me, who my dad did like.

I also spent time with my best friend, John, and his family, whom I loved. I felt like an honorary part of John's family. His mom and dad were kind, engaging, and very welcoming. John's older sister Jean was in my high school class, and his younger sister Mary was still in high school with John. John and I played guitar together at his house, often at the request of his family. We also played casually at parties, enjoying singing in harmony and filling out the songs with catchy guitar riffs. It was all such a wonderful time. While it was cold in Massachusetts, I put up with the weather knowing it was temporary. Snow, ice, and steel-gray skies were common in the winter, and I knew I would be back in sunny Florida soon enough.

Bea and I spent as much time together as we could, but we both felt the strain that being so far apart was causing. When at Bea's house, we could talk privately and comfortably in her bedroom. Her family's modest two-story house was set back on a half-acre lot on Washington Street, the busy main road through town. While sitting on Bea's bed facing her in a chair, Bea reiterated that her parents would almost certainly not permit her to move to Florida, given she was not 18.

Even though I understood the concerns her parents would have had, not to mention the legal ramifications of taking a minor out of high school and moving her hundreds of miles away from home, my heart still ached at the thought of being separated from Bea. I wish we had talked about it with her parents, or at least given some thought about how we could move her down to Florida when she graduated from high school. My number one priority was finishing college and realizing my dream of working for NASA. For better or worse, that focus limited my scope of vision. With all the obstacles facing us at that age, I couldn't comprehend how we could have made it work for both of us.

We loved each other, and again our hearts broke as we parted for my return to Florida after Christmas. I enrolled in a full load of five classes for the spring semester, one of which was Statics, my first core engineering class. I enjoyed learning the methods and equations required to analyze the forces, stresses, and strains on structures like trusses, bridges, airplane wings, etc. I also had Physics II and a math class. Physics was very interesting, as we covered electricity, magnetism, fluid flow, thermal dynamics, optics and more. The computer programming class I took the semester before was okay, but it wasn't something I would want to do as a career. I had another computer class this semester, and it would be important for analyzing structures that were too complicated to analyze by hand. I discovered I did like writing computer code.

Bea and I wrote letters to each other, but we didn't seriously discuss having her come and live with me once she graduated from high school. The reservation I silently harbored about her moving down was that I was scared I wouldn't keep my grades up and that our relationship might interfere with my dream of working for NASA. My fears were valid, but unfortunately, I let my concerns prevent me from discussing this with Bea or even asking advice from people I trusted. I recognize now that expanding my thinking might have really helped.

I opened a letter from Bea one afternoon as I was walking across campus to the university center. It was a beautiful spring day, and the air was warm. I think I had numbed myself over the weeks to what I knew would likely happen at some point. Bea told me she had met another guy. I stopped walking and read the letter in its entirety. His name was Gary, and she was feeling their friendship growing into something more. I knew I couldn't hold her in our now floundering relationship. Because I was so far away from her, I wasn't a very involved boyfriend, and I knew it. With a heavy heart I accepted her wish to date him.

At that time in my life, I didn't have the wisdom gained from experience to see what I was losing, nor the maturity to make our relationship blossom. Bea and I had seemed perfect for each other as we fell in love over the summer and carried on through the fall.

My focus on achieving a dream career at NASA, though, was still very much alive. During the mid-semester spring break, I took a bus tour of NASA's Kennedy Space Center an hour away. I wanted to see the brand-new Space Shuttle *Columbia* on the launch pad at Kennedy which was scheduled to blast into orbit in a week or two. This would begin the new era of the Space Shuttle program. As the bus crawled slowly by the launch pad, I took a photo of this amazing shuttle, majestically poised and waiting. I wanted to be a part of this program with every bone in my body.

*Space Shuttle Columbia on the launch pad for her maiden voyage, Spring 1981*

Fast forwarding a couple of weeks, fifteen other students and I struggled to maintain focus on our instructor as the clock ticked agonizingly closer to *Columbia's* planned launch time while the TV in the corner sat lifeless. As promised, our instructor turned the TV on five minutes before the launch, and we all breathed a sigh of relief.

This was a historic moment for NASA. *Columbia's* launch was the inaugural flight of the Space Transportation System (STS).

# BEATRICE

*What would the launch look like?* I wondered.
*Will we be able to see the shuttle rise through the sky outside?*

The Space Shuttle was designed to enter Earth orbit eight minutes after launch. Once in orbit, *Columbia* would begin two days of testing of the shuttle's systems, including opening the cargo bay doors to space. After the orbital checkout phase of the mission, *Columbia* would embark on the most dangerous part of its mission – re-entering the atmosphere at 17,000 miles per hour. This would put the tile heat shield to the test. The shuttle would reach 2,700 degrees Fahrenheit and then glide unpowered through the lower atmosphere and land on a runway. This mission was designated STS-1, representing the first flight for the Space Shuttle program.

Holding my breath in the dead-silent classroom, the three main engines ignited and seconds later the shuttle leaped off the pad when the two solid rocket boosters blasted to life. Clapping and cheering, our eyes were glued to the TV as *Columbia* cleared the launch tower and rocketed upward. Given we were only 60 miles north of the launch site, we all raced onto the concrete sidewalk just outside the classroom to see if we could view the shuttle race skyward. My eyes grew as big as saucers when the shuttle appeared right in front of me to the south, blasting a thick plume of white vapor in its wake. The shuttle rose swiftly upward in an arc, on its way to meet the edge of space somewhere well beyond the clouds.

Like many of the other students, I stood there amazed and proud of what NASA was doing. I fervently wanted to be a part of this program.

When the semester was over, I had successfully completed my sophomore year and was on my way back home to Massachusetts to work at Doug's wood shop again in the old shoe factory during the summer.

By that time, Bea was dating Gary seriously. I didn't know much about him, except that Bea liked him, he lived near Holliston, and he was working full-time. Bea and I spent some time together but being just friends was hard for both of us, as we both felt the love between us was still alive yet drifting away from us like a ghost. I couldn't help grasping for the support I needed to keep from losing her forever. Bea was out of high school by that point. I dared to imagine the huge change of having Bea living with me in Florida and venturing into a happy, loving life together.

One evening while visiting with my dad, I approached him with the idea. To my utter surprise he abruptly shut it down. I felt as if all hope for Bea and I was gone. I expressed my feelings for her, but Dad wasn't happy with the idea of Bea and I living together. Lacking the self-confidence to follow my own heart, I felt powerless to broach the idea with Bea. Instead, I looked to the future, knowing that I would one day fall in love with someone else in Florida, or after graduation from college.

Later in life I discovered, like many people do, that I often gave more credence to other people's opinions about women I was interested in rather than following my own heart. This was especially true throughout the first half of my life, and I did this repeatedly. The result was I could barely get out of my head and approach these opportunities with my heart.

My relationship with Bea revealed to me the qualities that a loving, healthy relationship embody. Although our time together was brief, the ease in which we related to each other, our common values and aspirations, and our undeniable depth of caring for each other painted the picture of what I wanted in a future relationship. Bea had a heart of gold. She was kind and compassionate, patient, and smart. Not only did I choose to embody these noble qualities within my own character, but I found I instinctively looked for these qualities in all my future relationships. At the same time, I couldn't help but let Bea go. Bea and Gary married in a couple of years and began a family.

It is also very clear to see that I had an unwavering commitment to becoming a NASA engineer as I forged on into my junior year of college. I recognized that a deep calling within me held every facet of my being focused on school and my dream. I stayed centered on this path and the fruits of my labor joyfully manifested in just over a year.

# 7

# INTERNING AT NASA

The 30-foot high, 15-foot wide, double doors to the testing room looked like they could withstand an atomic blast.

*What's behind these doors?* I wondered, staring up at them.

*Nothing in this test complex is small,* I thought as I looked at two other equally large doors along the wall, and at the huge domed, cylindrical chamber in the corner of the room.

Stew Meyers, the man who hired me for this NASA internship over the phone, brought me to this complex to support his sounding rocket nose cone ejection test. A sounding rocket uses a variety of scientific instruments to measure conditions in the upper atmosphere or space for about 20 minutes during its quick sub-orbital flight.

Amazed at what I saw in this test complex, I was eager to learn about it. I'm glad Stew allowed me to just take it all in ... and there was a lot to take in. I walked a few feet from the door and peered into another tall, expansive room. Twelve-foot-wide blue chambers filled the room. Each chamber had a huge circular door. One chamber with bundles of wires plugged into the side was audibly venting a white, quickly dissipating gas into the air, making the scene perfect for a science fiction movie. At the far end of the room was a wall of green, opaque windows, which I would later learn were part of a large cleanroom used to assemble spacecraft.

"Stew, what are those chambers for?" I asked curiously.

"The blue ones and that huge one in the corner are thermal vacuum chambers," he said.

My eyes got wide as I realized the enormity of the dome-covered chamber. Stew said the chamber extended down 15 feet to the floor below. The chamber had many large metal ventilation ducts arcing down from its lower section, giving it an eerie spider-like appearance.

The thermal vacuum chambers simulate the vacuum and extreme temperatures of space. All spacecraft and science experiments bound for low Earth orbit or beyond eventually find themselves in one of these chambers, or similar smaller ones, for functional testing.

Looking down to the other end of the hall was another huge room. I had been told that the largest cleanroom in the world, by volume, stretching eight stories high, was in there.

*I'd love to see what's in THAT cleanroom!*

NASA Goddard Space Flight Center, in Greenbelt, Maryland, consisted of about 30 buildings at the time, and I was standing at the center of its four-building Integration and Test Complex. I only saw three of the four large buildings from where I was standing. In these buildings, sounding rockets, scientific instruments, and large spacecraft can be assembled and test-verified for every phase of their mission to ensure their survivability and functionality, starting with the intense vibration of launch.

Our sounding rocket sat cradled on its dolly outside the tall doors. About 12 feet long and 18 inches in diameter, this was the "payload section" of the sounding rocket. It would contain scientific instruments and a parachute. The two 10-foot long rocket fuel stages, also called "boosters," holding the aerodynamic stabilization fins were not attached. Our gold-colored pointed payload section was dwarfed by the size of the room, and it appeared to be the only flight-bound item in the area.

Stew had me following every phase of this rocket's mechanical development, and I was excited to know I would be following it to NASA's Wallops Flight Facility on Virginia's eastern shore in a couple of months to witness the launch.

One of the test facility technicians and I rolled the rocket dolly away from the large doors when they were ready to be opened. After moving the rocket, he joined another technician to pull on the doors' big, round plungers that latched the doors together. Leaning back hard while holding the plungers with outstretched arms, the technicians pulled the behemoth doors slowly open. The room inside was as tall as the doors, but modest in depth. I walked to the railing six feet inside of the door line and looked down to see what I was told was a vibration table. A three-foot diameter drive motor was connected to the left side of a large, square, steel-looking table.

"Anything flying into space goes through a vibration test to verify its ability to survive the intense launch vibration caused by rocket engines," the technician asserted.

I was excited to be in this test complex. The huge doors, the strange-looking vibration table, the thermal test chambers, and everything about it was intriguing.

The technician brought over a beefy-looking Kevlar lifting strap and placed it on the floor by the dolly. Using a handheld controller, the technician maneuvered an overhead crane out of the testing room, or "test cell," and lowered the crane hook to within reach. Soon the rocket payload section was rotated upright using the crane and then lowered down to the vibration table and securely fastened to it using large bolts.

I felt like a kid seeing Disneyland for the first time, as I looked down at the 12-foot-tall rocket standing straight up on the vibration table. I knew this was where I was meant to be.

I'll pick up with the countdown for this exciting nose cone ejection test later in this chapter.

My tenure at Goddard started a month earlier. Because of the high security associated with NASA Goddard Space Flight Center, my initial stop was the badging office. Within a half-hour the office had me ready to go.

"Here's your temporary badge, Mr. Martins. Your permanent badge will be ready in a week or two, and you will be notified," the female security officer said with a welcoming smile.

I clipped the badge to my shirt pocket and walked toward the office exit, pulling on my coat. Outside, I stood with the other newly badged students in the mildly cold January air. A large American flag waved gently overhead 20 feet away, marking the entrance to Goddard. Under it stretched a large flat concrete panel proudly displaying the famous NASA meatball logo with the words "Goddard Space Flight Center" spelled out next to it in bright blue letters.

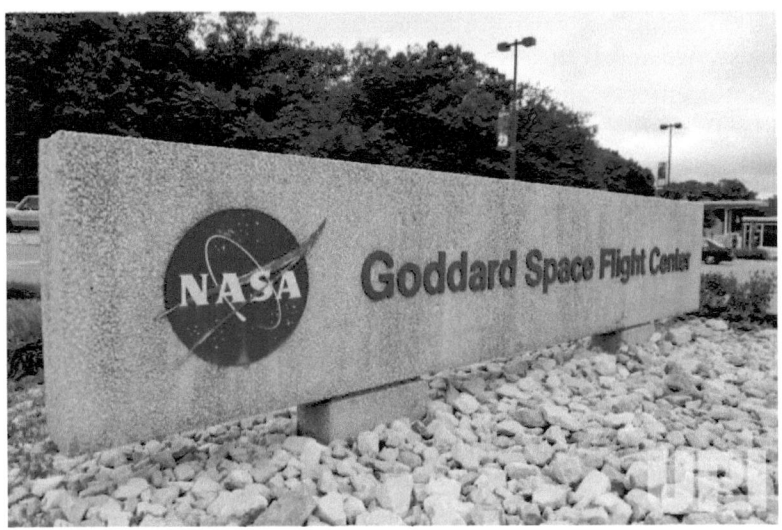

*Goddard's main entrance sign (Photo credit: NASA).*

With about twenty other students, I took a seat in one of the chairs lining the conference room walls, while other students sat at the long mahogany conference table. We were in Building 1, the Human Resources building, for our orientation. The experience felt surreal. I excitedly looked around the room at the other equally excited interns and took in the pictures on the walls – rocket launches, headshots of some of Goddard's past center directors, photographs of spacecraft missions and buildings at Goddard. The room expressed the tall mystique of NASA.

*I made it to NASA Goddard,* I thought proudly. I embraced the reality, smiling from ear to ear, in gratitude and near-disbelief.

The Human Resources branch head welcomed us to Goddard, sharing that Goddard's internship program was a major pathway for hiring college graduates. As he exited the room, I knew I had made the right choice to delay college graduation by a semester to get my foot in the door as a NASA intern. When I brought up the internship idea with Dad a couple of years before, he accepted my choice to apply to the program, even though he felt graduation was a higher priority. I'm glad I listened to my gut feeling and applied for internships every semester.

Next, we received a 45-minute orientation detailing our internship requirements and the opportunities available for learning about Goddard's work on-center. "As you may know," the presenter began, "Goddard is home to one of the nation's largest teams of scientists, engineers, designers, and technologists. Here we innovate cutting-edge science instruments and spacecraft to study the Earth, the Sun, our solar system, and the Universe!"

I was thrilled beyond words. I was being handed a world of opportunity.

Soon I was back in my car driving up the street to meet my boss, Stew, in Building 5. Walking along the sidewalk toward the side of the building, I could see the building had been in use for a long time. Weather and sun gave its pastel yellow color a worn, yet enduring appearance. The front of the building was brick with dozens of large windows lining the three floors, providing the regal look I imagined for such a prestigious center.

When I found my destination, Room W34, my heart started pounding. I peered in the door at the large open area. A 10-foot long, wooden conference table occupied the center of the room, while office doors lined the walls. I walked in and found Stew's office in the far left corner. As the Mechanical Engineering Branch Head for the Special Payloads Division, Stew's office was the largest.

My expectation of what a branch head's office would look like was instantly shattered, as I saw him at his desk and knocked on the door. I imagined his office would be neat and well-organized. Instead, tall, well-balanced stacks of paper and folders consumed the tables and chairs almost everywhere. Various metal parts filled the remaining spaces, including the tops of his filing cabinets. I walked toward him with a smile.

"Hi, I'm Greg Martins, reporting for work."

"Hello, Greg. Welcome!" he said as he stood, reaching out to shake my hand.

He was happy to see me, putting me at ease. Stew gestured toward one of the unoccupied chairs, chuckling as he apologized for the state of his office.

Stew had a kind face. He wore thick glasses, and had short brown, slightly graying hair with a small, straight mustache. Sporting a pot belly, he was dressed very casually, as evidenced by a worn-through elbow on his aging sweater.

"I have another Embry-Riddle student interning here – Alan Lindenmoyer."

"Yes, I've seen Alan in some of my classes," I said, enjoying the brief bonding moment with Stew.

I felt motivated to start working when he said the branch had a lot of new, very interesting work.

"The staff is now developing reusable carriers to take sounding rocket experiments into space using the cargo bays of the new Space Shuttles, and I'd like you to become familiar with them. We're doing this in addition to our usual work of designing, assembling, testing, and launching sounding rockets," he said with a confident attitude.

*Working on Sounding Rockets AND Space Shuttle projects – great! I can't believe my luck,* I thought.

The nose cone ejection test Stew referred to during our pivotal call last semester would be taking place in a month.

Stew then graciously gave me an hour of his time showing me around and introducing me to people. I was happy to meet two other interns who were now having their second internships with Stew. The three of us were the only young folks in the branch. The remaining dozen or so staff members were male, senior engineers, designers, and draftsmen, except one who was in his 30's. Everyone seemed relaxed and happy, offering me genuine smiles and welcoming attitudes.

Down the hall was the fun stuff – sounding rockets. Stew opened the double doors to the "Integration Room," as it was called, and I saw three sounding rockets in various levels of assembly. They were gold colored, about 15 inches in diameter, and of varying lengths, each resting on a work stand that doubled as a wheelable dolly.

*I'm finally getting to see the real thing,* I marveled as I walked in.

I would have been happy to spend the rest of the day there.

"These are sounding rocket payload sections. They hold the experiments bound for the upper atmosphere or space," Stew said. "The long rocket boosters will attach to the lower ends of these."

Two technicians were busily working on the rockets but took time to welcome me to the branch with a smile.

*Example sounding rocket "payload section"*
*(Photo credit: NASA)*

The sounding rocket payload section in the image above is an assembly of several canisters which are bolted together at the visible rows of holes. A lifting sling is attached in two places near the nose cone.

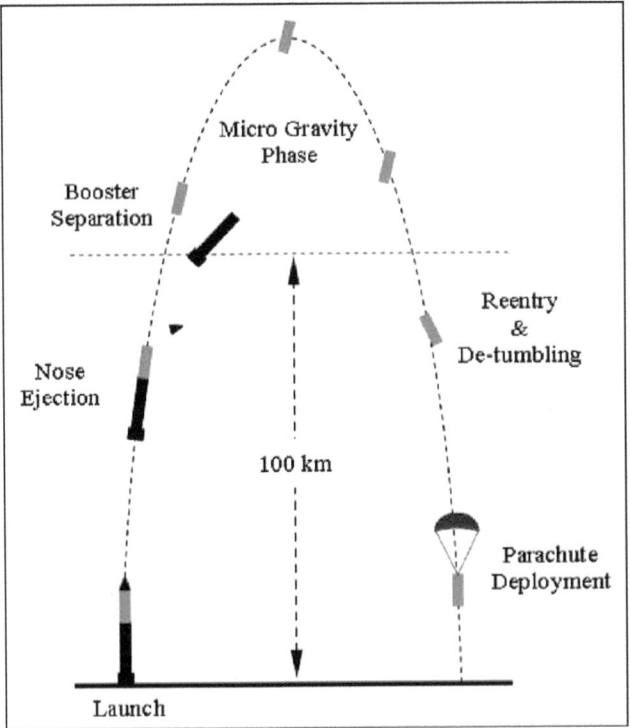

*Example of sounding rocket mission profile (www.researchgate.net).*

    A sounding rocket flight can take between 30 to 60 minutes from launch to parachute deployment, and may travel down range 40 to 100 miles, depending on how high the rocket flies. The rocket boosters that carry the fuel will drop back to Earth when they are empty, leaving the payload section to continue rising until gravity stops it and pulls it back to Earth. The payload section's path is similar to how a baseball travels in an arc when thrown into the air.

    Fast forwarding a month to the sounding rocket nose cone ejection test, I offered to help where I could, and I was invited to come down to the floor below where the rocket was mounted to the vibration table. The vibration test cell smelled of machine oil. Everything in the room, including the control room, appeared old, but solid and functional. The tall walls of the test cell and the control room were painted a light pastel green.

"Why are the test cell doors so thick," I asked a technician during a break in the preparations.

"Sound suppression," he replied.

"At full test levels, the closed doors keep the vibration test noise down to an acceptable level up on the main floor. It's amazing how loud a random vibration test can be," he said, grabbing and waving his earmuffs.

When the ejection test was moments away, I went back up to the landing on the floor above where the nose cone was nearly at eye-level.

After a short countdown on the lower floor, two explosive charges let out a bang. The nose cone separation band flew out into a net, and the nose cone sprang straight up and away. Then the nose cone slowly fell back a foot or so, dangling safely by the cable attached to its tip.

*Wow, that was awesome.* I smiled with admiration.

That test might have been just another day in the office for Stew, but it was a test I will never forget. I knew I was in the right business. The test was fun and satisfied my techy, engineering-oriented brain. I felt confident that with training and experience, I could someday run tests like this.

Much of my work for the semester centered around managing the fabrication and storage of sounding rocket parts. Manufacturing occurred in the huge machine shop at the other end of the building. The shop was equipped to manufacture large spacecraft. Much of the large Solar Maximum Mission spacecraft, which launched into Earth orbit in 1980, had been manufactured there. Thanks to this sounding rocket project, I realized how much I enjoyed working with people, hardware, and managing segments of projects. Years later, I also realized that what I learned about parts manufacturing, inspection, and processing from this experience would benefit me in many future projects.

In addition to my sounding rocket work, I happily assisted with two other projects scheduled to fly in Space Shuttles within a year or so. Each Space Shuttle had a cargo bay, also referred to as a "payload bay." It was big enough to hold something the size of a school bus and was used to fly science experiments, technology tests, and satellites into orbit.

I enjoyed Stew as a boss. He was laid back, highly experienced, and competent. By the way his peers interacted with him, I could see he had gained their respect as an engineer and a leader. Stew had some captivating hobbies as well. On occasion, he drove me home in his tiny MG sportscar, which he said he liked working on. He was also an aviation enthusiast, and he revealed that he enjoyed flying in the back seat of open-air biplanes. Fortunately for me, Stew's interest in airplanes led him to appreciate Embry-Riddle Aeronautical University and its intern applicants.

I finished my Spring co-op assignment by witnessing the launch of our sounding rocket at NASA's Wallops Flight Facility on Virginia's eastern shore, four hours from Goddard.

*Our sounding rocket on launch rail at NASA Wallops Flight Facility, Wallops Island, VA (Photo credit: NASA)*

At Wallops, I learned how sounding rockets get fully assembled and launched. The black and white rocket boosters with fins in the image above contain the solid rocket propellant for thrusting the payload section to the desired altitude. The image shows the rocket mounted to its launch rail. When the rocket was ready for launch, the building's walls and ceiling were rolled back on tracks, exposing the rocket and the launch system. The launch rail was then rotated to the proper launch angle.

At Wallops I was given some minor work to help with launch preparations, but I often had down time which I spent listening to others discussing the work at hand. I grew to appreciate the complexity of the mission.

Launch was scheduled for a few hours after dark. A camera mounted on the end of the payload section would bring the view of Earth to our video monitor once the second stage rocket booster was pushed away.

After a brief countdown, the rocket shot off the launch rail in a blaze of light, quickly entering the thick clouds of the night sky. My heart pounded as I silently cheered the rocket on. As I stared out at the launch pad, I was momentarily transfixed as I watched the rocket smoke float slowly downwind. I managed to take a photo of the launch through the window next to a video monitor. See below.

*NASA Sounding Rocket launch I witnessed, Wallops Flight Facility*

Unfortunately, when the second stage rocket booster jettisoned away from the payload section, the electrical connector did not separate, causing the electrical cable to tear apart. The force from this imparted a huge torque on the payload section and caused the rocket to spin uncontrollably.

My heart sank as all ten rocketeers sadly acknowledged the mission was a failure. Looking at the video screen, it was clear that the payload section camera was rotating around and around over the sunlit Earth.

I felt better hearing the lead experimenter and NASA mission manager discussing a re-flight.

Despite the disappointment of the failed sounding rocket mission, I left Goddard for the semester feeling very happy with my internship. The fascinating projects and the outstanding folks at Goddard made it a great place to work. It's not surprising that Goddard was rated one of the best federal agencies at which to work. Stew's staff also enjoyed training us interns to be the next generation of branch engineers. Stew was pleased with my progress and invited me to come back in the fall for another internship. I gratefully accepted!

# 8

# REMOTE VIEWING AND ASTRAL EXPLORATION

I climbed into bed, eagerly anticipating my girlfriend Katherine's "astral" arrival. We agreed that she would attempt to astral project to me this week from her home miles away, and try pulling me, in my astral body, out of my physical body.

*I hope this works,* I thought eagerly, as I surrendered to the moment.

I was working at NASA during my first internship, and I was at my apartment in Silver Spring, Maryland. Katherine and I were both interns and we had met at NASA a couple of months before.

I hadn't been able to achieve an OBE on my own, so Katherine was going to try to help me out ... literally!

Experience told me that my consciousness would go with my astral body, so this would be my first conscious OBE if we were successful.

*I bet she will come tonight. She's more psychically active during the full moon!*

With the moon as my silent ally, I planned to stay awake as long as possible in hopes of her arrival.

I knew that her attempt to pull me out of body would be successful only if I was deeply relaxed and had loosened my astral limbs within my physical body. As I described earlier in my "developing intuition" chapter, I learned I could move my astral limbs with my breath or simply with my intention.

After relaxing and going through my preparatory steps, I was ready for Katherine. I was lying on my back, eyes closed, when suddenly I felt a distinct tug on my astral foot.

*Katherine is here!* I rejoiced, even as I did my best to temper my excitement. Another tug followed, then another. With each tug, my astral foot and leg moved upward by a few inches and then slowly fell back to my body like a feather.

*I know it's her astral hand pulling on me, but I can't sense her individual fingers, or my individual toes, for that matter. I do feel the pressure of her hand.*

Katherine then tried pulling my astral foot straight out the bottom of my physical foot. I sensed my astral leg stretching like rubber. I was familiar with this feeling from my past experiences, so I lay quietly like a patient having a medical exam. The stretching is an odd feeling, but not unpleasant. Unfortunately, only my astral foot and leg were moving with Katherine's repeated tugs. I was hoping that, instead, my entire astral body from head-to-toe would move with her tugs and I would slide easily out of my body like a hand from a glove.

Next, my astral hand became her focus, rising upward with her invisible pulling motions. My forearm followed along, mimicking what my physical body would do if pulled on. As with my foot, my hand and arm slowly fell back when she let go.

Katherine pulled on a few more body parts. We laughed the next day when recounting her pulling on one in particular.

I resigned myself to the obvious conclusion that I wasn't going to slip out of my body, despite Katherine's persistent efforts to pull me out.

I fell asleep in awe that Katherine was psychically advanced enough to astral travel to me and perform our little experiment. This was the first time that someone I knew had pulled on my astral limbs. Her presence had felt peaceful and comfortable. In the past when unknown astral beings pulled on my loose astral limbs, I never felt negative or disturbing energy from the beings, but I sometimes called on Jesus Christ to be with me for protection anyway.

The next day we met for lunch and excitedly described our experiences from the night before. Our recollections matched in every detail, validating the existence and capabilities of our astral bodies.

When Katherine and I met at NASA Goddard in early 1983 during my first internship, we clicked immediately. We both had strong interests in spirituality and metaphysics and were naturally drawn to each other. Katherine was very easy to be with. She was kind, happy, engaging, and we quickly grew to care about each other very much.

Katherine was interning in the Human Resources office as an employee development specialist. It was evident to me that Katherine cared deeply about what mattered to people. There was a big age difference between Katherine and me. She was 18 years older than I was and a world ahead of me, given she had three children. Her youngest daughter was eight at the time, and her middle son was in high school. The three of them lived in a stable, happy home environment together, though Katherine had weathered a challenging marriage that ended in divorce a few years prior. Her oldest had recently moved out of the house and was now doing well.

I was impressed that Katherine had shown the determination and ability to pursue a bachelor's degree in psychology and get accepted into the highly competitive intern program, all while raising her children as a single parent.

I was keeping a personal journal at the time and wrote down dozens of our experiences in practicing psychic skills together. Astral projection and remote viewing were two of our favorites. Remote viewing is seeing an event or object in the mind's eye that is not physically within sight.

By March the weather was often nice, and Katherine and I enjoyed having lunch together outside.

"Today involved another enchanting lunch," I wrote in my journal referring to Katherine. "I feel today, as I have lately, very psychically in-tune, very happy – like I'm living a fantasy. Life is beautiful. We're bringing out so much in each other."

A romance with Katherine was quickly developing.

One evening in April, I imagined my consciousness being in Katherine's house to see what she was doing. Katherine gave me permission to check in on her this way whenever I wanted. I was attempting remote viewing.

*This scene appears real enough. I'll just record what I'm seeing. She is cutting up paper at her dining room table. I'm glad she is standing, so I can see what she's wearing. I wonder why she's wearing an apron.*

Talking to Katherine on the phone a couple of hours later, we both delighted in the accuracy of my remote viewing.

"I was doing exactly that, Gregory. You were spot on."

Katherine had been in an apron cutting paper with scissors, preparing for her daughter's birthday party.

Katherine liked to call me Gregory sometimes, which was rather formal sounding, but it was endearing, and I liked it because only she referred to me that way.

This remote viewing session clearly demonstrated to me how detailed and accurate a clairvoyant experience can be. I didn't know Katherine was going to be preparing for her daughter's party or working with paper, further validating the experience.

Remote viewing has been used by the military for intelligence gathering and perhaps more so by police for helping to find missing children.

For example, in 1979 a remote viewer in the classified intelligence program, called Stargate, was able to help guide the CIA to a downed military aircraft. The remote viewer's success led the CIA to continue recruiting remote viewers into their Stargate program.

In 2011, a California court convicted a swindler of murder in a case that was solved partly, the lead police investigator said, with the help of remote viewing. Remote viewers saw the swindler had fled to the British Virgin Islands. He was indeed found there, arrested, and convicted.

I have found that remote viewing exercises are often only partially accurate. Still, I had some remarkable successes, and the examples I present in this chapter are my most accurate experiences.

After completing my first NASA internship, I ventured home to Massachusetts for a brief, but relaxing visit before returning to Embry-Riddle for a full summer of courses. One evening in Massachusetts, I had a particularly funny experience that spoke volumes about what others may have thought about me – or anyone else for that matter – working at NASA. My best friend John and I went out to a local restaurant that night. While ordering a couple of beers at our booth, John excitedly said to the young waitress, "My buddy works for NASA!"

She said "Ya, sure," and walked off to get our drinks.

I burst out laughing while John's excitement drained away in disbelief. I was surprised by her response, as well. I'm still not sure if she found it hard to believe that anyone roaming around our small town would work at NASA, or that I, in particular, worked there.

John and I enjoyed playing our guitars together for the week or two I spent at home. We especially enjoyed playing at parties with other friends who were also back from college.

As I started back to school that summer, I had eight more courses to take before I could graduate. Six were core engineering classes. I planned to take two classes in the Summer A term and three during Summer B, each term being seven weeks long. The compressed schedule and the highly technical nature of the classes I was taking meant I would be very busy, so I wouldn't be able to work at the math and physics tutor lab, or grade Physics 1 homework papers as I had done during my junior year. I was grateful to have had those jobs since they reinforced my education and I got to work from home or on campus.

I rented a room from a former roommate at a Daytona Beach apartment complex I enjoyed as a junior. Everything was falling into place and Katherine and I kept in touch regularly.

Because Katherine had given me permission to practice remote viewing with her as my target any time I wanted, I spontaneously decided to try another remote viewing session to her house one weekend morning. I closed the door to my bedroom and sat on my bed with my back against the wall. The sun was streaming in. I can't recall if I kept my eyes open or closed, but sitting up was my preferred position for alertness. I relaxed my body and opened each of my seven main chakras to enhance my intuition.

I put my mind on Katherine hoping to see what she was doing. I saw her fixing the ruffled white collar of a purple shirt she was wearing. Since I hadn't seen Katherine wearing a ruffled collar in the past, I thought I may be seeing this wrong. She appeared to be wearing a dark skirt, as well. I kept my attention on Katherine for about 15 minutes.

Later, when I told Katherine over the phone what I saw during my remote viewing session, she excitedly affirmed my experience – she was wearing exactly what I had seen! She said she had bought a new dress with a ruffled white collar, a purple top, a belt, and a lower portion that was black. This was an exact match for what I clairvoyantly saw. I was amazed.

This experience reinforced my belief that our consciousness and mind can travel instantaneously with the speed of thought. I did not feel any of my astral body leave my physical body to travel to Katherine's house for this exercise.

In the fall I returned to NASA for my second internship with Stew Meyers and the Mechanical Engineering Branch of the Special Payloads Division. As in my first internship, I roomed with the same two NASA interns I lived with previously at a high-rise apartment complex in Silver Spring, Maryland. The Point apartments consisted of three huge, T-shaped, 20-story buildings adjacent to a wooded neighborhood 20 miles from NASA. We occupied a three-bedroom apartment on the 16th floor. My roommates had the same basic schedules as I did, and we got along great. I was particularly happy with the location of our apartment. I discovered a nearby wooded trail that led down to a quiet stream, and a large shopping complex was available right across the street.

At NASA I was thrilled to be immersed in developing Space Shuttle payloads. One of my projects was serving as the liaison between our branch and a university preparing a scientific experiment to fly in the newly created Get Away Special (GAS) program. The GAS program used uniquely designed canisters to inexpensively fly experiments into space in the Space Shuttle for students and scientists. The photograph below shows three GAS canisters with the extra functionality of opening lids. The university students and faculty I spoke with were as excited about the mission as I was. Our discussions centered around the electrical and mechanical interfaces to the GAS canister, as well as hardware development, and documentation.

*Three Get Away Special payloads in Space Shuttle Columbia's payload bay in orbit, STS-62, March 1994 (https://archive.org)*

My main project was in the newly developed Spartan program, which provided a low cost, quick turn-around method for placing scientific instruments into low Earth orbit for several days via the Space Shuttle. The Spartans were designed to operate autonomously in orbit for several days without the presence of a Space Shuttle nearby. The Remote Manipulator System (RMS) arm in a Space Shuttle would be used to put a Spartan overboard and retrieve it before returning to Earth. Spartans would be secured in the Shuttle Bay using a mechanism activated from inside the Shuttle's crew cabin.

This greatly increased observation time was very attractive to sounding rocket experimenters who were used to getting only about 20 minutes of observation time using sounding rockets.

My boss told me that GAS and Spartan projects would require branch engineers to access the Space Shuttles and the Shuttle launch pads while preparing the payloads for flight. I excitedly looked forward to doing that.

My task in the Spartan program during this internship was calculating the weight, center of gravity, and mass moments of inertia, collectively known as mass properties, for the Spartan 1 X-ray astronomy spacecraft. This payload was in the fabrication phase and was scheduled to fly in the Space Shuttle *Discovery* on the STS-51G mission in less than two years. The photograph below shows Spartan 1 during that mission while it was held on the end of *Discovery's* arm before being temporarily released into orbit.

*Spartan 1 spacecraft during STS-51G mission, June 1985*
*(Photo credit: NASA)*

To fulfill my task, I needed to determine the mass properties for every part or assembly in the Spartan spacecraft, which I dutifully logged into the pages of a large 3-ring binder. I learned about the materials, functionality, and detailed design of Spartan 1 in the process, which helped me in developing future Spartan missions in the years to come.

Meanwhile, Katherine and I were once again enjoying the romantic relationship we started in the spring. One weekend, Katherine and I went shopping at a mall and spent half the time going off in different directions.

*Katherine, I'm going to the mall grocery store,* I told her in thought, while she was off somewhere in the mall. By this time, we'd been separated for a half hour or more. I telepathically sent her an image of the grocery store as well, thinking she might receive the image more easily than if I simply sent her my thought. I felt fairly confident Katherine would sense my message, since we were in tune with each other's energy.

In the men's clothing section a while later, I stopped for a moment and stood motionless, attempting to tune into Katherine's whereabouts. I cleared my mind and let go of any tension in my body, putting my attention on my inner sight with eyes open. In a moment, my inner sight showed her in a Junior Miss clothing section of what I intuitively sensed was the Sears department store.

*She must be looking for clothes for her daughter. Well let's go there and see if I picked up on her correctly,* I thought with a smile.

I felt my chances of correctly sensing her true location were at least 50-50. When I arrived there, she wasn't anywhere to be seen.

*Drat. Oh well. It is possible she had been here, and I missed her,* I reassured myself.

Later when Katherine and I reunited in the mall, I told her about my remote viewing attempt. She smiled and jubilantly affirmed that she <u>did</u> go to the Sears Junior Miss department and bought several items.

"Ah, awesome," I chimed in, mentally giving myself a high five.

Katherine also revealed that she had intuitively picked up on me being at the grocery store earlier. I assumed the telepathic message and image I sent her helped with this.

We acknowledged that we were making good progress in our intuitive development, since we were having success even in the busy mall where other people's energies surrounded us everywhere. It was exciting to realize we no longer needed to rely on having a quiet, energetically clear environment for intuitive accuracy.

"Katherine, let's plan for you to astral travel to my apartment this weekend to see if we can observe each other's astral bodies."

"That sounds great. When do you want to try it?"

We planned for this to take place on Saturday at 9:30 a.m. I was excited for this experiment because I'd rarely seen astral forms, and when I had, the experiences were often very brief.

With my eyes open, I sat on my bed against the wall. I quickly achieved a centered, meditative state by relaxing my body and mind, and briefly clearing each chakra. In this state, I would be more energy-sensitive and intuitive.

I couldn't help but get excited anticipating Katherine's arrival when my clock reached 9:30. With a subdued morning sun blanketing the room, I suddenly felt an energy pressing firmly down on my crown chakra. It was slightly after 9:30.

*Katherine, I can feel you pressing down on my head,* I excitedly reported telepathically, thinking I might hear her voice in my head in response.

I didn't hear a reply, but I felt her press down on both of my hands immediately afterward. I felt this cycle repeat a couple of times.

Talking with Katherine on the phone later, she confirmed that she was brushing her hands down the sides of my energy field, starting at my head.

"Ah, that matches what I felt," I said with delight. "Although I didn't sense you brushing your astral hands against the sides of my body."

Katherine also saw my energy field. She reported that my heart chakra glowed pink, and my crown and third eye were a purplish/white color. I reported that I unfortunately didn't see hers. She must have been right in front of me, given she was using both of her astral hands to brush down the sides of my body. I found all this very exciting, regardless.

"Katherine, you're amazing," I said with admiration.

To this point, I've focused on remote viewing and astral activities that were intentionally initiated. This isn't the only way these events can occur. Sometimes we might find ourselves remotely viewing a location or astral traveling without our knowledge or focused intention. I experienced this firsthand in 2000.

I was a student in the five-day Gateway Voyage program at the Monroe Institute just south of Charlottesville, Virginia. The program was aimed at expanding our abilities to access multiple levels of consciousness. Robert Monroe, the institute's founder, was internationally known for his work using audio frequencies and sound patterns that can lead the brain to various states ranging from deep relaxation or sleep to highly expanded levels of consciousness. Having read Monroe's three books about his fascinating, often corroborated, OBEs, I wanted to further explore what the institute had to offer.

During one of the morning sessions, our group of students was treated to a surprise visit from Joe McMoneagle, one of the nation's most renowned remote viewers.

Joe shared his fascinating involvement in remote viewing as a member of the classified military intelligence program known as Stargate, which I mentioned earlier. This program spanned nearly two decades and was centered at Fort Meade in Maryland. Joe continued his work with remote viewing after the program ended. Of course, he wanted us to try remote viewing during our time together. I was seated a few tables back from the front, putting Joe about 20 feet from me.

Joe wrote the latitude and longitude on the white board for a location he wanted us to remote view. People were chatting, and Joe was about to start speaking.

*Wow, I wonder if I can do this. I've never attempted this using coordinates.*

Then, as I sat quietly waiting for Joe to speak, I saw the iconic yellow double arches of McDonald's fast-food restaurant in my mind's eye.

"Oh, are we going to that McDonald's again?" I jokingly blurted out.

Joe stared at me for a moment but didn't say anything.

Joe then gave us some encouraging guidance for our remote viewing attempt, and everyone began. The room went silent. I can't recall what I sensed over the next few minutes.

Then Joe revealed the location of the coordinates: the Gateway Arch in St. Louis, Missouri.

I was dumbfounded. I realized I had picked up on the Arch immediately, albeit what I sensed was only a partial perception. My experience that day illustrates how effortlessly our consciousness can remote-view a location without our focused intention. The McDonald's double arch was familiar to me, so my brain quickly showed me that.

*Gateway Arch, St. Louis, Missouri (https://places.travel)*

My remote viewing and astral practice sessions greatly expanded my understanding of these phenomenon. Katherine and I had vividly experienced the presence of each other's astral bodies and repeatedly demonstrated the validity of remote viewing. We also demonstrated that with practice, we could enhance our remote viewing ability.

At the end of my second internship at NASA, I shared with Katherine that I wanted to change the nature of our relationship from being romantic to more of a friendship. Because of the significant age difference between us, I was concerned this would prevent me from having the opportunity to start a family of my own someday. Katherine was heartbroken. I had mixed emotions about my choice because I cared deeply for Katherine.

Regrettably, I didn't have the awareness and insight to see the pain Katherine hid after our breakup. Instead, I went instantly to "just friends" mode, and I didn't treat her with the sensitivity she deserved regarding the loss she was feeling. Years later, it was clear to me that I owed Katherine an apology, and I offered her one. Katherine accepted my apology with tears in her eyes, and we talked about how we felt at that time. This belated apology offered at least some healing. I have long known Katherine as a true, deeply committed soul friend, and it's clear she weathered this trying time in our life-long relationship with an inner strength I can only admire.

Our relationship taught us the value of having a partner who is also interested in spirituality and metaphysics. It's how we both are wired, and our joy and sense of well-being is founded on it.

Thankfully, Katherine had other special relationships after ours, and she is very happily enjoying her children and grandchildren.

I'm grateful that Katherine and I have remained special friends, even after both of us retired from NASA and now live in different states. I always enjoy and appreciate our communication. Katherine is a model of integrity, unconditional love, and positive thinking.

I completed my second NASA internship in December 1983, having thoroughly enjoyed preparing several Space Shuttle payloads for flight. Stew and I both looked forward to my coming on board full-time in the spring after my final semester at Embry-Riddle.

# 9

## VISION QUEST

What do you want me to be aware of, Creator? What do you want me to be doing at this time in my life? This is the heartfelt prayer I offered frequently during my first Vision Quest, a profoundly meaningful ceremony at the beginning of my life-long walk with Native American spirituality.

Vision Quest sounded like a great idea, and I was gratefully experiencing one, praying alone on a blanket in the quiet, cool, sunlit woods of New York's Catskill Mountains. I was 27 years old and the next 24-hours were mine to peacefully and humbly connect with Creator, known by many as God, by myself. I had prepared for this traditional Lakota Sioux ceremony for a couple of months, following the gentle instructions of Mary Thunder, a very wise Native American elder I was blessed to encounter. As I learned more about her teachings during her deeply spiritual talks and events, she sparked a strong desire within me to actively participate in what she described. The Vision Quest naturally drew me.

Vision Quest ceremonies have been foundational to my spiritual path; I have attended many throughout my life. I love Vision Quest. Over the decades, this ceremony has repeatedly blessed me with profound awarenesses, guidance for my life, and spiritual connections with beings aligned with my soul purpose – extraterrestrials included. Vision Quest also often revealed personal issues I needed to look at while the healing energy of mother nature and the ceremony supported me. With Vision Quest, my life has been far more full, complete, and rewarding than it would have been otherwise.

I was raised Catholic, and my interpretation of Christ's teachings felt easily compatible with Native American spirituality. Both Christianity and Lakota spirituality emphasize one God, compassion, love, healing, and honoring all of God's creatures, God-loving spirits included.

During my Vision Quest, I gave Creator and nature my full attention, wanting to experience a deeper connection with them. I felt compelled to dive fully into the mysteries of life and create the space for Creator to show me whatever was mine to do, or to know.

Animals roamed those woods, but I felt completely safe. I had no food or water to tempt them, and I felt I would attract only what was for my highest good. I had come to trust Mary Thunder to lead ceremonies in safe, uplifting ways. If a bear came by, I could make some noise to dissuade it, or pray, or do both. Sitting alone on my blanket, I felt calm, peaceful, and happy to have an undistracted time with Spirit. The term "Spirit" encompasses Creator and all the spirit helpers who assist us.

I stayed awake for as long as I could, humbly praying, and often being without focused thought, as I opened myself to experiencing nature and Spirit from my calm, quiet state.

The sun was headed down a few hours after I got to my blanket, and the woods were quiet except for the movement of birds, small creatures, and the rustling of trees in the cool spring breeze. As night approached, the owls made their calls, and I drifted off into a deep, deep sleep.

It was then I had a special dream that stayed with me throughout my life. In the dream, I am on my blanket but it's daytime, with sunlight dancing on the ground and blue sky visible through the trees. All is peaceful. To my surprise, Mary Thunder is quietly sitting on a blanket just a few feet from me! She isn't looking at me, but she is smiling serenely, enjoying the peaceful setting as much as I am. This is special, having her here with me, because she is usually in the house in her sacred space maintaining her spiritual connection to all the Vision Questers. I see she has a few personal items neatly arranged on her blanket. In her presence I feel protected, cared for, and empowered.

When I awoke with the sunrise, I recalled the dream with a smile. I knew I had been blessed with an informative, positive, empowering dream. It showed me that Mary Thunder was clearly an inspired choice as a guide for my budding relationship with Native American spirituality. I always felt happy and cared-for during gatherings and ceremonies that she facilitated, so the dream was understandably affirming.

I was one of perhaps 10 others who went on a Vision Quest that week. It was Spring of 1988, and Mary Thunder had been providing this ceremony in the spring and fall for a couple of years. We were in a small town, ironically called Big Indian, at an old, rustic retreat center named Rudi's Big Indian Center.

*Rudi's Big Indian Center main house*

Swami Rudrananda – a renowned, American-born East Indian spiritual teacher known as "Rudi" – founded the property as an ashram in 1968. An ashram is a spiritual hermitage or a monastery in Indian religions. It became a simple retreat center around 1980, several years after his passing. Sacred, spiritually energetic Buddhist and Hindu statues and a 50-foot-tall stupa still occupied the property. A stupa is the most sacred monument found in ancient Buddhist countries. Filled with Buddhist relics and other holy objects, stupas emanate blessings and peace.

# VISION QUEST

*Me in front of the stupa at Rudi's Big Indian Center, 1988*

I was at least partially familiar with what to expect when I went on my Vision Quest because I supported a Big Indian Vision Quest six months earlier. In that role, I enjoyed clearing trails and Vision Quest sites in the woods and gathering wood for the Sweat Lodge fires. "Thunder," as we called Mary Thunder, said she loved Vision Quest because it offered a way for people to gain transformational insight into their lives in a short amount of time.

First-year Vision Questers, like me, went out on their blankets for just 24 hours, while second-year questers went out for 48 hours, and third-year questers spent 72 hours in the woods. I don't recall if there were any fourth-year questers who would have gone out for four days.

Folks coming to the ceremony were encouraged to arrive several days before it started to help prepare the land, Sweat Lodge, and facilities. I arrived at Big Indian several days before I was put out on the hill for my Vision Quest, giving me time to decompress from my busy day-to-day life and get accustomed to the energy of the land.

Thunder was kind, compassionate, wise, and humorous. I heard her speak to audiences a number of times and found her to be masterful at communicating a message of self-empowerment as she shared her own challenging past with acceptance and compassion.

Mary Elizabeth Thunder was part Cheyenne, part Irish, and adopted Lakota. She spent her early professional years as an administrator and counselor at various service organizations, including being assistant to the mayor of Indianapolis, Indiana. In 1981, she suffered a heart attack and had a near-death experience. In response to this, and at the bidding of her elders – Wallace Black Elk, Grace Spotted Eagle, Leonard Crow Dog and Rolling Thunder – she left her job in Dallas at the Urban Inter-Tribal Center of Texas to begin a life on the road as a teacher.

When I met Thunder, she had been on the road in her van for a couple of years with her partner, Jeffrey Hubbell, following Creator's guidance. She traveled across the country, providing talks, workshops, and ceremonies as a spiritual service to those who invited her. She was a Sundancer in the Lakota tradition and had spent almost two decades learning the ways of her elders and being in service to their needs.

*Mary Thunder and Jeffrey Hubbell, Mary's partner, at Rudi's Big Indian Center during Vision Quest, 1988*

# VISION QUEST

Mary Elizabeth Grimes received her spiritual name "Thunder" from Chief Leonard Crow Dog, who adopted her into his family as his niece in 1975. Chief Leonard Crow Dog, a renowned spiritual leader and Native American rights activist, lived on the Rosebud Indian Reservation in South Dakota. Thunder recounted him saying that Spirit said she had the ability to see, hear, and interpret for the spirits and that she came into this life to be a powerful bridge between cultures and assist people in becoming the best they could be. The word "spirits" refers to non-physical beings. Over the years, I grew to see just how fitting Chief Leonard's vision of Thunder was. More than once, she had been referred to as a teacher's teacher.

In those days, Mary Thunder's chosen path was full of difficulty. Even with the support of her full-blood Lakota elders, Thunder endured significant rejection and hardship from many Lakota for carrying a Sacred Pipe, or "Canupa" in the Lakota language (pronounced Chah-nu-pah), and for attending ceremonies on the reservations. Women and non-full blood traditional Lakota people had it pretty tough.

Additionally, most Lakota did not support sharing their spiritual ways with non-natives. This was understandable, given the religious and U.S. government oppression they'd endured for well over 100 years. It wasn't until 1978 that the American Indian Religious Freedom Act (AIRFA) was passed into law. The AIRFA protected the rights of Native Americans to exercise their traditional religions by ensuring access to sites, use and possession of sacred objects, and the freedom to worship through traditional ceremonial rites. Before 1978, Native American religions were openly discriminated against.

Vision Quest, called "Hanblecha" in Lakota language, is one of the seven sacred rites, or ceremonies, of the Lakota Sioux nation. The seven rites are central to the Lakota for maintaining health, happiness, and a strong connection with the Creator, also known as the Great Mystery and Great Spirit, in the Lakota's words. "Wakan Tanka" is the Lakota way of referring to this one creative, higher consciousness in the Universe.

The seven rites of the Lakota were presented long ago by a supernatural being referred to as the White Buffalo Calf Woman, at a time when the Lakota were struggling and in need of much help. She came to them as a maiden, attired in white buckskin, carrying a bundle wrapped in buffalo hide. As the foundation for these seven rites, she brought them the Sacred Pipe, or Canupa. in Lakota language.

"Follow the way of this sacred Canupa, and you will walk in a sacred way upon the Earth," was the White Buffalo Calf Woman's guidance.

A Pipe Ceremony creates a powerful connection with Creator in ways that are truly mystical. The effects of the ceremony are often subtle but highly supportive, based on my experience.

The original Pipe still exists in South Dakota, under the care of Arvol Looking Horse. He is the current keeper and guardian of this sacred instrument, which has been passed down for generations in the Looking Horse family. The sacred Pipe is the holiest of items in Lakota tradition, and is always treated with reverence, per the instructions from the White Buffalo Calf Woman.

A Canupa's maroon-colored bowl is made of pipestone (catlinite), which is found only in Pipestone, Minnesota. The stem is made of wood. The bowl represents the female and the blood of the people. The stem represents the tree of life, the roots of our ancestors, and the male. When the two are connected, the Pipe becomes subtly active, acting as a strong link to Creator. Once connected, the Canupa is then filled by the Pipe carrier with a non-hallucinogenic blend of herbs. A traditional Lakota Pipe filling song would be sung during the filling, asking Creator to hear the words and hearts of those in the Pipe Ceremony. Lakota elders sometimes remind us to be careful of our thoughts when a Canupa has been filled, because every thought is a prayer.

The Vision Quest Ceremony and Sweat Lodge Ceremony, or "Inipi" Ceremony in Lakota, are two of the more common sacred rites.

The Sweat Lodge Ceremony is for purification and prayer. Hot rocks are brought into the lodge to produce steam and assist in the spiritual nature of the ceremony. A Sweat Lodge is typically made of slender pliable saplings, ideally from willow trees, that are secured into the ground, bent over, and tied together to form a dome shape. An opening is left in front as a door. Blankets are used to cover the lodge so it will be dark inside when the door flap, also made of blankets, is lowered over the door. Typically, the Pipe Ceremony is included in the Sweat Lodge Ceremony. Lakota sacred songs are sung in the lodge as well, including spirit-calling songs, Pipe-honoring songs, prayer-songs, thank you-songs, and more.

I have always found the Lakota sacred songs, Pipe Ceremonies and Sweat Lodge Ceremonies to be transformative and uplifting. When sung with heartfelt intention, the Lakota songs create a noticeable atmosphere of purity and connection to spiritual energy. Combining the songs with a Pipe Ceremony or a Sweat Lodge Ceremony brings additional health, help, and purification on mental, emotional, and physical levels. I have sometimes gone into Sweat Lodge Ceremonies with a weighty personal concern or emotional stress, and by releasing my concerns in the ceremony, I came out feeling much clearer and closer to a solution for my concern.

In the several days prior to my Vision Quest while at Big Indian, I could feel the sacred energy building. There were many causes of this.

To begin with, some questers had already gone out for their multi-day Vision Quests, so the Sacred Pipe had been filled and would stay filled until the last quester had completed their quest. I learned the Pipe's energy had a subtle spiritual influence on all of us, as that is the nature of the Pipe Ceremony.

Adding to the spiritual sense that surrounded us, the Sweat Lodge fire was burning, and it would stay lit until the last questers had returned from their Vision Quest. The fire was an energetic anchor for all the questers on the hill. It maintained the Vision Quest energy in conjunction with the Pipe's sacred role and Thunder's connection to the questers and Spirit.

Along with this, we were all participating in brief Sweat Lodge purification ceremonies each evening before dinner, which helped participants gently purify mentally, physically, and spiritually.

Another element was our being together at dinnertime. We all gathered in the large dining area each evening for an amazing meal, light socializing, laughter, and storytelling with teaching gems from Thunder. This helped us bond as a group.

"The kitchen is where the heart is," Thunder always said.

*An evening mealtime at Big Indian.*
*Thunder is standing in the center of photo between two seated women.*

The food was prepared with love and the sacred energy of the event was also supported every evening after dinner. Questers who needed to finish preparing for their Vision Quest would spend time in the large gathering room preparing "prayer ties" and other items. There, the purifying energy of burning sage, our inspired spiritual focus, the light conversations we engaged in, and the laughter we shared were fun, relaxing, and spiritually uplifting.

Each quester needed to secure 101 prayer ties on four separate yarn strings for their Vision Quest. The strings of prayer ties would be placed on the forest floor along the edges of the quester's blanket for their Vision Quest. Each prayer tie consisted of a small piece of cotton cloth with a pinch of tobacco.

When I made my prayer ties before coming to Big Indian, I placed a prayer, or prayerful thought into each pinch of tobacco. Because the prayer ties had prayers in them, I knew the four six-foot-long strings I was making would keep my blanket surrounded with positive energy and would also be a tangible material from which Spirit could sense my prayers and intentions. Questers would remain on their blankets for their entire Vision Quest.

There were more than 20 of us at this Vision Quest. Some were supporters, some were questers, and some traveled with Thunder and worked closely with her. Questers always helped as supporters before going up on the hill for their Vision Quest. Some folks worked solely in the kitchen, preparing nourishing meals, and some helped care for the children of questers and other supporters. Others, including me, cleared trails and Vision Quest sites, and gathered wood to use in the Sweat Lodge fire.

*Gathering wood for Vision Quest Sweat Lodge fire, 1988, with Butch Hennigan, a supporter who traveled with Thunder and Jeff.*

On the day of my Vision Quest, I formally asked Thunder, with tobacco in hand, if I could Vision Quest. Offering tobacco is customary in the Native American tradition when ceremony is involved. As with all questers, Thunder was looking for assurance from Spirit that the timing was right for me to go out on Vision Quest. Tobacco is sacred to the Lakota people, and it holds the prayers and intentions of the person who prays with it. While alone with her and her helpers, and after I silently prayed with the tobacco for my Vision Quest, she held my hands with the tobacco, and closed her eyes to see what Spirit would say. She opened her eyes, smiling, and said yes.

"Spirit is happy you're going out on Vision Quest, Greg."

Before going to the Sweat Lodge as my last stop before my Vision Quest, I prepared my bundle of items that would go with me to my Vision Quest site. I rolled out a thin plastic painter's tarp and spread my blanket on top. Then I unrolled my sleeping bag on it, placing my prayer ties and backpack of warm clothes, sage, and other items onto my sleeping bag. I folded the plastic over it all and secured it with rope. At my quest site in the woods, a portion of the tarp would keep the bottom of my blanket dry while the rest of the tarp was available to pull over me if rain came.

I excitedly went to the Sweat Lodge, bundle in hand, dressed in cut-off shorts with a towel flung over my shoulder. The Sacred Pipe that had been filled days ago had been brought from the house and placed on the Sweat Lodge altar as the central spiritual anchor for the ceremony.

Inside the Sweat Lodge, I sat with several other questers and supporters, plus Thunder, Jeff, and a singer/drummer. Thunder asked the fire tender who was standing just outside the door to bring in seven hot rocks. One-by-one, the rocks were brought in on a pitchfork and placed in the shallow pit centered in the lodge. At least the size of grapefruits, the rocks were heated in a fire a short distance outside the Sweat Lodge door. The Sweat Lodge central pit, door, altar and fire were traditionally arranged along a straight line in this order.

Once the bucket of water was placed inside the door next to Thunder, she asked for the door flap to come down, and the lodge went dark as night except for the orange glow of the rocks. We were ready to begin. Thunder wasted no time raising the energy with a few upbeat, wordless, vocalizations while feeding water to the hot rocks with a buffalo horn. The water exploded into steam as it hit the rocks, bathing us all in heat and moisture. Jeff and the singer began fervently beating their drums and singing earnestly in the ancient Lakota language. They sang several songs in a row, letting Spirit know we questers were coming to seek guidance for our lives and help with our prayers.

Once the singing stopped, Thunder said, "Honey, would you please pray for the questers."

It was then Jeff spoke to us in English.

"Great Mystery, please watch over these questers coming to you for guidance and support in their lives. Take care of them while they're on the hill…and I pray that the jackalopes stay away."

I heard Thunder chuckle, as Jeff continued.

"You know there's been sightings here of those horned beasts."

I was shaking my head, smiling in disbelief — laughing silently in the dark as sweat rolled down my face. I wondered if any of the questers would buy his story. I knew a jackalope was a fictitious creature having a jackrabbit's body and antelope horns.

Thunder then spoke out with a surprised, chuckling reprimand.

"Honey! Don't tell 'em that!"

Jeff's laughter likely alleviated all concerns the other questers might have had.

Thunder then asked a woman supporter in the lodge to pray for the questers. Her prayer was as heartfelt as Jeff's, but without attempting to arouse our insecurities. Next, Thunder asked me to pray.

"Greg, would you please pray for your Vision Quest?"

"Creator, Great Mystery, I come to you humbly seeking your guidance. Please watch over me and show me what you want me to be aware of."

An unexpected splash of water suddenly assaulted my face. Thunder had expertly hurled the water at me using her buffalo horn dipper in the pitch dark to assist her in connecting me more deeply with Spirit, my Vision Quest, and her energy. By doing this, she would always be subtly aware of my energy during my quest. All the questers got a chance to pray and connect with Thunder and the Vision Quest energy in this way.

We laughed, prayed, and passionately attempted to sing along with the Lakota songs, to embrace the experience, even though we didn't really understand 90% of the Lakota words. In no time, the door flap was opened, and it was time to go.

Outside after the brief Sweat Lodge Ceremony, I quietly changed into a clean shirt and pants behind a hanging tarp, avoiding eye contact with anyone nearby. Avoiding eye contact allowed us to maintain the deeper connection with Spirit made in the Sweat Lodge. I was excited, yet peaceful, and centered. All this felt very natural and integrative to me.

I was led by a man and a woman up the now familiar mountain path to my Vision Quest site. They were in a support role at that time, and they knew where my Vision Quest site was located. Thunder liked to have a male/female balance when the questers were led to their quest sites. My blanket was spread out waiting for me, with my four strings of prayer ties outstretched on the ground just outside the edges of my blanket. I was happy to finally arrive at my spot in the woods for my reverent time with Spirit.

It was that night when I experienced the special dream I described earlier in the chapter. I spent the next day on my blanket appreciating the good weather and being prayerfully open for further guidance or messages from Spirit. The sky was pure blue, spotted by clouds that slowly sauntered by. Like the clouds, meandering thoughts often floated through my mind.

Occasionally I heard the voices of those near the house off in the distance. All the questers on the hill would be coming down off our Vision Quests later that afternoon. It was an exciting day for that reason, and I imagined the overflowing energy of the people at the house. I knew the closing of the week's ceremony with the Pipe would happen around sunset, followed by the celebration dinner. I eagerly looked forward to both.

My thoughts came back to the woods as I was drawn to a deer jumping into view in the distance. The deer didn't see me. I watched it, my mind quiet. I was at peace. I didn't want to be distracted by my idle thoughts. Instead, I wanted to focus on the fine, gentle energy flowing though me. A subtle message or experience could reveal itself at any time, and I was paying attention. My experience the rest of the day was like that, sometimes redirected by significant thoughts and emotions about my life – the happy ones and the challenging ones. I did my best to let my true feelings arise as a gift of awareness. I didn't have any "aha" moments of sudden, unexpected realization, as I didn't come on this Vision Quest with any pressing questions about my life.

Sometime in the afternoon, a male and female supporter slowly approached my blanket.

"Aho, Greg. Are you ready to come in?" the man gently asked.

He said "Aho" as a way of acknowledging my presence and wanting to get my attention.

"Yes, I'm ready," I said in a grateful, peaceful tone while gazing downward in their direction.

I bundled up my personal things and left them there to be picked up later. The two helpers and I then walked silently to the Sweat Lodge where I changed into my shorts for a quick sweat to disconnect me from my Vision Quest state of being.

After seven rocks were brought in the Sweat Lodge and the door flap went down, the lodge leader excitedly shared celebratory, welcoming words for us returning questers. Thunder wasn't in the Sweat Lodge this time. The laughter and light-hearted comments we shared made me smile. We were all glad to be back off the hill. The rocks glowed orange and sizzled to life when the cool water hit them. Steam rushed into my face and body and sweat instantly began rolling off my chin. A couple more tosses of water onto the rocks from the buffalo horn and the drumming and singing began by the closed door. I realized this was a thank-you song being sung to Spirit for gently taking care of us while we were on the hill.

Once the song finished, the lodge leader addressed one of the questers.

"Would you please pray."

"Thank you, Creator, for taking care of me and all the questers who went out on Vision Quest. Thank you for my insights and answered prayers." he said with an empowered, sincere tone. He began to say something else when a dipper of water splashed onto his face, and everyone laughed. We could tell by his suddenly broken sentence that the water was well aimed. The water splash was done to break the connection the quester had with the vision energy in which he'd been anchored.

"Greg, would you please pray."

"Aho, Great Mystery, Creator, thank you for hearing my prayers. Thank you for blessing me with your guidance."

Water suddenly splashed against my forehead.

"Did I get you?" the water pourer asked.

"Yup, direct hit," I muttered.

Everyone laughed. We were all full of positive energy and gratitude. We had all been on a journey together, whether we were a quester or a supporter. Because we were all immersed in the Vision Quest energy that week, everyone was receiving Spirits' blessings in some way.

All the questers got a chance to pray and share thanks. The darkness in the lodge was suddenly replaced by daylight when the door flap was flung upward at the end of the round. I locked eyes with a quester across from me. We were both smiling. When I exited the Sweat Lodge, I felt grounded, and I was happy to look at people again. I enjoyed being quieter than usual for a number of hours afterward. I did everything more slowly and gently; my energy was calm and clear.

All the remaining questers on the hill came down that evening and went through a similar Sweat Lodge Ceremony.

"Greg, Thunder's ready for your talk-in now," Sparky said, after finding me in the kitchen where I was having some watermelon to break my fast.

Sparky was one of Thunder's best "warriors." She watched out for her well-being, as did the others who traveled with her.

"Okay," I said enthusiastically.

I was going to share what I experienced on my blanket with Thunder, as was customary for each quester. I walked the creaky wooden steps up to the third floor where her room awaited at the top of the stairs. I knocked and a couple of voices beckoned me in. Thunder was sitting on the opposite side of the room, smiling happily at me as I approached the empty seat beside her. Sparky and another supporter, Bonnie, were sitting beside her. Bonnie had pen and paper in hand for note taking. The energy in the room was noticeably high, and I understood why, given Thunder was holding the energy of the quest in that room for its duration. The Pipe was always there with her except when it was briefly placed on the Sweat Lodge altar.

I sat down and Thunder kept smiling. I was very happy to see her, and I just wanted to start gabbing like old friends would. Although we hadn't spent a lot of time together in the past three years, I felt like I'd known her longer.

"So, how'd it go, Greg?" she asked.

I told her about my dream.

She shook her head in acknowledgement, smiling.

"Well, I just love you, Greg," Thunder said, viewing me with eyes that seemed to look right into my soul.

We were happy to be in each other's lives. I shared about the rest of my quest, but the dream was the main piece I wanted her to know about. I was very happy with how my Vision Quest turned out and I felt like I had gone through a gate of initiation, as brief as it had been. After a short time, I stood and thanked her again, and she reached up for a hug. We embraced and I left the room so she could do her talk-in with the next quester, who I found standing outside the door.

In a couple of hours, everyone at the event gathered in a large circle outdoors. Thunder stood with us, smiling, Sacred Pipe cupped by her left hand with the stem leaning on her shoulder.

"Spirit came to each and every one of you that went out on Vision Quest," Thunder said with an assured look. "Thank you for seeking a vision for your life and for the people. All people will benefit from what you gained on the hill."

Vision Quest was supportive on many levels. In addition to receiving guidance about our prayers, what needed to be emotionally and spiritually healed in our lives also commonly came to our awareness during ceremony. Over the years, these ceremonial ways helped me and others to grow into better, more awakened, versions of ourselves.

Thunder spoke with gratitude for the efforts that everyone put in to make the Vision Quest a success, and she gave thanks to Creator and Spirit for gently embracing all of us.

"You are all like new babies," she said, looking out at us questers. "Be gentle with yourselves. Keep your experiences close to your heart. Don't share them with others for a while, so they have time to integrate into you."

Thunder lit the Pipe and reverently blew a puff of smoke to each of the four cardinal directions, then a puff for Creator, then Earth Mother, and then for all that exists. She then passed the Pipe for each person to briefly hold and take a puff. When the Pipe came to me, I gratefully puffed it, silently giving thanks for this Vision Quest ceremony. I noticed the Pipe's high vibration. I had a deep respect for the Pipe and these Native American ways. They were healing and reminded me that all life is sacred and connected.

Once the Pipe finished going around the circle, the last puff was smoked and then Thunder held the pipe out horizontally. She was about to disconnect the bowl from the wooden stem, which would conclude the link to Spirit for the Vision Quest ceremony.

"Thank you, Creator, for all of your blessings, and may all be blessed today," Thunder said with love and gratitude. Then she gently pulled the bowl from the stem and lightly thrust them forward in a gesture of appreciation.

"Let's go feast" was the direction after that. We all went to the large dining room and enjoyed a delicious, homecooked, celebration meal. The conversations were lively and joyful. The children enjoyed playing with small toys, eating, and listening to everybody with curiosity.

Gifting was a tradition at the end of a Vision Quest ceremony, so the questers had a little something to share with everyone, especially Thunder. I had an assortment of small gifts to hand out that I'd gathered during the few months prior. Many people worked hard during the Vision Quest and I, like the other questers, enjoyed personally thanking and gifting everyone.

I had met Thunder and her partner Jeff three years earlier at a large gathering in Alabama arranged by a humble, visionary Native American man named Sun Bear. This gathering was called a "Medicine Wheel Gathering" because it brought people of all ages and from all walks of life together for a spiritual purpose. Sun Bear had a vision indicating it was time to bring Native American teachings to people of all different backgrounds and beliefs to break down walls of cultural separation and aid in the spiritual healing of all people. The gathering included an exciting blend of Native American speakers, crafts vendors, ceremonial leaders, and food vendors. I went with a friend, George, to further explore Native American culture and spirituality, having quickly developed an interest in it through my friendship with a Cherokee woman in Maryland named Two Feathers.

One night during the three-day medicine wheel gathering, I participated in a Sweat Lodge Ceremony that Jeffrey Hubbell, Mary Thunder's partner, attended. I had already met Jeff at that point. The ceremony was led by Lakota elder Grandpa Wallace Black Elk, who years earlier had adopted Thunder, in a spiritual sense, as his daughter. When we got out of the Sweat Lodge, Jeff surprised me by dumping the remaining bucket of water over my head. I did not see that coming, given it was dark. I let out a surprise shriek, while Jeff laughed and gave me a big hug. Our friendship was starting.

I spent some of my time at the gathering working to help defray the cost of attending. During a closing event on the last day, I was to receive a T-shirt commemorating the gathering – a small gift from the gathering's facilitators for attendees that worked there. On stage, Grandpa Wallace was sitting with Thunder, Jeff, and others who traveled with them. As I walked toward the stage after my name was called, Thunder and I made eye contact. She was looking at me intently and said with a smile "Aho Greg."

I felt a peaceful comfort inside me as I smiled back. I felt compelled to get to know her and Jeff.

*Mary Thunder's Compelling Story*

As with all the questers at the Vision Quest, I received blessings and good energy in many ways from Spirit, Thunder, and mother nature herself. When I left Big Indian that spring, my heart was full of joy, love, and appreciation for my life, people, and Native American spiritual ways. I was thrilled with my first Vision Quest and silently set my intentions to return in the fall to support the next Vision Quest.

I happily participated in many more Vision Quest ceremonies with Thunder at Big Indian and later at her property in Texas. I was also blessed with being able to participate in additional Lakota ceremonies in various states with her, and in later years with her son, Chief Richard Grimes.

Sadly, in 2017, Mary Elizabeth Thunder passed away from natural causes, taking her journey to the Spirit World. She is missed by many, but her family continues her life's work, and I continue to be involved in the activities she lovingly brought into our lives.

# 10
## AKASHIC RECORDS

I began my amazing journey accessing the Akashic Records (ARs) in 1993 when I was 32 years old. I had witnessed my close friend, Leah, access the records countless times over the years while giving classes, seminars, and intuitive readings, and I realized I could likely develop the ability to give intuitive readings using the records, too.

Every person has an Akashic Record. "Akashic" is derived from the word "Ākāśa," or Akasha, a Sanskrit term that has several related meanings: (1) the primordial substance or spiritual essence that pervades all space; (2) it is Space itself; (3) the fifth cosmic element, Aether; and (4) the "tablet of memory" that records all events.

The Records are the non-physical energy imprints of every action, event, and life in human and extraterrestrial history. The "Hall of Records" is the name used to describe the organized energy library that holds access to every record.

I had a flash of inspiration to make this an important part of my life. I eagerly wanted an activity that would bring me a more personal connection with the ET phenomenon, and this was a tantalizing approach. I realized my service could be especially beneficial to those who had experienced unsettling, or even scary, UFO and ET encounters and wanted clarity about them. I also imagined myself retrieving home world and Oversoul information for people, as Leah did.

*Their records would have all the information. I could access the Akashic Records like Leah. After all, I've developed my intuitive senses and*

*I've had a lot of experience accessing dimensions beyond the physical realm during meditation and OBEs.*

My confidence in the usefulness of the ARs was bolstered by recalling the broad success Edgar Cayce — a well-known American intuitive, or psychic, from the early 1900s — achieved in helping people by accessing the Akashic Records. Mr. Cayce accessed clients' Akashic Records, or "soul records," while in a deep trance-like state. He used the records to determine the cause of, and remedy for, their health issues and to answer other questions. The accuracy of his diagnoses and effectiveness of the treatments he prescribed for body, mind, and soul gave him high credibility in the world of medicine. The details of his 14,000 intuitive readings are available to the public at Edgar Cayce's Association for Research and Enlightenment (ARE) in Virginia Beach, Virginia.

A couple of weeks after my flash of inspiration, I approached Leah with the idea of doing Akashic Record readings during a trip to her place in West Virginia. Leah had recently moved to this rural location from Maryland with her husband and son. We sat at a picnic table by the house, appreciating the warm, sunny afternoon on the quiet mountain. Leah was instantly excited about my idea, thinking it would be a great way for me to be of service, since ET connections were right up my alley. She checked in with her spirit guides, and mine, to see if they felt the same. To our delight, a green light was instantly given.

"Let me see if they will provide you with a reader of the records," Leah said to my surprise.

There are librarians, so to speak, in the astral or etheric realms. These non-physical beings maintain the Akashic Records and help people with noble intentions access the records. Although I'd witnessed Leah call on her reader of the records countless times when she wanted information, it hadn't dawned on me that I'd be offered a similar assistant.

"Karl is being assigned to work with you, Greg."

I felt deep gratitude well up within me. I was being given an abundance of support for my new pursuit.

"Karl was chosen, with his agreement of course, because his energies are similar to yours, Greg, which will help you two telepathically communicate."

Karl would be providing me with AR information through my intuitive senses of sight, hearing, feeling, and knowing. I left Leah's the next day smiling ear to ear, excited to begin my new adventure.

I met Leah Stansell in 1985 at a monthly presentation in Bel Air, Maryland that she and three of her business partners had organized. The topic was Native American spirituality. Leah's business was called the "At-One Center," and the presentations were held at a Friends meeting house. This was a nondescript building owned by the Quakers — people who belong to the Religious Society of Friends, a Christian denomination. I learned about the presentation after meeting one of the At-One Center founders, Glenda, at her store nearby.

Sitting in an aisle seat a few rows back from the front, I waited patiently for the evening's speaker to come forward. While people were chatting, Leah walked over to welcome me. She introduced herself with a smile, and we talked briefly. Before excusing herself to the back of the room, she put her hand on my shoulder and said something endearing, expressing that she felt a connection with me somehow and looked forward to getting to know me.

Leah and I have been close friends ever since. She held metaphysical classes at her house in nearby Edgewood, Maryland on a regular basis. I looked forward to those classes, since the topics centered around metaphysical and spiritual development.

Leah was kind, gentle, and appeared to be very experienced with the material she presented. I felt at home there, sitting around the small table in her finished basement, exploring the topics of the class with the others present. Her husband Joe and preteen son, James, chose to stay upstairs during class, and on occasion I enjoyed chatting with them before classes.

*Leah Stansell's informative book about our higher selves and spiritual principles*

For as long as I've known Leah, she has continually offered classes, workshops, and individual consultations on a myriad of spiritual and metaphysical topics. Leah and her guides stress that we are all equal in the eyes of Creator and that we are all connected through unseen levels of consciousness.

Leah has accessed the ARs hundreds of times for clients and a number of times for me over the years regarding relationships, spirit guides, past lives, ET connections, and more. I found the information fascinating, as it intuitively rang true and was useful in my life.

Leah has students throughout the United States, England, and Canada. Her reputation for accuracy and reliability is such that she also assists the police as a psychic investigator in missing persons cases.

I practiced accessing and experiencing the Akashic Records alone with Karl, my assistant, for more than forty sessions before I felt comfortable providing readings for clients. This training period lasted 15 months. During that time, I developed my proficiency at reading records and communicating with Karl. Some sessions were frustrating because my intuitive abilities seemed to be on vacation. Most sessions, however, were engaging enough to record in my notebook.

I sometimes say to people that my initial 15 months of AR practice sessions offered great material for science-fiction stories and Star Trek episodes – Star Trek being the popular TV and movie series about exploring the galaxy.

Seventy-five percent of the practice sessions Karl chose for me were about star systems, planets, and ETs. The other 25 percent addressed countries and cultures, other time periods, and more.

During one practice session, Karl brought me to three different books in succession. Using my sense of feeling and knowing, I determined the first two books were about Jerusalem and Egypt. I was moved from one book to the other once I sensed their general contents. The third book captivated my attention with vivid pictures of dinosaurs. I recall turning the pages, taking in the scenes of their natural settings. Another fascinating session was sensing prehistory in which human-looking ETs from our Eocene epoch, roughly 40 million years ago, were studying the DNA of early primates.

I initially accessed the Hall of Records and Karl through my crown chakra. Later I explored hearing Karl through my right ear and accessing the Hall from the front of my body where more of my chakras could connect to it. This follow-on approach was more productive and left me feeling more grounded.

It is truly amazing to feel, and intuitively see, the Hall of Records appear in front of me. Two large, stout, wooden doors, flanked by nondescript walls, appear to me within seconds when I ask to connect with the Hall. The Hall has a distinct feel to me. It's peaceful and vibrant with a calm energy that opens to me in the form of knowledge and experiences if I simply ask. Karl also introduced me to a large purification fountain inside, not far from the entrance. I enjoyed moving into the energy of the fountain as part of my beginning ritual, where my energy rose to a higher level of vibration and my sense of selfless service deepened.

When I access the ARs these days, I simply telepathically call on my reader of the records – a spirit named Abraham – and ask him to open the client's soul record. I found this to be more efficient than going into the Hall of Records. If the client is not with me in person or on the phone, I provide Abraham with their birth name and birth month and day. When I feel the record open in front of me, I ask Abraham a question and wait for intuitive responses. This direct approach to accessing the records works well. Abraham became my reader of records after a number of years when my spirit helpers felt I should begin working with someone different because my intuitive sense of feeling and knowing had become more prominent.

Over the years since 1994, I have felt honored to do hundreds of readings for clients. In my early days of doing readings, I often asked Leah for confirmation on the information I received during those sessions. Leah's reader of the records agreed to check the information, which built my confidence and taught me about common errors that can occur during readings.

Experience has taught me that the Akashic Record readings I do fit into three categories: (1) Questions about people's ET and UFO experiences; (2) General readings about any personal topic; and (3) Information about people's star connections, home star system, and Oversoul.

The first reading I want to share addresses a Mutual UFO Network (MUFON) field investigator's extraordinary encounter with a UFO and a physical extraterrestrial being. Founded in 1969, MUFON is an international organization that investigates UFO reports from around the globe.

I met Sandra (not her real name) in 2018 at a small UFO conference in Bowie, Maryland, a couple of towns away from where I lived at the time. Presenting her story to a riveted audience at an Elks Lodge, she shared that the husband and wife owners of a large ranch in a rural eastern town had called MUFON to investigate nightly visits of low-flying, distinct UFOs on their property. It was apparent to the owners and Sandra they were UFOs because the craft didn't have wings or helicopter blades or any other apparent means of maintaining flight. Although Sandra and a junior field investigator managed to activate their electronic recording equipment as the UFOs flew over them one night, the equipment failed to record. As a former Department of Defense employee trained and certified as a private investigator, Sandra was used to running the equipment. These electronic malfunctions were frustrating, though not uncommon near UFOs.

Even more compelling, while she and her MUFON partner walked down a dark, quiet, dirt road with the landowner one night, flashlights in hand, their attention was suddenly brought to the sound of movement in the adjacent field. Their flashlights swung over and there, about 30 feet away, was an equally startled being staring back. The being looked humanoid, much like the "Grey" ETs that are often depicted as part of the Roswell Incident in 1947. The being was about four feet tall and had black almond-shaped eyes. Sandra told the audience that she and her two companions immediately ran in complete terror, emphasizing that the deep, penetrating feeling of fear and the involuntary compulsion to run were overwhelming. She stressed that she had no explanation for these overpowering sensations.

*Grey alien, general illustration (Source: Myminifactory.com)*

I introduced myself to Sandra after her talk and asked if she'd like me to investigate the case on my own, using the Akashic Records. Sandra was very pleasant and easy to talk to. She eagerly agreed, wanting answers to her perplexing encounter. She told me that she felt like she failed the distraught owners because she couldn't answer why the UFOs had been significantly active over their property on a nightly basis for weeks.

A few days after the conference, I sat down by myself to investigate Sandra's experience using the Akashic Records. I called in Abraham and asked him to open Sandra's soul record and any record that could help with my questions. I then telepathically explained to him the event and the state where the investigation occurred. What Abraham expressed to me was that the Grey and the occupants of the UFOs were benevolent. They were flying over the property to measure and record its condition using some form of energy. I felt water was involved in why they were there. I sensed that the ETs felt unthreatened on the property and thus repeatedly returned. I also felt the Greys operated within a "collective" consciousness – meaning they were constantly connected telepathically and made decisions through some sort of hierarchy.

I asked Abraham what caused the unusually deep sense of terror Sandra and the other two people felt when they saw the Grey. I was told that it was largely due to the fear the Grey ET and his companions felt as Sandra and her friends were unknowingly connected with the Grey telepathically. The Grey was telepathically connected to his companions and his fear resulted in his companions also experiencing fear, resulting in a collective, magnified response. In my mind's eye I saw a shaft of light going up from the top of his head to his companions, wherever they were, reinforcing my intuitive sense that the Grey was telepathically connected to them.

After completing my reading for Sandra, I called Leah and asked if she and her reader of the records would critique my findings. I wanted to be accurate for MUFON. Leah and her reader of the records agreed with my findings. I breathed a sigh of relief. Leah added that those particular Greys are from the Antares star system. Accessing the ARs later about Antares, I intuitively felt strongly that was correct.

When I presented the information to Sandra during a twenty-minute phone call later that week, she said the information made sense and then proceeded to share some previously unrevealed details about the case.

"The land where the event occurred had been flooded under six-to-eight feet of water prior to the frequent UFO activity there. The flood was considered a 1000-year flood, and it affected an area around 200 miles long," she said in near disbelief.

I listened intently and was glad to hear I was on-target about water being highly relevant.

"The land where the event occurred has cattle and crops. After the flood, the UFOs flew in every night. The client said he and his relatives lived in a very remote area. He grew up in a place where miles stretched between neighbors. I came out to the area once the roads were passable."

Sandra concluded by saying, "No additional UFO visits were noticed for 60 days after I finished my investigation."

"Perhaps the Greys were afraid to return after having their close encounter in the field?" I offered.

We talked a while longer and soon felt complete in our conversation. Sandra emailed me a heartfelt follow-up message a few days later.

"Greg!!!! I wanted to spend a moment and truly thank you for this amazing reading! I sincerely believe I now have better answers that, for the first time, make sense! All the best to you for such a wonderful gift of comfort and information!!!!

Happy Holidays, Sandra, MUFON Field Investigator"

I also do quite a few Akashic Record readings addressing personal questions from clients, often dealing with relationships, past lives, health concerns, and jobs. I've discovered that not only can information be retrieved from a client's soul record, but that a particularly intuitive client can feel the energy associated with the reading as it is being communicated. One reading I performed in June 2016 even went a step further when the client, my friend Sienna (not her real name), accomplished her own healing by neutralizing some of the emotional trauma she felt from her revealing, past-life reading.

Sienna, a doctor of naturopathic medicine, asked me what I thought about a lengthy portrayal of her in Greece, as shared with her by an intuitive friend. She wasn't sure if it represented something she was called to do or something that happened in a past life. Surprisingly, she felt such an emotional reaction to it that she was considering traveling to Greece to find out more.

"Sienna this is a lot of information," I said, wide-eyed. "It sounds like a past life to me. You don't need to go to Greece to address this," I told her with near certainty. "I'd be happy to try doing an Akashic Record reading for you about this, if you'd like. I've never used the ARs for a general reading, but I presume the process for gathering information would be the same."

"Yes, I'd love that," Sienna replied eagerly.

When I arrived at her home a few days later, I set up a small altar to make a high vibration space for the reading, and we centered ourselves in peacefulness. I cleared my energy field using my mind and we called in our spirit helpers and angels. Sienna's dog lay curled up at her feet.

*Here we go,* I said to myself as I trusted in the process.

I silently called in Abraham and asked him to open Sienna's soul record. Feeling her record open promptly, I asked Sienna to start talking about what she wanted answers to.

I accessed her AR with my eyes open, maintaining a clear connection with Abraham and the record as Sienna and I talked. Sienna often jotted down notes as I revealed information. To my amazement, she intuitively felt and saw much of what I sensed as I shared it, saying that it felt correct. I was breaking new ground with this reading, and I was happy to see it going so well.

The records revealed that Sienna and a small number of other girls her age were in special metaphysically-oriented trainings in ancient Greece. I was surprised to sense that the teachings included ancestral lineage going back to the stars. A mother-like figure was their trainer and custodian. The children were about seven years old, and I saw them happily playing, wearing white robes.

In one instance, as I felt the energy of the woman and children, I asked the energy I was feeling to move into Sienna's energy field to see if she could also feel it.

"At last," Sienna said exuberantly. "This truly feels like home — something I haven't felt in a long time."

*Awesome*, I thought enthusiastically.

During the reading I clairvoyantly saw Sienna in Greece as an outgoing, happy, adult teacher and energy healer. An energy healer is someone who can positively affect another person by working with life-force energy. In that lifetime she was aware of the constellations and used her connection to Pleiadian ET ancestors as she ministered to others.

I believe that we all have animal spirit helpers, and in this reading, I intuitively saw that she had an orange, striped tiger spirit helper back then. Sienna said she could feel the tiger as I talked about it.

While Sienna was outside with her dog during a small break in the reading, I retained my connection to her Akashic Record, and it was then that I saw a noose hanging down.

In a few moments, Sienna returned with her dog, appearing relaxed as they settled back in. Before I could say anything about the noose, Sienna spoke up.

"I feel like they tried to strangle me," she said to my utter surprise.

"Well, I didn't want to share this with you," I said, "but since you felt that, I saw a noose while you were outside. A local government, or prominent group that didn't like you helping less fortunate people, wanted to kill you."

Sienna stared at me with a dejected look. She then shared that throughout the reading she'd been having neck discomfort. Now she knew why. I remembered seeing her crack her neck a few times during the reading.

"Fortunately, I feel you were saved by your supporters, Sienna," I said confidently.

"This explains why I have felt so intimidated when meeting with government officials or even just going into government buildings," Sienna said emphatically.

While sitting comfortably on the couch, we talked about how we would attempt to clear the traumatic feelings Sienna experienced in that lifetime that related to strangling and life-threatening oppression. Neutralizing the energy of the trauma could eliminate its influence in Sienna's current life. For my part, I imagined the energy from that experience disappearing from her soul record. Sienna silently visualized clearing the traumatic event in her own way. I could literally feel layers of energy come off Sienna as she did this.

Fortunately, I saw that Sienna did escape the danger to her life with the help of her supporters. I saw her safely back at her home attending to her usual activities somewhere in Greece after the scare.

We chose to end the session there, feeling complete. I thanked Abraham and asked him to close Sienna's soul record. I promptly felt it close, and with that the energy thread to her record vanished.

Rubbing my legs briskly, I took a deep breath and smiled. We had been on a long, amazing journey together for two and a half hours. I was thrilled by how visual and tactile the reading had been for both of us.

To ensure we were fully disconnected from the energy of that lifetime, I asked out loud that all dimensional doorways that were opened during the session be closed. We both felt a number of invisible energy openings in the room close down. With that, the room felt clear, and we both felt grounded. We gratefully thanked our spirit helpers and angels, concluding our session.

A number of significant events occurred for Sienna regarding this reading and her friend's strong visuals of Sienna being in Greece. First, Sienna neutralized the effect the strangling-like trauma from her life in Greece was having on her in this life. Also, Sienna awakened memories and abilities of being a healer and teacher of ancient knowledge. She now has access to those energies which she can incorporate into this life. In addition, the AR reading awakened in her a strong sense of having lived in Greece, and that it felt like home.

I also conduct Akashic Record readings addressing peoples' home star systems and home planets. Although we are born on Earth, Earth may not be a person's home planet. Surprisingly, all the clients I have read for, so far, are from other worlds. I imagine there are many other people who have Earth as their home world, however.

Although this concept of originating from a world other than Earth is new to most of us, numerous indigenous cultures, including Native Americans, have had these beliefs for hundreds of generations.

Furthermore, many indigenous spiritual leaders around the world have experienced visions or strong intuitive guidance that the time has come for them to speak openly about their most closely held oral traditions regarding our star origins. They are inspired to do this to help humanity survive and flourish. Their traditions include revealing their origins from the stars, and the influence of Star People visitors on the formation of their culture, spiritual beliefs, and ceremonies. They also describe the imminent return of these Star Nations.

My experience with the Akashic Records indicates there does not have to be a DNA connection between star beings from our home world and our bodies here. We can simply incarnate on Earth while our home world connection is at a non-physical, soul level.

In the 1990s, I benefited a great deal when I intuitively connected with what I came to believe is my home planet. Leah suggested that a particular planet in the Andromeda galaxy might be my home. Andromeda is our closest neighboring spiral galaxy, located 2.5 million light years from our Milky Way galaxy. Each time I intuitively checked in on the planet Leah had suggested, my energy field strongly resonated in the affirmative. It truly felt like home and my intuitive abilities shifted to a higher level in a matter of weeks. The topic of my home world and its effect on my abilities is fascinating, but too much to describe right now. I will go into greater detail about this in a later chapter.

*Andromeda Galaxy (Source: Pixelstalk.net)*

I can tune into my home world existence at any time. This implies that I exist here and there simultaneously. When considering the implications of reincarnation, it also means that I exist there during all other lifetimes.

An example of me existing in two places at the same time are my Out-of-Body Experiences (OBEs). In my OBEs, my physical body was lying comfortably in bed while I was operating elsewhere in my astral body with full cognitive ability. The "astral body" is a quasi-material energy body, made of something called prana, also known as life-force energy.

Science supports this paradigm, too. Quantum physics has shown there are undeniable, measurable, connections between subatomic particles across great distances here on Earth. This supports the idea that the different parts of my soul are connected, regardless of the physical distance between them.

When I discuss the concept of existing on my home world through all my lifetimes, this raises the prospect that perhaps all my lives are happening simultaneously. This may seem impossible, but quantum physics, quantum entanglement, and plank theory tell us this is a real possibility. I find it hard to wrap my head around this mind-blowing concept because – like all of us – I live in a time-based reality. I prefer to simply appreciate connecting to my home world and leave it at that.

The Akashic Records also indicate that most people operate at a higher vibration and level of consciousness on their home world than they do here on Earth, increasing the likelihood that they exist in a higher dimension there. This makes sense because many of the home star systems I have found while conducting Akashic Record readings for other people are either too young or they emanate too much radiation; either of these conditions eliminates the likelihood that physical life as we know it evolved there.

The existence of other dimensions is postulated in the field of physics called String Theory. Additional support for the existence of other dimensions comes from people who have had near-death experiences. Dr. Eben Alexander is a neurosurgeon who wrote about vividly recalling being in another dimension with full cognitive ability during his near-death experience. One of the many compelling aspects central to his experience is that he discovered later that his physical brain was incapable of imagining or creating his experience, given its unresponsive, inactive condition at the time.

Adding support for the existence of other dimensions comes from when my friend Katherine visited me in her astral body. I could feel her hands running through my energy field, but I could not see her. She was in her astral body, operating in what's called the astral plane. The astral plane is described as a nonphysical realm of being – a dimension of existence that transcends our physical world.

I approach these topics with an open mind. We are just beginning to understand the non-physical components of our existence as human beings.

Returning to the subject of the Akashic Records, the home star system reading I performed for my friend, Mandi (not her real name), in 2023 is a good example of connecting with our home world selves because the corroborations with her go well beyond coincidence.

"Mandi, do you want to know where your home star system is?" I asked as we both gazed peacefully at the stars one night in my driveway.

"Sure!" Mandi replied.

It was Spring of 2023, and we were enjoying the balmy air of south Florida with the Orion constellation, the Pleiades, and Sirius in plain view.

I decided to just open to my intuition and see if the answer would come, instead of reaching for the Akashic Records. I rarely tried that approach for home world information.

My intuition was drawing me to the Sirius star system. I looked over at Sirius – the brightest star in the sky – and told Mandi what I was sensing.

"I've always felt a special connection to Sirius." Mandi responded, making me smile.

Later in the month while I was giving her a long AR reading in my living room, I asked Abraham, my reader of the records, a number of questions about her home world. The star Sirius B was clearly given to me as the answer, delighting me as it confirmed my earlier notion. Mandi accepted this because she felt it rang true in the core of her being. She had been developing her intuition over the last year, so she had this tool as a guide.

I asked Abraham for a description of her home planet. In a moment I saw lots of water. I strongly felt dolphins and whales there. I have rarely felt the presence of whales on another world, but I have often seen water and dolphins on planets around Sirius A and B.

During several of my Native American Vision Quests, I briefly saw a dolphin and a whale against a starry background within my mind. Those repeated experiences strongly suggested that dolphins and whales are present on other worlds.

I asked Abraham what Mandi's appearance was on the planet on which she lived orbiting the star Sirius B. She appeared as a vibrant energy form – a shaft of light. I also sensed she could take on a denser form if she desired. She could walk on land, swim in the water, or fly over the water, as she desired. I shared all this with Mandi.

This is consistent with what I experienced when I did readings for other people having Sirius B as their home star system. It was apparent to me that on Mandi's home world she likely lives in a dimension with a much higher vibration than our Earthly physical realm since she exists there as an energy form that can shape shift.

"Mandi, I'm experiencing something rather odd now, but I'll share it because it may truly be significant," I said, trusting the process.

"I'm seeing an octopus-like creature that feels male. He is a mentor, of sorts, to you on your home planet."

"Oh my God, I've always felt drawn to octopuses," Mandi gasped in amazement, her eyes wide, displaying a big smile.

"Oh good," I replied, breathing a sigh of relief. I was happy I wasn't misreading.

"I even have octopuses on my pajamas," Mandi excitedly revealed.

At my request, Abraham gave me the name Mandi can use to telepathically call on her octopus when she desires. When I repeated the name to Mandi, both she and I felt it resonated with her energy. Mandi's sense of clairsentience, or intuitive feeling, was strong. The octopus certainly works with Mandi on her home world, and I assume he can help her here on Earth, as well. He could help guide her when she has questions, assist her in connecting to her form on her home world, and bring her comfort on Earth when she asks. From my experience, I can attest to the value of connections like these for people who want to cultivate them.

There is strong evidence that beings from the Sirius star system have been present on Earth in the distant past. An article produced by the Gaia platform uncovered some extraordinary findings regarding the Dogon tribe in West Africa. From their website:

*The Dogon tribe have demonstrated a knowledge of beings from Sirius A. The Dogon inhabit an area of Mali in West Africa, called the Bandiagara Escarpment, a stretch of sandstone cliffs nearly 100 miles long, reaching up to 1,500 feet high. The tribe built their homes into the side of the cliffs during the 3rd century B.C. and have remained there since.*

*Dogon tribe in Africa (www.Behance.net)*

*It wasn't until the 1930s that French anthropologists discovered their strangely advanced astronomical knowledge, despite maintaining a very primitive lifestyle.*

*The Dogon are incredibly familiar with the Sirius star system, where they indicated aliens travelled from and imparted them with knowledge hundreds of years ago. These beings, known as the "Nommos" to the tribe, were amphibious beings, coming from the same star system as the Egyptian god, Isis.*

*While Sirius A is visible to the naked eye, its companion white dwarf, Sirius B, was not discovered until the 1950s with an advanced telescope. The Dogon, however, were well aware of its presence, as well as its orbital period, and told anthropologists of its existence before it was confirmed by modern telescopes.*

*It has been said that their knowledge of the Sirius star system is represented in 400-year-old artifacts, and they have an understanding of subatomic particles, and their theory of the Universe's creation is similar to today's mainstream Big Bang scientific theory.*

Furthermore, according to Egyptian mythology, the gods descended from the star system Sirius and the belt of the Orion constellation. Ancient Egyptians firmly believed that Isis, a prominent Egyptian goddess, came from Sirius.

The Sirians may have come to the Dogon from a dimension that has a much higher vibration than Earth's. To communicate with the Dogon, they would have either appeared in spirit form, or lowered their vibration to appear in physical form. I don't have a sense of how they would have lowered their vibration enough to become physical.

Mandi is not the only client I've found associated with the stars Sirius A or B. I find it very compelling that my AR readings about the Sirius star system are supported by the Dogon tribe's oral history and the ancient Egyptian stories of Isis.

The Akashic Records have continually astounded me with fascinating information for clients that reinforces their own experiences and intuition. Whether their questions are about past lives, personal relationships, UFOs, or ETs, the Akashic Records typically provide clarity, peace, and often optimism to those who seek them.

# 11

## NASA SPACE SHUTTLE PAYLOAD

"Good morning, Curt. We really have to thank you and the Space Shuttle *Endeavour* crew for the spectacular show at about 5:35 AM local time, as we first got a view of the Spartan inflatable antenna passing overhead. It was the brightest orbiting object I think most of us had ever seen. Three minutes later we saw a faint little Spartan streaking across the sky with *Endeavour* in hot pursuit."

These were the words from the Mission Control Center at NASA's Johnson Space Center (JSC) in Houston, Texas, to the Space Shuttle. The tennis court-sized, highly reflective Inflatable Antenna Experiment (IAE) had passed over NASA JSC before sunrise, dazzling onlookers as the brightest object moving among the stars. Minutes later, the bright reflection of the Space Shuttle *Endeavour* came into view 175 miles up as it closed in on the much smaller, unmanned spacecraft called Spartan. Spartan had jettisoned the IAE moments before, and *Endeavour* was closing in to retrieve the remaining Spartan carrier and stow it in the Shuttle's payload bay where it had been just a day earlier.

*Spartan IAE with antenna experiment fully deployed in orbit*
*(Photo credit: NASA)*

Spartan provided the means to get IAE into orbit and support both phases of its experiment. Inflating the three 100-foot-long struts and the 50-foot-diameter lenticular-shaped inflatable antenna was the experiment's first milestone. The lenticular shape consisted of two surfaces. The silvery, reflective antenna surface facing the Spartan carrier was metalized rubber. The other surface was a simpler, clear, transparent barrier between Spartan and the antenna.

The second phase of the experiment required a pattern of laser pulses to survey the shape of the antenna's surface. The pulses traveled from the IAE box structure to the reflective antenna surface, where they bounced back to Spartan and were detected at the IAE box structure and recorded on Spartan's data recorder. After the laser pulse survey, the experiment was complete, and Spartan jettisoned away the IAE. The drifting IAE box structure with its three inflated struts and antenna would soon deorbit and burn up in the atmosphere.

A California-based company, L'Garde Inc., developed the antenna experiment to verify that their design would inflate into the desired shape in zero gravity. With a successful flight demonstration of the

IAE, inflatable antennas could be considered as viable alternatives to some heavier, metal antennas being designed for spacecraft at that time.

As the lead mechanical engineer for the Spartan spacecraft, I was one of several people from NASA's Goddard Space Flight Center (GSFC) sitting in a mission-support room at NASA JSC listening to the communication between mission control down the hall and the Space Shuttle *Endeavour* crew orbiting the Earth. If anything went wrong while the Space Shuttle was handling Spartan, we might be asked by mission control for guidance in resolving the problem.

I loved working in the Special Payloads Division at NASA Goddard where I led the development of the Spartan IAE carrier. I was proud to be instrumental in advancing the world's technical capability and scientific knowledge in space exploration. Working in the space program was full of challenges and risks, but science enthusiasts around the world supported NASA's mission, and I was thrilled to be a part of it. The CNN nightly news shared our sentiments by airing a video segment of Spartan IAE orbiting the beautiful Earth below, as shot from *Endeavour*.

Spartan IAE, an 1,800-pound spacecraft, was put overboard from *Endeavour's* payload bay using the Shuttle's Remote Manipulator System (RMS) arm, which was controlled from inside the crew cabin. Once released from the arm, Spartan acted autonomously, using an on-board timer, internal commands, a data recorder, three torque rods for spacecraft rotational control, and battery power.

Shortly after being released from the Shuttle's arm, Spartan's timer initiated the commands for the IAE box structure doors to fold down and then fill the folded antenna to its fully deployed shape using the pressurized nitrogen gas stored onboard.

*Spartan IAE being deployed on-orbit*
*(Photo credit: NASA)*

The laser pulse survey of the antenna's reflective surface was then performed, completing the experiment.

Once the jettisoned antenna was a safe distance from Spartan, *Endeavour* closed in on Spartan and retrieved it using the Remote Manipulator System (RMS) arm. Soon after, the small spacecraft was lowered down onto its support structure in the Space Shuttle bay and latched into place using an electrical signal from the crew cabin. I breathed a sigh of relief as I sat back in my chair in the mission support room. All had gone as planned.

This project was a dream come true. I had progressed at Goddard to the point where I was the lead mechanical engineer for this Spartan mission. I could not have been happier. Having been at Goddard full time for 12 years by now, this was my second project as a lead mechanical engineer for a large, primary, Space Shuttle payload. The first project was a dream job as well, but Spartan was even more thrilling, given it was designed to be deployed overboard from the Shuttle.

This Spartan had two distinct sections: the Inflatable Antenna Experiment and the Spartan carrier. I was responsible for the design, manufacture, and assembly of the Spartan carrier. Once IAE arrived at Goddard, I led the team integrating IAE to the Spartan carrier's four jettison posts – successfully completing this complex task was an exciting milestone. Following this, I led the spacecraft testing, shipping, and handling operations at Kennedy Space Center. It sometimes felt overwhelming but I had support from designers, technicians, structural analysts, test engineers, and crane operators, as needed. Where I lacked experience, such as in vibration testing and strength testing Spartan, senior mechanical engineers were assigned to lead those tests, and I took a support role.

The Spartan IAE mission was one of my favorites during my 35 years at NASA. From start to finish, the Spartan IAE project spanned two-and-a-half years. The quick turn-around time at Goddard was made possible because the Spartan service module portion of the carrier had already been developed as a standard design for most Spartan missions.

*NASA Goddard Spartan IAE team members posing between the Space Shuttle's solid rocket boosters on the launch pad at NASA's Kennedy Space Center in Florida. The bottom of the liquid fuel tank is visible above us. I am standing next to the person crouching down.*

The mission-unique, four-post jettison system incorporated complex mechanisms. I had the pleasure of devising this system with a colleague of mine named Don. Don was my lead engineer for developing these posts, and he made the design and test effort look easy. He was as bright as engineers come. Each post had two halves secured together with an intricate clamp. The jettison system worked flawlessly as the clamps released and a spring-loaded push-rod in each post simultaneously pushed IAE away.

If the jettison system had jammed, the IAE would have remained attached to the Spartan carrier, preventing the Shuttle from retrieving the carrier. If that happened, Spartan would have deorbited due to drag and burned up as it reentered the atmosphere, resulting in the loss of an expensive, hard-to-replace piece of equipment that was designed to be reused.

*Spartan carrier, post-flight at NASA's Kennedy Space Center. Three of the four jettison post push-rods are visible at the very top corners of the box structure. (Photo credit: NASA)*

This Space Shuttle mission was designated STS-77, where "STS" stands for "Space Transportation System."

The STS-77 mission commander, John Casper, and the Remote Manipulator System arm operator, Mario Runco, came to look at Spartan IAE at Goddard a few months before shipping it to Kennedy Space Center. I spoke to them about Spartan's mechanical interfaces to the Space Shuttle and answered questions, as did others on the Spartan team. They were easy to talk to and the visit was a pleasure.

Commander Casper had been a USAF pilot flying the F-100 Super Sabre during Vietnam and logged more than 10,000 flying hours in 52 different aircraft. He was the Shuttle commander for three of his four Space Shuttle missions, with STS-77 being his last. Mission Specialist Runco served in many roles as an officer in the U.S. Navy and flew on two Shuttle missions prior to STS-77, one of which included a four-hour spacewalk. Runco completed his career as an astronaut with STS-77.

I wished everyone on my team at Goddard was that easy to work with. One of my biggest challenges as the Spartan IAE lead mechanical engineer was a personality clash with my lead mechanical technician. Ben (not his real name) was an intimidator. I talked with him daily during integration of Spartan's parts and assemblies. Humility and respect were not his strong suits. Many of my interactions with him were met with sarcasm and an obvious sense he felt imposed upon.

I spoke to my supervisor, Craig, about this. Unfortunately, Craig had never worked with Ben, so he didn't have any first-hand experience he could share. Craig sympathized with me, and we both agreed that the best course of action was to be professional, ensure that everything was done properly, and to make certain that any personality conflicts didn't interfere with doing the job right. I did my best to get through the project with Ben, and ultimately it was a success. Unfortunately, he continued his passive-aggressive behavior for the rest of the mission. A few years later Ben had a heart attack. At that point, I think he realized he needed to change his attitude for his own well-being. He lightened up significantly, and talking to him actually became a pleasure.

The Spartan IAE Release Engage Mechanism (REM), which secured the Spartan to its support structure in the Shuttle payload bay, needed to be checked a day or two before flight. This was a matter of routine for such devices. We were required to verify the REM securely held Spartan in the locked position for launch. The check would be done while the Shuttle Bay doors were still open in what was called the "Payload Changeout Room," or PCR. The PCR was a cleanroom in a vertical building that had been rotated over to the Shuttle on the launch pad and had formed an airtight seal around the Shuttle's payload bay. An extendable platform in the PCR would be used to access Spartan for the inspection.

Three of us from Goddard were there to perform Spartan's REM inspection. I had been in the PCR years before to access a "Hitchhiker" payload, for which I was the lead mechanical engineer. A Hitchhiker was another type of large Shuttle payload carrier provided by the Special Payloads Division. I was equally in awe inside the PCR this time around, looking up at all the payloads in the Space Shuttle. It was a larger-than-life experience.

*Endeavour in the vertical position on the launch pad with its payload bay doors open in the PCR. Spartan IAE is clad in copper-colored thermal blanketing. (Photo credit: NASA)*

At one point, the three of us were on the floor-level of the PCR, looking up at our Spartan payload, admiring what we had accomplished at Kennedy. My supervisor, Craig, said, "I can't believe they let us do this." We were only in our mid-thirties. We had to pinch ourselves occasionally – the work really was surreal at times.

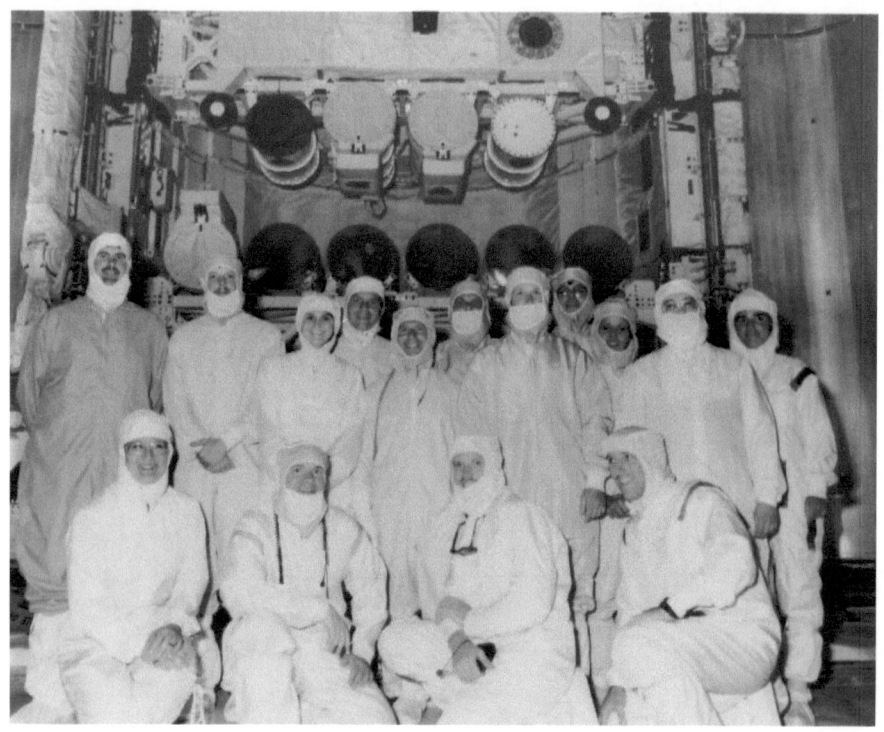

*NASA Goddard and Kennedy Space Center personnel supporting Spartan IAE. Photo taken in the launch pad PCR at floor-level, pre-flight. I am the short guy in the center of the middle row. (Photo credit: NASA)*

The photo above represents an excellent cross-section of just some of the team that successfully supported the Spartan mission. Clad in cleanroom garments, it includes the Spartan IAE NASA Mission Manager, mechanical technicians and engineers, an electrical technician, a thermal engineer, KSC safety and quality engineers, and more.

Many Get Away Special (GAS) experiment canisters, which I briefly mentioned in my NASA Internship chapter, are visible in the photo above. In addition to Spartan and Hitchhiker carriers, the Special Payloads Division (SPD) also offered GAS canisters for flying small experiments aboard the Space Shuttle.

Assembly of the International Space Station (ISS) in low-Earth orbit began in 1999, three years after the Spartan IAE flight. Space Shuttles were the main work horses for transporting ISS components from the ground. Understandably, this led to a significant reduction in the amount of room available in Space Shuttles to fly experiments. Making a far greater impact on the SPD, the Space Shuttle *Columbia* tragically broke up during the heat of re-entry in Earth's atmosphere in early 2003, resulting in the deaths of seven astronauts. Space Shuttle missions were then suspended for more than two years during the *Columbia* investigation. This sadly brought an end to the SPD's era of flying experiments in Space Shuttles.

NASA Goddard's Special Payloads Division accomplished a tremendous amount during the 21 years from 1982-2003. During that time, the SPD flew more than 200 payloads, using 108 Space Shuttle flights. The experiments flew in Get Away Special canisters, Hitchhikers, and Spartans.

The SPD's Shuttle Small Payloads Project Office, which managed these missions, offered an invaluable, low-cost proving ground for science and technology. It was also one of NASA's most fertile training grounds for developing young engineers and future program leaders. My experience as a mechanical systems engineer with these types of payloads opened a world of exciting opportunities for me.

Despite the winding down of the Shuttle Small Payloads Project Office, there were still a wide variety of exciting projects I had the opportunity to work on in the SPD. My next major project would be an extendable mechanical boom on a spacecraft destined to study the Sun.

# 12
## THE OVERSOUL

I felt my consciousness begin to travel as Karl, my reader of the Akashic Records, initiated the practice session. I didn't know what the session's topic would be but based on past sensations in the Hall of Records, I understood I was being brought deeply into the energies of a record. Occasionally when I access the records, it can feel like I'm traveling, and the travel associated with this particular session felt familiar. My mystery destination had a home-like feeling – safe and pleasant. After a moment, I realized I was entering the energy of my home planet in the Andromeda galaxy. It was a couple of years prior that I became aware of my home world and my appearance there. I didn't know if this traveling sensation was simply a journey into my own record and soul essence, or if part of my consciousness was actually traveling to Andromeda, 2.5 million light years away.

When I stopped moving, I felt taller and realized I was hair-covered. From past experience, I knew I was perceiving my form on my home world. I felt unusually content and peaceful. I vaguely saw a being in front of me who was also hair-covered. On my home world we look somewhat like Chewbacca in the *Star Wars* movies, but our hair is straight and flat, and our facial structure is different. I had experienced myself in my home world form to a limited degree a handful of times before and vaguely observed other similar looking beings – almost always while I was in a meditative state.

The hair-covered extraterrestrials in the dream I shared earlier in this book represented the beings from my home world. When I had that dream, I had been aware of my form there for years, but I hadn't been thinking about them, or the Andromeda galaxy, for months. I believe this eliminates mental preoccupation with the subject as the reason for the dream. I was astonished during the dream because I knew the beings represented my home world people.

All these experiences have added to my confidence in the existence of these beings.

A person's Oversoul is a critical part of his or her existence in the Universe. It is the part of the soul that is intimately connected with their home world. The Oversoul is also the link in the chain of our existence that works the most closely with us throughout our lifetimes. I am excited to share this concept in this chapter because of how I and others have appreciably benefited from this knowledge.

My mentor, Leah, told me Kezia is the name of my home planet in the Andromeda galaxy. When I tune into Kezia, it always feels like home. I feel this at the core of my being, and the resonance is strongest in my gut.

I also have learned I have one particularly important parent on Kezia. I look similar to him, as everyone in our species has the same general, hair-covered form. I discovered his name is Sumara – a name I received from him during a meditation. He has a female partner. We are of high enough vibration on Kezia that I was not physically born but came into being there through thought in the form of a young adult. In essence, I was created through divine intention by my parents.

In addition, on Kezia the energies that make up an offspring's consciousness come directly from one of the parents. When they wanted to create me, they decided Sumara would be the one from whom I would be manifested. With their divine intention and desire, and with the blessings of their individual angels and the will of God, some of Sumara's aspects of consciousness were used to form my consciousness without ever separating them from himself. I was given my own unique identity and free will. It was then that my life began. On my home world, I can stand in front of Sumara as a separate being, yet my consciousness and soul essence remain a part of him.

# THE OVERSOUL

I refer to Sumara as my *Oversoul* because I am part of his soul. There is no separation of consciousness between us. I also believe there is no separation between Sumara and the Creator. Sumara's aspects of consciousness are part of Creator, or God, and therefore my aspects of consciousness are as well. Thankfully, this supports my long-held belief that we are never separate from God.

My experience with the Akashic Records indicates that each person has an Oversoul and a body, or form of some kind, on their home planet. The Oversoul concept has consistently rung true with me since my introduction to it in the early 1990s.

We incarnate on Earth but can telepathically communicate with our Oversoul at any time.

As an offspring of my parent, I have a unique identity and higher self that is connected to all my past lifetimes on Earth and elsewhere, along with my life on Kezia. My higher self is also active as I operate on multiple levels of consciousness and in multiple dimensions. We can define the higher self as the unlimited, loving, spiritually centered side of our consciousness. Sumara is clearly the higher part of my soul, and I imagine his influence is present when I'm thinking and acting from my higher self. Although all aspects of my consciousness are part of my Oversoul, I am responsible for my personal soul growth, my actions, and the resulting impacts on my life. Fortunately, I am told that each of Sumara's offspring have their own higher self and lives to lead, and they don't mix with mine. We can, however, meet other offspring from our Oversoul. I have been fortunate to meet and create a great friendship with another of Sumara's offspring right here on the East Coast of the United States. I will describe this fascinating connection a little later.

I don't have a sense of how my lifetimes influence my Oversoul. From my experience, he oversees my activity, and I believe he and my angel have an influence on where I incarnate from lifetime to lifetime.

Experience has shown me that my Oversoul is my best spirit guide because he knows me completely and loves me unconditionally. He also knows what's best for my highest good. Plus, since I am part of him, I can easily connect with him.

My understanding of how Oversouls end up in various dimensions and on various planets is based on what Leah and her guides have said. My understanding is that all souls came into being at the same time, which was when our Universe was created during the Big Bang, billions of years ago. Some souls wanted to remain fully awake, that is, they wanted to maintain full consciousness at the God-level. These beings are in the angelic realm. As the Universe formed, Oversouls took up residence in various dimensions on various planets. Some dimensions are at a much higher vibration than our Earthly dimension, so we likely cannot see these planets or their inhabitants with our physical eyes. My Oversoul tells me that people who have Earth as their home world have their Oversoul present primarily in the higher dimensions of the Earthly realm.

Leah and her guides say that an angel is assigned to each Oversoul, and that each offspring in the Oversoul has that angel, as well. That angel is present throughout all lifetimes and activities, and in all realms.

I also understand that an Oversoul can choose to incarnate part of their essence elsewhere while maintaining full functionality on their home world. The incarnation would not be considered an "offspring" creation, like me, or one of my soul siblings. Instead, the incarnation would be considered a partial Oversoul. Sam – a man I did an Akashic Records reading for – is an example of such a partial Oversoul.

Sam (not his real name) reached out to me by email after learning about my services with the Akashic Records. After some brief email discussions and an AR reading addressing a long-standing question he had, Sam asked me to find his home star system in the ARs. I sat in front of my Native American altar alone, armed with his full name and birthdate, ready to check his soul record. To begin, I burned sage to purify my energy field, and I performed some chakra clearing using my intention. I asked Abraham to open Sam's record and waited until I felt the record open. Then I asked him to retrieve Sam's home star system, followed by a request for his home planet's name. Sam's home planet is elsewhere from Earth. The names I received had affirming energy to them, so I continued.

When I asked for the name of Sam's Oversoul, I suddenly felt Sam's presence in front of me, which I found odd. Even though Sam and I had never physically met, my intuition clearly indicated it was Sam. I'd never felt the energy of *any* client appear to me while I performed their home world reading.

"He is the Oversoul," Abraham said.

I almost fell off my cushion. I'd never read for a client who manifested on Earth at the Oversoul-level. Every client I'd read for was an offspring of their Oversoul.

Feeling Sam's energy appear in front of me makes sense because it answered my question of who Sam's Oversoul was. Sam's Oversoul would have a unique name on his home world, but Abraham did not provide that.

"He came to Earth to assist humanity," Abraham said.

Given how challenging life on Earth can be these days, this made perfect sense. Sam was highly intellectual, caring, and spiritual.

My Oversoul also manifested part of himself on Earth as a Native American more than a century ago. I became aware of him as my spirit guide in my early twenties, at least a decade before I heard about the Oversoul concept. He is such an important part of me that now I sense him within me, so I don't typically see his face. On the rare occasions when I do look at him, he is in his Native American form, smiling with bronze-colored skin, wearing a beautiful eagle-feather head dress. I believe I incarnated with him in that lifetime. For as long as I can remember I've called him White Buffalo. I also call him Sumara, the name he shared with me years ago when I asked him if he also went by another name. Whichever name I use, he is the same being residing on my home world where he is hair-covered like all Kezians.

On one particular occasion, I saw White Buffalo's Native American face in exquisite, clairvoyant, detail. I was participating in a group guided visualization on the island of Bimini in the Bahamas. It was a beautiful September morning in 2018, and 10 of us were lying on the floor of the small activities room at the Wild Quest retreat center. I was enjoying a week-long group retreat centered around snorkeling with pods of wild dolphins in the open ocean.

The guided visualization was intended to connect participants with a past life. Following the gentle guidance from the leader, in my mind I walked along a wooded path where I found myself as a Native American in his twenties praying alone in a small gazebo-like structure. At one point, from my perspective as the Native American, I recognized White Buffalo walking up to the structure to greet me. We were very happy to see each other.

I approached him and our eyes locked, as if in a long-awaited embrace. He had deep, soulful eyes that reflected his joy and wisdom. I saw his face vividly — every detail — as if I was looking at him with my physical eyes. His skin was dark and extensively wrinkled from decades of outdoor living. I'd never seen his face with such clarity before then. I will always remember that special moment. This surprise intuitive experience supported my belief that a part of my Oversoul and I shared a life together as Native Americans.

As I told Leah about this experience months later, she intuitively sensed the elder was my Oversoul, even before I mentioned his headdress and who I thought he was.

My introduction to the idea that White Buffalo might be my Oversoul occurred while driving with Leah from West Virginia to Maryland in May 1991. I was 30 years old. My curiosity about the Oversoul concept had simmered for years, having heard Leah talk about it many times, but I hadn't given it any priority due to my workload at NASA. I was pleasantly surprised and intrigued when Leah revealed that she felt my spirit guide, White Buffalo, was my Oversoul. I was captivated by this gem of insight.

Excited by the prospect, I made a special effort to meditate on the idea several times during the following week to see how it resonated with me. While in meditation, I simply asked my higher self if White Buffalo was my Oversoul father. My energy responded by gently focusing in my abdomen while my chakras became enlivened. I also felt a heightened, positive, heart-centered vibration in my overall energy, while my sense of inner knowing resonated in the affirmative. These responses told me the answer was yes. I was humbled, honored, and excited to think I was cultivating such an important, personal connection with the higher part of my soul.

In the week that followed, I often called on White Buffalo to feel him in my energy field. I noticed, surprisingly, that my seven main chakras seemed out-of-sorts at the end of that week. They felt especially unsettled. They weren't their usual calm, steady, comfortable energy centers. After feeling this way for a full week, I reached out to Leah on the phone. I was perplexed and worried.

"Leah, why are my chakras out of sorts? They feel so wonky and unsettled. It's an uncomfortable feeling."

"Your chakras are attuning to a higher level of vibration since you're consciously integrating with your Oversoul," Leah matter-of-factly responded. "They will settle out in about a week."

She was right. In another week, my chakras settled down and felt calm and integrated. I breathed a sigh of relief. I was thankful for the reprieve, and optimistic for what this new level of chakra attunement might offer. In the weeks following I noticed my intuitive senses had become slightly more perceptive and I felt a subtle, but noticeable, deepening in my sense of wholeness.

I discovered that intuitively calling on White Buffalo while emotionally stressed offered significant comfort. I had to come from my heart, with humility, though. I needed to quiet my mind the best I could, so I could sense his calming influence. Knowing that White Buffalo is always centered in love and high vibration, l called on him occasionally while walking between buildings at NASA during work. His presence would become subtly noticeable in my solar plexus as a high vibration, peaceful energy. I always felt better.

It was some months after discovering White Buffalo was my Oversoul that Leah suggested my home world is the planet Kezia in the Andromeda galaxy, which is also her home world. I had learned to trust Leah's intuitive insights, so I received this intriguing suggestion with gratitude. Lacking an understanding of the value of knowing my home world, I first considered it an interesting novelty. Curious, however, I asked my Oversoul on a number of occasions if Kezia was my home world. I always felt an affirmative resonance. The strength of the resonance varied from day to day, but it was always affirming and brought what felt like a connection to my deeper self, especially in my solar plexus. It felt like home.

When I want to connect to Kezia, I always ask my Oversoul to connect me to it, as opposed to attempting to connect to it myself. I do this because I discovered he can connect me easily, quickly, and safely. When I feel my Oversoul's presence upon calling him, I simply ask him to connect me to Kezia. I feel the connection to Kezia emerge in my solar plexus; it feels like a long cord connecting me to the planet. When I intuitively connect to other worlds, they don't feel like home. When connected to Kezia, I feel a sense of wholeness, well-being, and gentle nourishment. My energy field gets a tune-up. It's akin to getting a good hug from that special someone, but less intense.

I found it curious that I felt a connection in my solar plexus when sensing my Oversoul or my home world of Kezia. Metaphysical literature describes a silver-golden cord that connects astral travelers to their physical body at the solar plexus, though it may be invisible to some travelers, as has been my case. It states that the cord contains a component that passes from the soul to the physical body. If true, this is amazing and would explain my solar plexus sensations.

From a distance, I see Kezia's sky as purplish. There are structures on the planet, but I haven't seen them clearly. I seem to see other people's home world settings more clearly than my own. Emotionally detaching enough to perceive the planet clearly can be a challenge because of my relationship with it. If we went to Kezia in a spacecraft, we may not see the planet because Kezia is much higher in vibration than we are here on Earth.

Going further, I feel confident that I have separately met two people – Laura and Angie – who have the same Oversoul I do.

I met Angie in the mid-1980's while attending metaphysical classes in Leah's recreational room downstairs at her home in Maryland. Angie described having a spirit guide that looked like White Buffalo. As the months progressed, Leah confirmed that indeed we both had the same spirit guide. I didn't know what to make of it. I'd never known two people who shared the same spirit guide. Years later, I asked White Buffalo if Angie was from his soul essence. When he said yes, I felt an affirming energy resonance.

I met Laura, my other soul sister, in November 2018 in a hotel lobby adjacent to the "AlienCon" convention in Baltimore, Maryland. I, and a few other people, were waiting patiently in the lobby that night for our individual opportunities to share our ET-encounter stories with a film crew upstairs. While we waited, Laura and I got to know each other a little. After hearing some of her story, I offered her a mini-reading about her son and her ET-encounters. Laura shared that she felt a connection with me, and I said I felt the same. After a while, Laura and I went upstairs and shared our stories with a small, and obviously tired, film crew. Unfortunately, our interviews didn't make it to TV.

In the days that followed, Laura and I kept in touch by phone. Laura was happily married, living in south-east Pennsylvania with her husband and son. Even on the phone, Laura and I felt a connection to each other. It wasn't long before our discussions led me to a hunch — I called in Abraham and asked him if Laura was White Buffalo's offspring. He clearly verified this as true.

I told Laura the news over the phone and explained the Oversoul concept to her. Excited, she was very receptive to my suggestion of meditating on it to see how it resonated with her. A few days later, Laura reported that this genuinely felt right. We were both excited, feeling we'd truly found the reason for our sense of closeness.

Thanksgiving, Christmas, and New Years came and went. We were both very busy – I at NASA and Laura as a schoolteacher. I phoned her in mid-January to catch up, and within a few minutes I sensed our Oversoul, White Buffalo, come into my energy field. I hadn't called on him — he simply chose to come in on his own. From my perspective, he was both in my energy field and standing with us. I sensed him in my crown, heart, and solar plexus chakras. The vibration was notably high and strong this time, and I could sense a home-like feeling. This evolved into my seeing my home world, Kezia, in my mind's eye, and then seeing a bit of my hair-covered form there. I told Laura what I was experiencing as it happened, and she got excited.

"Laura, do you want to connect with White Buffalo, too, while he is here?" I asked encouragingly.

I could sense that Laura and White Buffalo were both excited with our reunion.

"Yes," Laura said eagerly.

*White Buffalo, would you connect with Laura as well, please?*

I felt his energy go to her while staying connected with me.

"I can feel him, Greg!" Laura said.

I was so happy to hear this. I felt very blessed to be witnessing the unfolding of their relationship and further validation of the Oversoul concept.

"My spirit is celebrating like a happy child!" Laura said with laughter in her voice.

"I don't feel a sense of home, but the connection feels very good and comforting."

I clearly felt White Buffalo was overjoyed with our three-way reunion. I could see him smiling ear-to-ear.

In the months that followed, I gave Laura some pointers on how to initiate and sense a connection with White Buffalo. I told her "Sumara" was another name for him, and she has always preferred this over "White Buffalo."

Laura and I have enjoyed a strong friendship since the day we met. We truly feel like family. We enjoy talking on the phone and getting together at least once a year. I get a kick out of referring to Laura as my "soul sister." We've given a much deeper meaning to the term!

As I described to Laura my interest in writing this book, she graciously provided me with the following testimonial regarding meeting me and our Oversoul.

*Greg and I met at AlienCon on November 10, 2018, in Baltimore, Maryland. It seems ironic that this is how the Universe brought us together. Nick Pope (a frequent speaker on the TV show Ancient Aliens) had asked the audience if they wanted to share any personal ET contact experiences, and a long line formed at the microphone. They ran out of time before everyone could speak so they announced that those who wanted to share their experience could meet in the lobby next door later that evening. I went to the lobby and there were several of us standing around. It turned out that Prometheus Entertainment was filming these interviews for the History Channel. We had to sign some paperwork and then we were called in pairs up to a room where they filmed our story. Greg and I were paired up, so we started talking before they took us up. Instantly, I felt drawn to him and wanted to talk to him. I can't quite explain the connection I felt but it was strong.*

*We were each filmed while sharing our experiences. When we were done, Greg and I continued to talk in the lobby. He gave me an intuitive* reading, answering questions about my son. I drove him to his car, and we exchanged contact information. During the whole drive home (we lived about two hours from each other), I just felt a connection like I knew him or that he was somehow very important to me.

Our connection: Over the next few days and weeks, Greg and I both felt this strong connection and started talking to figure it out. I had the sense that maybe we were Twin Flames. A number of days later, I saw an image in meditation of two egg yolks in an egg, and I also saw a mirror. It felt like an overwhelming love, and it was confusing to me because I am happily married. Greg introduced me to the concept of the Oversoul. I was already familiar with guardian angels but had never heard of the Oversoul. Greg felt that we share the same Oversoul and angel when I told him I saw us as "two yokes in the same egg." He said he'd asked his Oversoul if I was one of his offspring, and his Oversoul gave him a very affirming response.

Greg asked me to mediate on it and try to connect to "our" Oversoul and see what I felt. I did, and it was amazing. We do share the same guardian angel and Oversoul! I had so many questions! How is this possible? How many people can an Oversoul and guardian angel look over at the same time? How did it all work? He was very patient with me and answered all of my questions until I had a clear understanding. Greg also taught me about home planets, and that we are both from Kezia in Andromeda. He has a natural ability to tap into the Akashic Records and do a "Home World reading" for people to find out where they are from in the Universe, and what their purpose is in this lifetime. As you probably know, we all have psychic ability, but some have a more developed sense and connection. Over the next few years, we got together a few times a year. When we are together, my psychic ability is enhanced. It's really cool! I now refer to him as my "soul brother" and love him dearly.

My Extraterrestrial connection: I have vivid memories of five separate alien abductions starting when I was about ten years old. They seemed to occur about every five years until I was 30. I can remember being taken from my room by small Greys, being on a metal table, and being experimented on. I have physical evidence of this as well. I have two small holes at the top of my ears on both sides of my head. I am adopted and did not have these at birth or when I was a very small child. The last time they *came for me they also left physical evidence on my cat — a small triangle shaved on his back. No matter where I was living at the time, they would find me, and I would have an abduction experience. It wasn't until I met Greg that I could ask questions about what happened. He got that I was part of a breeding program and it felt correct. He also sensed that there was a Grey named Parbo that looked after me and that I could try to connect with. I greatly valued Greg's input and information. He always has the purest intentions and wants to help people.*

I asked Laura if she would answer questions for this book regarding her experiences with our Oversoul, Sumara. Here are my questions and her replies:

My question (Q): When you connect with Sumara, which of these intuitive senses are used: Feeling, seeing, knowing, or hearing?

Laura's answer (A): Feeling, mostly. I always get the feeling of love and protection. Sometimes, I also use "knowing" as it seems that when I ask a question, or ask for guidance, the answers are given as a knowing. It's more like communication without words — basically telepathy. There are times when I just get images shown to me in response to questions I ask. For example, Greg, when you first confirmed to me that we share the same Oversoul, I was shown two pictures. One of an egg and the other of a two-sided mirror. These were both confirmations for me that the information was correct.

Q: How often do you feel you've connected with Sumara?
A: I've connected with Sumara's energy hundreds of times. Each night before I go to sleep, I try to connect to give thanks and ask for protection and healing for my friends and family. The signal is sometimes stronger than others, but anytime I ask, I am able to connect.
Q: Did your chakras or energy field go out of balance when you first started connecting with Sumara?
A: I'm not sure if my chakras or energy field went out of balance when I first started connecting with my Oversoul. The feelings were very strong when I was with you and we connected to Sumara

together. It's like the signal was stronger and easier since we are both connected to the same Oversoul.

Q: Did your intuition increase since establishing a connection with Sumara?

A: I haven't noticed an obvious increase in intuition since I started connecting with my Oversoul.

Q: Why do you connect with Sumara? What benefit do you get?

A: I connect with Sumara because he is part of me and my connection to my higher self. I know he can see "the big picture" and is always on my side and comes from Source, God. The benefit I get is knowing someone has my best interests and gives me a feeling of great love.

I have used the Akashic Records to help numerous other clients gain awareness about their Oversouls and home planets. I recently provided a client, Laurel Ann, with her home star system (Sirius A) and her Oversoul's name. Laurel graciously agreed to provide answers for my questions to use in this book.

My question (Q): Does the Oversoul name (Rena) I retrieved for you intuitively resonate?

Laurel Ann's answer (A): Yes.

Q: Have you been able to sense a connection with your Oversoul?

A: Most definitely.

Q: If so, which of these intuitive senses are used: Feeling, seeing, knowing, or hearing?

A: Feeling and knowing.

Q: How often do you feel you've connected with your Oversoul's energy?

A: Daily. Sometimes multiple times during the day.

Q: Have your chakras or energy field gone out of balance since you started connecting to your Oversoul? They will stabilize, if so.

A: I feel stabilized now.

Q: Has your intuition increased since establishing a connection with your Oversoul?
A: Yes.
Q: Anything else you'd like to share?
A: I am experiencing so much love and support coming from Rena. I am getting downloads from any question I ask — so much clarity.

I believe the concept of the Oversoul has consistently stood the test of time. Throughout all the home world readings I have given over the decades, whether I am retrieving a client's Oversoul name, or personally connecting to a client's Oversoul, or having a client connect to their Oversoul in my presence, my intuition has always affirmed its existence.

# 13

## ALPHA CENTAURI

It was the middle of the night. I was alone in the woods on my Vision Quest in the fall air of Indiana. Twenty years had passed since my first Vision Quest, and I had enjoyed at least a dozen more in that time. Now 2008, I was 47 years old. While comfortably asleep in my sleeping bag, with my Chanupa — my sacred Pipe — held to my chest, I had a dream of being in a small bedroom somewhere unfamiliar. The walls of the A-frame bedroom were made of sturdy, unadorned planks of wood. Standing just inside the door, next to a small, nondescript bed, I faced an empty wall at the opposite end, wondering why there wasn't a window there, given its ample size. There were no windows anywhere in the room.

In the dream, I was talking to my close friend, Brent, on my cell phone. He said something and I didn't reply, so he disconnected from the call. When I looked at my phone to call him back, I was shocked to realize I was no longer on my Vision Quest blanket. I had always honored the guideline that Vision Questers remain within the safety of the prayer ties surrounding their blanket. I got very concerned. I hadn't yet realized I was simply dreaming.

Curiously, my dream body began to shake all over, and I began hearing a slight roaring in my ears. I was familiar with this feeling and sound – it happens when my astral body is close to leaving my physical body. My awareness immediately returned to my motionless physical body, and I found my astral body was still shaking. The roaring in my ears had increased. I was very glad to discover I once again was on my blanket, and I had only been dreaming.

Next, to my surprise and excitement, I found myself swiftly exiting my physical body through a tunnel at my third-eye chakra. I was propelled through an unfamiliar light blue, ever-curving, circular tunnel no larger than a few feet in diameter — and I was enjoying every moment of it. I had never experienced an OBE like this, and it was thrilling. My consciousness was fully present in my astral body as if I were there physically. I knew that what happens on Vision Quest is especially meaningful, so this OBE had a significant, yet unknown, purpose.

After 10 seconds of travelling, I suddenly stopped moving and found myself instantly floating upright in midair in the center of a well-lit cylindrical room. The room appeared to be about 30 feet in diameter, and I was facing one end of the cylinder, which was spherical. The surface of the cylinder was made of flat, rectangular, backlit panels, alternating black and white in their arrangement. I marveled at this spectacle, the likes of which I'd never seen or imagined. The triangular panels making up the spherical end of the cylinder maintained an attractive alternating black and white arrangement that fit precisely together.

I estimated I was about 25 feet away from the end of the cylinder. I noticed I did not have my Chanupa, and I was dressed in my usual street clothes. The energy of the room felt neutral, and I felt calm and self-confident.

*Okay, now we're getting somewhere.*

I was excited and eager to see what was going to happen next. I surmised I was in a spacecraft. Unfortunately, no one interacted with me, and there were no signs of activity.

After about 20 seconds, my awareness faded from the room and resumed in my physical body in my sleeping bag. Chanupa in hand, I was still positioned as I had been before my OBE. While I was elated that I had this OBE adventure, I was disappointed that no one interacted with me while I was out of body.

Sometime the next day, while still on my Vision Quest, I intuitively sensed I had been on a spaceship associated with the Alpha Centauri star system – the closest star system to Earth.

My experiences with beings from Alpha Centauri are a significant part of my life. Most importantly, I enjoy connecting with these engaging, benevolent beings who have chosen me to be an ambassador of sorts as we expand the important connections between our two species. I am eager to share how I initiated and developed a relationship with my friends from Alpha Centauri and how their methods of connecting with me go way beyond interacting in dreams or meditation. I also feel that sharing about my experience does them and us a service because they are mostly unknown and rarely mentioned in ET discussion groups. The lack of awareness surrounding the Alpha Centaurians is puzzling because they are located in the closest star system to Earth.

I first learned about these beings from Patricia Smith about a year prior to my Vision Quest experience. In her book, *Emergence*, Pat details her life-long journey of discovery centered upon the Alpha Centaurians and her realization of her soul connection with them. Two of the ways I have interacted with Alpha Centaurians were during unexpected Vision Quest OBEs – one of which I just shared. The other way was through meditation. The OBE experiences were substantiated by the intuitive experiences of others involved in the Vision Quests.

Chief Richard, Mary Thunder's son, led the Vision Quest I just described. After I came down from my blanket and returned to the camp site, Chief confirmed with me that I had indeed been in an ET spacecraft.

Chief Richard began Vision Questing in the mid-1980s along with many of us in Thunder's close group of friends and supporters. Chief Richard's path led him to become a facilitator of traditional Lakota ceremonies. His experience, training, and permission to lead these ceremonies came primarily from his mother, Mary Thunder, and Chief Leonard Crow Dog. Leading Vision Quests was one of the ways Chief Richard chose to serve people. He also used his carpentry skills to make a living and support his family. I liked Chief Richard. He was personable, social, and interested in ETs, given his experiences with them earlier in his life.

Our Vision Quest camp was primitive, yet well-functioning, with a propane-run outdoor kitchen, a sweat lodge, porta-potties, tents, and ample room for the 20 or so vehicles. The few children that accompanied adults were happy being a part of the gathering, and we all enjoyed the beautiful rural setting and view of the rolling hills.

Sarah (not her real name) Vision Quested the same day I did, and to my amazement shared an ET-related experience associated with me that she had on her Quest.

"I saw two spirits walking through the woods while I was on my blanket, Greg. My gut told me they were ETs, and they were looking for you."

I was flabbergasted. I knew Sarah was an intuitive who could see spirits, and I listened intently.

"One of them had a green energy field and the other had a blue energy field with a very prominent sine wave in its head. Maybe the sine wave was a symbol that my mind used to indicate it was a robot, I don't know. I kept my head down to appear as if I couldn't see them. I had enough to contend with on my Vision Quest and I didn't know where you were located anyway."

I stared at her wide-eyed, taking in her incredible story.

"One of them tripped over an elemental who grumbled at being stepped on."

I burst out laughing, while Sarah shook her head in disbelief.

Elementals are spirit beings who inhabit the natural world. In many cultures, they are known by different names, such as fairies, pixies, sprites, nymphs, and more. Each type of elemental has a unique personality and role within the natural world.

"How ironic," she said. "ETs can come halfway across the galaxy but can't see right in front of them!"

"Sarah, that's an amazing story," I replied with surprise. "Thank you so much for sharing it. This explains why I telepathically heard a being excitedly say to me 'We're here!' a few hours before sunset. Sarah, I bet they were responsible for somehow initiating my OBE to their craft."

As I stood on my blanket facing west with my Chanupa the day after my OBE, I sensed spirits thanking me for pursuing the role of helping star people and Earth people with their star connections. The spirits said it was an important role that needed filling, and I felt they had confidence in me. I didn't have a sense of who they were, but I felt they were not Alpha Centaurian.

As my Vision Quest drew to a close, I knew the time on my blanket would soon end, with two people coming to bring me back to camp. To complete my time with Creator and the spirits that helped, I faced each cardinal direction, Chanupa in hand, and gave thanks. I also asked spirit to communicate if anything more needed to be done to complete my Vision Quest. While standing facing north, I felt an energy come to me that included several spirits. I realized the gentle, heart-centered beings felt Pleiadian. Each different star group I have sensed over the years has a unique energy to them. I humbly felt them honor me, dress me in spirit clothes and give me a full-body energy infusion. I felt very honored. Shortly after, I received intuitive confirmation that they were Pleiadian.

From the time I began planning to attend the Vision Quest, I never entertained a thought about connecting with ETs during the ceremony. I always go to Vision Quests with the sole intention of praying for people and asking Creator to show me what he wants me to know or do. Sometimes I go with specific questions.

When I asked my Oversoul about my OBE several days after my Vision Quest, I felt like a student passing a test when he confirmed the beings were from Alpha Centauri. I was pleased I had discerned my VQ experience correctly. With that, he said it was okay for me to communicate directly with them and the relationship would be ongoing. I always feel these ETs are centered in their upper chakras when we connect, indicating they have a spiritual, heart-centered intention.

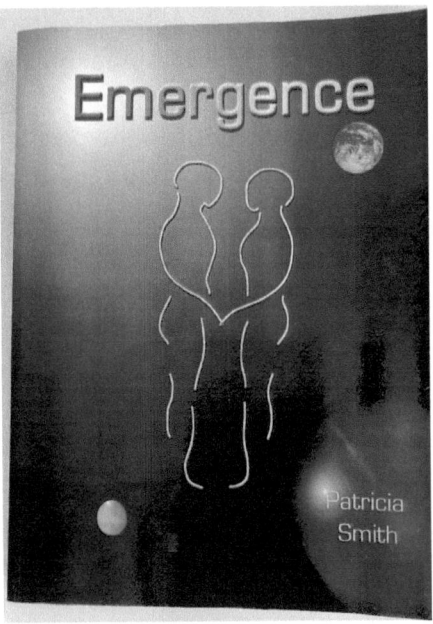

*Patricia Smith's book about her encounters with beings from the Alpha Centauri star system*

Patricia Smith served for more than 32 years in military and government positions. Her educational background includes business management, intelligence analysis, and criminal justice. Unfortunately, Pat is no longer with us today, as she passed away in 2023 from natural causes. She became actively interested in the UFO field at a very young age after observing a strange craft near her home. She was further drawn into the subject after realizing she had experienced interactions with extraterrestrials.

Pat and I met at the Monroe Institute in Charlottesville, Virginia area during a day-long class about exploring and experiencing expanded states of consciousness. Bob Monroe, the founder of the institute, developed methods for altering consciousness using sound frequencies combined in complex, yet restful ways, and I wanted to explore this avenue. There, Pat told me about her life-long experiences with the Alpha Centaurians. I was intrigued by her tales of these beings I had never heard of before.

Early on in our friendship, Pat said she felt Alpha Centauri was her home star system, and I verified with Abraham, for my own benefit, that this was correct.

Pat wrote *Emergence* to share her involvement in the Alpha Centauri-human genetics hybridization program, and to extensively describe the makeup of these beings and their benevolent intentions to assist humanity in realizing our full spiritual and mental potential. Their hybridization program combines human DNA with their ET DNA to birth a being that is a mix of the two.

From what I've found in the Akashic Records during intuitive consultations with clients, the Alpha Centaurians and the Grey ETs have been successfully implementing hybridization programs on Earth for centuries.

The Greys are commonly associated with the star system Zeta Reticuli, though in my intuitive experience they also come from other star systems. Given this, I'm not surprised to see them as having a variety of body structures. Their most common appearance is four feet tall with gray skin, large black almond-shaped eyes, and a small slit-like mouth. I have also seen them as much taller. During two separate eye-opening intuitive consultations I gave clients about their experiences with the Greys' hybridization program, I was visited by an adult Grey in spirit form. They each gave me their name and let me know they had been involved with the client's hybridization program activities throughout the years in an oversight capacity. They were kind, helpful, and interested in their client's well-being.

My understanding of the hybridization process is that ETs impregnate a woman using an "in vitro" type process involving her eggs, human male sperm and ET DNA. The embryo would grow in the human female as if it were purely human. For hybrids that are intended to look human, the pregnancy would go to full term and the baby would be born on Earth. Over the years the child would not likely see physical hybrid traits. The mother may or may not recall her interaction with the ETs. For hybrids that are designed to have noticeable physical ET characteristics, the hybridization process can be rather unsettling for mothers. The fetus disappears early in the pregnancy — taken from the mother by the ETs and brought to term in their care — likely on their spaceship. Although the mother may not have any memory of the ETs taking her fetus, she will likely know she was pregnant and find the disappearance disturbing.

One night on the phone Pat shared details with me about her experience in the Alpha Centaurian hybridization program.

"Greg, the Alpha Centaurians are a dying race. One day they will all be gone and only their hybrids and the co-existing race on their planet will be left to inhabit their beautiful green world. Human-looking hybrids are born on Earth and grow up in human society. The hybrids that look more like the full-blood Alpha Centaurians are brought to term on their world, where they grow up. Certain pre-selected human-looking hybrids have been chosen as emissaries for when the Alpha Centaurians openly make their existence and presence known on Earth."

The questions surrounding the future of the Alpha Centaurian race – specifically, why Pat said they are "dying" – remain unanswered for me. I'm also unsure as to the nature and characteristics of the race that coexists with the Alpha Centaurians on their home planet.

"Pat, your story about seeing one of the hybrid children is amazing."

"That was a surprising, and initially unsettling memory, I must say," Pat said emphatically. "All of us women in the hybridization program became involved by our own choice, too. It took me a long time to accept that and understand how it works. None of us were forced into this, apparently. Typically, most of us don't remember making these choices or agreements because we make the choices on higher levels of consciousness. Over the years, I've released the fear I had about the Alpha Centaurians, and now I feel their benevolence."

"I don't believe I'm an Alpha Centaurian hybrid, Pat. I feel confident of that."

"I don't believe you are a hybrid either. Your role is different."

The main reason I became inspired to connect with the Alpha Centaurians was Pat's sharing in *Emergence* that the Alpha Centaurians are looking for people to help them get the word out surrounding their benevolent mission to help humanity evolve. These ETs say they accepted this assignment at the request of the Divine Source, known to many as God.

*Well, I can likely connect with them. I could help them spread the word regarding their presence once I learn about what they are doing to help humanity. This would be really interesting and would help me develop my skills in connecting with ETs.*

I was enthusiastic as this seemed like a perfect fit. I wanted to get approval from my Oversoul, however, before offering to help the Alpha Centaurians. If my Oversoul felt this effort was in harmony with my soul's path and my highest good, then I was all for it. The idea of assisting them felt safe and appropriate because I had strongly sensed these heart-centered and unintrusive beings around me while reading *Emergence*. At one point while reading the book, I even felt my third-eye chakra perk up and I could vaguely see the outline of one of their faces. Their humanoid appearance is very different from what we are comfortable seeing, according to Pat. I haven't seen them clearly enough to draw a sketch. This aside, I have always experienced them as compassionate, welcoming, and loving.

My Oversoul, plus the Pleiadian Council and the Andromedan Council, each gave me the green light to support these Alpha Centaurian beings, feeling their goals were altruistic. The councils are the main governing bodies of their starry realms, and I communicate with them by asking my Oversoul to connect me to them. Impressively, he can make the connection upon my request.

The Alpha Centauri star system is the closest star system to our solar system at just four light-years away. Theirs is a three-star system, consisting of Alpha Centauri A and Alpha Centauri B orbiting each other, plus Alpha Centauri C (also called Proxima Centauri) orbiting those two at quite a distance. To date, no planets have been found around these stars that can likely support life.

There is a planet approximately the size of Earth orbiting Alpha Centauri B, but it is extremely close to that sun, making it a poor candidate for supporting life as we know it. There are planets orbiting Proxima Centauri, which is a red dwarf star that emits X-rays and ultraviolet radiation. This high level of radiation makes those planets poor candidates for harboring life, according to a 2018 article referencing NASA's Chandra x-ray observatory. NASA has said, however, that according to computer orbit simulations, other planets might exist with stable orbits in the Alpha Centauri A-B system that could possibly harbor life.

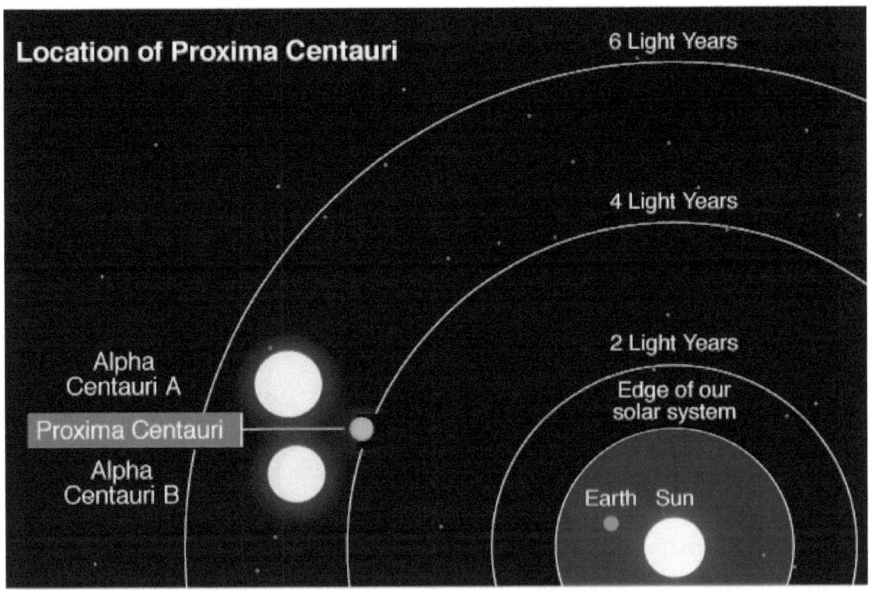

*Location of the Alpha Centauri star system with respect to Earth (Source: EarthSky.org)*

If any Alpha Centaurian beings have a very high vibration rate, they might not normally be visible to us in our dimension. In this case, they would have to somehow shift into our dimension for us to physically interact with them. We might be able to see the planet they reside on, but not see them. It is also possible that their planet is in a different dimension from ours.

An excerpt from Pat Smith's book, *Emergence,* illustrates the level of detail she shares about life at Alpha Centauri.

"Sentient life evolved on only one planet in the Alpha Centauri System...These beings originate from a world they think of as the Emerald Planet that rotates around Alpha Centauri...The temperature fluctuates between 70-and-115 degrees Fahrenheit...The population is comprised of two different races..."

I shared my Vision Quest experience with Pat on the phone a month after returning from the Indiana Vision Quest.

"Pat I'm feeling like we and the Alpha Centaurians are having a little reunion here on the phone."

"Yes, Greg, I feel it too," Pat responded emotionally. "I'm so happy to hear about your Vision Quest experience with them, but I don't have any recollection of the black-and-white cylindrical room you experienced."

"I was hoping you'd know all about it," I said half-jokingly. "Pat, I sometimes experience difficulty intuitively connecting with them during meditation though."

"Perhaps the difficulty occurs when they are not in Earth orbit, Greg. Sometimes they pull back from Earth for various reasons. Their ships have families onboard and they might pull back if they feel a threat from Earth."

Pat and I ended our conversation with warm hearts and a feeling of camaraderie.

In the months following my Vision Quest, I connected with Alpha Centaurians many times during meditation. One particular experience provides interesting details about our relationship.

While lying on my bed, I performed my usual chakra-clearing effort and then connected with my Oversoul. Unique to this meditation, I felt the benevolent energy of several unknown beings come up against my right side, and then my left. I sensed they were likely not Alpha Centaurians. I felt no urge to inquire about their identity because they felt non-threatening, and I wanted to stay focused on my objective. I asked my Oversoul and angel to help me connect with the Alpha Centaurian beings associated with my Vision Quest.

I called on the Alpha Centaurians through my heart chakra, while using my crown and third-eye chakras as monitors for their energy. In about 30 seconds, I saw several of them in my third eye, and I felt their familiar energy in my heart chakra. I sat up at that point because I didn't want to get sleepy. With that, I felt our energetic connection significantly increase and I sensed they were grateful for my interest in assisting them. I responded by sending them love. Our intuitive connection was strong. I felt their presence and vaguely saw their faces as if they were right in front of me.

I asked them if they wanted to communicate on a regular basis – every few days or so – and I was happy to sense an affirmative response.

For the next 10 minutes we didn't communicate much, as I sensed them energetically working with my crown chakra and some other areas of my energy field.

Afterward, they told me they had ships in Earth orbit. I saw Jupiter in my mind's eye and wondered if this is where their ships pulled back to if they felt a threat from Earth.

Shortly after, my inner senses of hearing, knowing, and feeling all indicated the Alpha Centaurians had chosen me to be something like an ambassador between them and humans. I felt honored and up for the task, figuring I could handle whatever that might entail.

I felt myself tiring soon after and requested we end our session. I thanked them and felt an abundance of love from them in return. In a moment, I didn't see or feel them anymore. Feeling that strong connection vanish validated that their presence was indeed real, and not a figment of my imagination.

Vision Questing at the same property a year later, I was again taken out of body to an Alpha Centaurian spacecraft. This fascinating experience included a personal interaction with one of them, though I never saw him. Chief Richard, who was leading the Vision Quest, and my Oversoul later validated this OBE and offered some clarity about it.

When I got to my Vision Quest blanket in the woods, I set up my altar by laying down an 18-inch piece of cotton cloth at an edge of the blanket and spiraling a long string of prayer ties on it. This is where I would place my Chanupa when I wasn't holding it. I also pulled sage, sweetgrass, cedar, and tobacco out of my bag – the four sacred herbs in Lakota tradition. I burned sage to purify myself and my belongings, and I gave thanks for this opportunity with Creator and Mother Earth.

With my Chanupa held to my heart, I humbly prayed and acknowledged the spirits in the four directions. I felt a peaceful connection with nature. The sky was clear, and the air warm. I often prayed without thoughts or words, but rather with intention and heart-felt unconditional love for family, friends, and others.

After a couple of hours, I noticed my inner sight showing me a silver spaceship hovering in a cloudy sky. It was a large disk, flat and thin, with two rows of many windows. The windows appeared closely spaced and very small, suggesting the ship was distant.

When I reclined for the night, I was comfortably dressed in warm clothes, holding my Chanupa to my chest, and lying on my belly in my sleeping bag. I had pulled a thin layer of clear plastic over me, as a light rain was falling.

Sometime in the night, I inexplicably awoke and opened my eyes. I felt alert, yet peaceful. Almost immediately, I heard an adult male speak as if he were right there on the blanket.

"We are going to take you out of body now," he said matter-of-factly.

"Okay," I responded telepathically. I was glad they — whomever "they" were — had come because I was eager to deepen my relationship with benevolent beings, especially ETs.

Next, I felt a very realistic hand come to rest on my left shoulder, as if the plastic cover on top of me wasn't there. The hand was warm and large enough to be an adult's. Another hand came to rest on my lower back. Then I was abruptly yanked completely out of my body through my lower back.

*Wow, that was a bit rough*, I gasped, as I felt myself being drawn away from my body.

*I guess they aren't used to taking people out of body*, I chuckled. I found the experience somewhat amusing. I wasn't afraid in the least, given I knew what being out-of-body was like, and I was confident they were caring beings.

I instantly found myself lying in the lower bunk of an upscale, yet simple, small room. The generous use of dark, reddish-stained wood reminded me of an old sailing ship. I surmised it was for upper-ranking crew or guests. I was eager to explore and still had no idea who had taken me out of body. Using my intention, I rolled out of bed in my astral body. Landing feet-first on the floor, I stood upright with the speed of thought. I felt a slight dream-like component to this OBE, unlike my OBE to the Alpha Centaurian spacecraft a year before. At this point, I wasn't aware that I was on another Alpha Centaurian spacecraft.

I looked around the room for clues as to where I might be, but there were no symbols, signs, wall hangings, or other indications.

I turned to face the stationary, wooden, swinging doors. I peered through one of the doors' oval windows seeing only a dimly lit, non-descript hallway. I willed myself forward through the doors and into the hallway, marveling at the feeling of passing through what felt like a dense material. To my right, at least 30 feet down the hall, a lit room quietly waited behind a similar set of swinging doors. Ahead of me, and to my left, were identical swinging doors blocking dark hallways. Figuring I had time to explore, I willed myself forward and through the doors ahead of me into a dark hallway.

"I'm here, and ready to work with you," I telepathically announced with enthusiasm.

There was no reply — and still no detectable presence of anyone. I floated 20 feet down the hall and suddenly sensed my consciousness begin to fade from the location. I felt so let down that this astral adventure appeared to be ending so soon. I hadn't yet met anyone or determined where I was. I knew I was likely fading back to my physical body in my sleeping bag.

Within a second or two, I found myself gently lowering into my physical body, its position unchanged from when I left it.

*Why didn't I go to the room with the light on?* I thought, discouraged. *Maybe they were waiting for me there.*

Chief Richard, who led my last Vision Quest, was leading this one, as well. I told him about this OBE when I was back at the camp a day later. I trust what Chief says about ET's during these ceremonies. He is very connected to Spirit and has led many ceremonies over the years.

"Yes, you were up on a spacecraft, Greg," Chief confidently said. "The ship you saw in your mind was likely the ship you went to."

"Chief, my mind might have made up that image of the ship in the clouds," I offered, looking for his intuitive sense about what happened.

Chief chuckled. "Greg, be more accepting of your connection to ETs. I think the ETs were monitoring your thoughts and actions in the ship."

"Perhaps they simply wanted to see how I would react to being pulled out of body and being in their ship?"

I felt fortunate to receive Chief's input about my experience while it was so fresh in our minds.

Chief also revealed to me how well protected the other questers and I were when I shared another topic with him — what I saw in the sweat lodge before going out to my Vision Quest site.

"Chief, In the sweat lodge before I was taken out to my Vision Quest blanket, I saw a Native American on horseback come from the west to the center of my view. He was facing the east on a sun-lit prairie, and he wore an eagle feather bonnet that went down his back. He carried a long staff in his right hand. An eagle's head next to him was facing me. Then my view was brought up close to the horse. The image faded away when a beautiful brown buffalo appeared, also facing east."

"What did you feel about the Native American?" Chief asked.

"I assumed he was going to take me to the spirit world on my Vision Quest."

Chief nodded in affirmation.

I assumed the Native American was going to guide me to the spirit world because years ago, while I was quietly leading several Vision Questers to their blankets for their Vision Quests, I was honored and awed to have a vision of a Native American spirit on horseback leading the way in front of me as we walked. The prominent vision appeared clairvoyantly in my third-eye chakra for about 15 seconds. During that time, my gut told me he was bringing the questers to the spirit world. We walked together.

"Greg, the Native American spirit you saw in the sweat lodge confirms what I saw in there," Chief Richard replied appreciatively. "He was one of four Thunder Beings that came into the lodge. There are four Thunder Being spirits in Lakota spirituality, and one carries a staff like you saw. They came to watch over the questers on the hill."

Two other questers shared with me and others later that they felt a guardian, or sentinel, protecting the entrance to their quest site while they were on their blanket.

In Lakota tradition, Thunder Beings are long-existing, revered spirits who come with thunderstorms. They are protectors and guardians, and I was amazed and appreciative that these beings came to support us.

While home in Maryland after my Vision Quest, my Oversoul added to my understanding of what occurred during my experience on the spacecraft. By this time, I had intuitively determined that the craft was Alpha Centaurian. He said that I knew the being who took me out of body — that he was an Alpha Centaurian-human hybrid assigned to work with me. His being a hybrid made sense because he seemed human. In addition, White Buffalo said the purpose of my going to the wooden bunk room and halls was to continue with my training. He added that I know that place. With that, I sensed that other folks and I used the beds on occasion while on the spacecraft.

I felt both surprised and encouraged by this realization. Later I wondered if I'd ever physically been on their craft and rested in the bunkbeds. I had no idea if my astral body would need to rest while there. I was very happy to hear White Buffalo confirm that the beings were associated with Alpha Centauri. His report was essential for me to have, given what I sensed about the profound nature of my experience – that I went onto a spacecraft run by beings from Alpha Centauri!

My last effort to confirm that I was truly with the Alpha Centaurians during my Vision Quest came when I connected with them in meditation at home. My brief telepathic communication with them confirmed my assessment of the Vision Quest. The verifications came mostly through strong affirming resonances in my energy field.

There's a reason why the Alpha Centaurians didn't interact with me consciously on their spacecraft, but I can only speculate as to their motives. Perhaps I received training, as suggested, or had other experiences that I don't recall. I can only trust that I will become fully aware of anything that may have happened when the time is appropriate. Until then, I can simply believe that the gentle and loving Alpha Centaurians had our best interests at heart, and I am grateful for the efforts they made with me.

These Vision Quest OBEs I've described are the most physically and astrally active interchanges I've ever experienced with ETs. To my knowledge, I have never been physically brought onto an ET craft. Based on my experiences during these two Vision Quests, though, I feel confident that productive interactions can occur with ETs through out-of-body travel to their craft.

Alpha Centauri, our next closest star system, harbors advanced, intelligent, benevolent life. We are blessed. I hope one day our societies can interact in peace with mutual appreciation.

# 14

## THE PLEIADES

I was excited to be on Vision Quest again. It had been seven years since my last quest in which Alpha Centauri beings took me out-of-body to their spacecraft. Now 2016, I was 55 years old. This Vision Quest was in Kentucky, and we were blessed with beautiful spring weather. I was happy to see Chief Richard Grimes as well, and little did I know, his presence would bring my connection to the Pleiades closer.

While standing on my Vision Quest blanket facing west at midday, praying with my Chanupa in hand, I sensed a spirit presence in the north. When I turned to face north, my inner sight saw a woman wearing a traditional Native American buckskin dress. I understood her to be quite real, but existing in a higher dimension. Grateful for the visit, I humbly acknowledged her. I sensed she was associated with the Pleiades. The Pleiades is an open star cluster of hot, young, blue-white stars about 440 light years from Earth. The "Seven Sisters," as they are also called, are easily visible in the fall and winter months in the northern hemisphere.

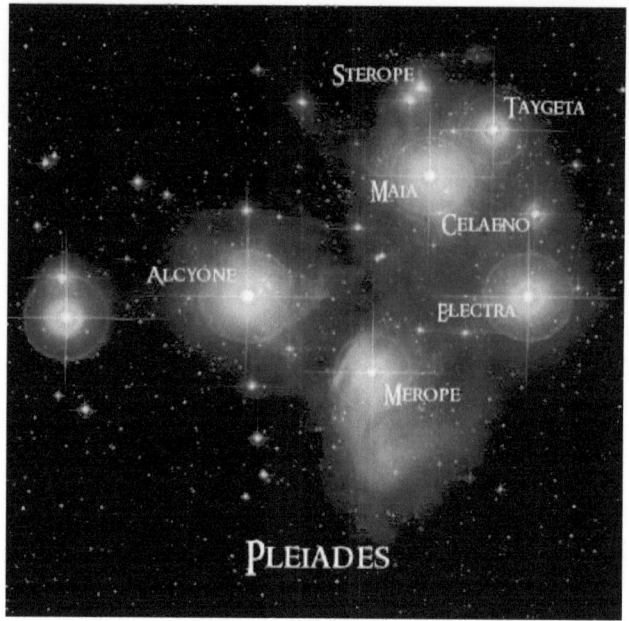

*The Seven Sisters of the Pleiades star cluster
(Source: Pinterest.com)*

The young woman told me she and several others were going to involve me with their spacecraft soon. Containing my excitement, I did not assume she meant this would occur during my Vision Quest, and I said I would be happy to go aboard.

*Maybe this will be the time I directly communicate with Pleiadians. Connecting in meditation is great, but having a face-to-face experience onboard their craft would be extraordinary.*

She described the leader of the ship as a male elder and referred to just one or two others onboard, leaving me with the impression their ship was small.

*She reminds me of one of the three Pleiadian women who wrapped a blanket around me at the end of my Vision Quest with the Alpha Centaurians. She seems very similar.*

I didn't receive further communication from her, and the sun soon dropped low on the horizon. As was typical for me during Vision Quest, I got very sleepy in the quiet, calm woods once the sun was down.

Soon I was comfortably lying on my back in my warm sleeping bag, looking up at the stars through softly waving trees. I was one of seven or so questers on the hill that night. The space between us and our distance from camp gave us the tranquility of silence. I was feeling great. The noticeably peaceful, sacred energy of my Chanupa held to my heart carried me into a gentle, sweet slumber, and soon I was dreaming.

My most special dream of the night came after a few earlier dreams. I was watching a group of folks talking and surmised they may have just finished a Tai Chi class, given the formal Tai Chi outfits two men were wearing. The group was about 30 feet from me. The two men slowly walked away from the group together and one of them looked at me and our eyes locked. With that, my energy body began moving slowly out through my feet. I realized I was going out-of-body.

*Oh, these guys are good,* I thought with admiration.

I was pretty sure I was being intentionally taken out-of-body, and whoever was causing this was very gentle. I was still dreaming and only noticed I was going out-of-body because of my past experiences with OBEs.

In the next instant, I was standing, fully conscious, watching stars go by as if I were on board a spacecraft.

*The stars look so clear, I must be looking at them from space. Wait, the stars just reversed their motion. That's odd.*

I continued looking straight ahead, trying to make sense of where I was. I noticed I didn't see stars beyond a particular distance in my peripheral vision, leading me to believe I was looking through a rectangular window.

As is disappointingly typical in my Vision Quest OBEs, my conscious experience on board the spacecraft seemed to last only briefly, and I didn't recall anything more related to the OBE or the Pleiadians after that. I also had no memory of returning to my body. In the morning, I clearly recalled the OBE and surmised from my past Alpha Centaurian OBEs that I likely experienced more on board the Pleiadian craft than I was remembering.

The Pleiades are central to the ancestral lineage stories of many cultures. I have personally experienced connections with the Pleiades and Pleiadians through dreams, meditation, Native American ceremony and in the OBE I just shared. In my perception, and that of many others, these ETs look like Earth humans in every way. I have always experienced them as gentle and patient. They have always been responsive and supportive to my requests for contact — answering my questions and even providing connection to their worlds while I meditate.

Taygeta (also spelled Taygete), Alcyone, and Maia are the three main stars associated with these spacefaring, highly evolved beings from the Pleiades. These stars are three of a collection of stars known as the Seven Sisters. Paradoxically, human beings would not be able to safely occupy any planets there in our physical dimension, given the high-radiation environment of the Seven Sisters.

My interactions with the Pleiadians have been a central part of my metaphysical growth throughout the years. For that reason alone, I want to share how they have interacted with me, describe what I have found in the Akashic Records of clients associated with the Pleiades, and talk about the relationship of the Pleiadians with their home worlds in the Pleiades system. Like the Alpha Centaurians and others, it's important to understand who the Pleiadians are and how they relate to us. From my experience, the Pleiadians want us to survive and thrive, and they are actively involved in helping humanity. Most importantly, by understanding them, we also acquire a greater understanding of ourselves and our place in the Universe.

My connection with the Pleiadians during this Vision Quest started unknowingly the day before my actual Vision Quest began. That was when I gave Chief Richard an intuitive reading to address ET connections and experiences he recalled from his early years. Thankfully, the information I received from the Akashic Records and Spirit resonated strongly with Chief, providing clarity and validation for his ET experiences. I felt the ETs in his life were benevolent and were assisting him along his spiritual path. During the reading, I didn't check the Akashic Records to see what star system the ETs were from because it wasn't a priority.

While in the darkness of the sweat lodge purification ceremony just prior to going out to my Vision Quest blanket, my inner vision saw a bald eagle, an owl, and a Pleiadian spacecraft. I was excited to see the craft, and I simply acknowledged its presence silently without fixating on it. The craft was nearly identical to the one I saw years ago in a dream, which I spoke of several chapters back.

The day after my OBE, the full scope of the Pleiadians' involvement in this Vision Quest became apparent. My Vision Quest ended in the late afternoon when I was brought back to camp. At that point, I entered the sweat lodge to share with Chief what I experienced and to disconnect from the Vision Quest state of consciousness.

"You did well on your Vision Quest, Greg," Chief said.

He surprised me with what he said next because nobody knew about it.

"Your out-of-body star flight was with Pleiadians, Greg. They are the ones we connected with yesterday while talking about the ET experiences I had."

My heart sang to hear this. They were interacting with both of us.

"The Pleiadians told me they would connect with you on the hill during your quest because you helped me understand their presence in my life."

I almost started to cry with gratitude that they would do that for me; I had helped Chief and the Pleiadians connect on a deeper level, and I was treated to a ride in their craft. My jaw was on the ground in awe.

"The Pleiadians told me you can contact them any time, Greg, and also act as an intermediary between them and me, since you connect with them more easily than I do."

"Yes, Chief, I'm happy to do this for you, and I thank the Pleiadians for this relationship."

My heart was full. I fantasized briefly about riding on their ship and having face-to-face conversations. I was excited knowing this was possible if there was truly a need for it.

Since that quest, I have experienced many non-physical contacts with Pleiadians – some I initiated, and some they initiated unexpectedly. These connections ranged in duration from just a minute to more than an hour. On one occasion, two years after the quest, I experienced a brief visit from them while alone during sweat lodge ceremony preparations on Virginia's Eastern Shore. Jon and his wife Kate graciously provided this Lakota ceremony on a monthly basis, and I went as often as I could. I always felt clean, clear connections with Spirit and experienced gentle purification of mind, body, and spirit at Jon and Kate's sweat lodge ceremonies.

On this particular Saturday sweat lodge, I was offering tobacco to each of the four cardinal directions with a humble, heartfelt prayer before preparing the ground to build the sweat lodge fire. My prayer simply acknowledged each cardinal direction individually, asking Spirit from each direction to be with us during our ceremony and to help folks arrive safely.

As I offered tobacco and a prayer to the north, I felt Pleiadian energy come to me from that direction. I had never felt ETs come in when doing this, so I was surprised and very honored. I saw a female wearing a Native American-style buckskin dress. I don't recall her saying anything to me, but I humbly acknowledged her presence and thanked her for coming to be with us for the ceremony. After a minute or so, I continued preparing the area where I would be placing the base logs for the fire.

Many Lakota believe their culture has connections to the Pleiades, and this seemed to affirm that connection. In doing home world readings, I have found many people are from Alcyone, Taygete or Maia in the Pleiades.

In 1997, I was practicing my skills at accessing Akashic Record information by giving intuitive readings to friends. One day, I conducted a reading for my girlfriend while walking with her in a wooded park on a clear, warm day. I finished the reading in the days that followed while home by myself.

"Bridget, I'm getting that your home star system is Alcyone in the Pleiades."

Bridget responded with a smile, "Wow, Greg, as far back as high school I've felt a kinship with the Seven Sisters."

*Whew, I got that one accurately, then.*

"OK, great. Let me see if I can get a name for your home planet."

A minute or so passed.

"Bridget, I'm not homing in on a name. I've got part of it, I think. Let me work on the name at home. I'll focus on what the planet is like."

A few moments later I spoke again.

"I'm sensing that green is associated with this planet. I'm seeing it as if I'm orbiting it now – it's a green planet. The planet has vegetation. I feel it is a sixth density planet, meaning it has a much higher vibration than Earth and may not be visible to our physical eyes if we went there in a spaceship."

Shaking her head with a smile, Bridget replied.

"Forest green has been my favorite color for a long time. I have always loved lush green foliage."

*Hmmm, I didn't know that. Good to know her favorite color.*

"I see you on the planet. You look human, as if you're from Earth. You're a member of a tribe."

I enjoyed seeing the image of her with her tribe and sensing what they were like.

"There you have fewer veils on your conscious awareness than you do here on Earth. I feel you're telepathic there and don't speak with vocal cords. Let me see if I can get a higher-self name for you."

I have found a higher-self name stimulates a person's connection with their higher consciousness and intuition.

"Bridget, 'Sophia' is what I'm hearing. How pretty."

"Oh my God, Greg, the name 'Sophie' has been a favorite of mine for years," she said excitedly. "The name is resonating in my chakras right now too — especially my crown chakra. This is so nice. Now I know why I've liked the name for so long."

I silently gave heartfelt thanks to Abraham, my reader of the Akashic Records. We were on a roll in this reading. We decided to end the reading there. While at home in the days that followed, I sensed the name of Bridget's home planet — Clandena — and the name of her Oversoul.

I have also come to understand that many people's home planets are located in a dimension, or universe, outside of our Earthly dimension. Although the Pleiades star cluster is located in our Earthly dimension, my Oversoul indicates that the Pleiadian people and their planets are

## THE PLEIADES

in a higher dimension. A person or planet in a higher dimension is not physically visible to us in our dimension.

During a meditation in February 2021, I found part of my consciousness unexpectedly heading to the Pleiades star cluster, and I soon realized I was receiving confirmation of where Pleiadians live. I felt a sense of traveling, but I also remained quite aware of being in my physical body the entire time. I was sitting in front of my Native American altar where the energy had an elevated vibration due to my Sacred Pipe being kept there along with other special items. In my mind's eye, I ended up among the stars in the Pleiades, as if I were in the star cluster itself.

*This is fantastic. I'm right inside the cluster.*

I felt grateful and excited to be experiencing this special trip.

*Well, I've been wanting verification about what dimension beings from the Pleiades live in, so I hope I get answers to this.*

I had never traveled "into" the Pleiades before. The energy felt uniquely high and very different from the energy at my altar.

I heard a voice speak in my head.

"Your understanding that beings live here in another dimension is correct."

I assumed a Pleiadian was speaking to me. Remaining emotionally detached to avoid clouding my intuition, I felt a strong energy resonance in my body that this statement was true. Soon after that confirmation, I brought my consciousness back. The meditation lasted about 45 minutes.

During an hour-long meditation a year later, I experienced further confirmation that Pleiadians live in a dimension beyond our Earthly plane. At the beginning of the meditation, I felt intuitively led to connect with our galaxy's council, referred to simply as the "Galactic Council." My experience in occasionally connecting with this council is that it functions as its name implies – to address matters within our Milky Way galaxy.

To start, I cleared my energy field with the purifying effects of burning sage. Sitting in front of my Native American altar, I continued with clearing my seven main chakras using my intention and intuition. When I was quietly centered in a receptive, high vibration state of consciousness, I asked my Oversoul to connect me to the Galactic Council. I knew he could do this swiftly and accurately. I felt an energy thread rise up from my crown chakra that soon connected with the Galactic Council. I asked my Oversoul and angel to continue facilitating my connection.

I sensed I was greeted by a being there. The "room" appeared vast and dimly lit. I saw a large hologram of our spiral galaxy floating in the room. I assumed the image was my mind's interpretation of what was there, and that the room may look different. I next saw a Pleiadian spacecraft in the council room at the left of my vision. Its appearance was strong and steady. I asked why it was there, and I sensed the answer was that beings in the craft were there to assist me with my questions. I was grateful for this opportunity, because for more than a year I had been interested in receiving multiple validations that the Pleiadians and their planets reside in a dimension beyond the physical Pleiades we see in the night sky. I assumed the ship was somewhere out in space and I was seeing it because the beings in it were reaching out to me energetically. I was captivated with this experience, appreciative that my silent question about the Pleiadians' origins was heard and important enough for them to address.

I asked my question: "Do Taygete, Maia and Alcyone in the Pleiades have planets in another dimension that are home worlds to many people on Earth?"

"Yes," I clearly heard in my head, without delay.

"I'd like to be taken out-of-body to the Pleiadian ship to experience clearer communication and ideally travel to the worlds in that dimension, if this is acceptable."

I tried my best to be humble yet confident in my request. I would not have been shocked if they took me fully out-of-body in their effort to give me an unmistakable answer.

Instead, I had the experience of feeling my entire energy body shift to a very high vibration while also sensing my consciousness shift levels or dimensions. With this, the energy in my third eye chakra and crown chakra both became highly activated. I stayed relaxed, allowing the processes to occur. This feeling of shifting lasted a minute or so before stopping.

# THE PLEIADES

*Well, this certainly feels like I'm in another dimension,* I thought with amazement and gratitude. I came to this conclusion based on how I felt in the past when connecting to other people's home worlds and during my numerous OBEs.

Without any words spoken by my Pleiadian friends, I felt and saw an energetic doorway open in front of me to a planet I understood to be orbiting Alcyone's star. From the air I saw an outdoor landscape bustling with people and activity. I was amazed at this experience. The people looked like humans, and their activity reminded me of an outdoor market.

Wanting to also check out Taygete and Maia, I boldly asked to sense the Taygete star system. I immediately faded away from Alcyone, and once again experienced a traveling sensation. Surprisingly, I sensed the name Taygete emerge, as if one of the Pleiadians was announcing our arrival. The traveling sensation ceased, and an energy doorway again opened to a planet. There was significant activity, and I sensed the energy present, although I don't recall specifically what I saw. My inner knowing gave me the impression that Taygete is the governing star system in the Pleiades.

Soon after my visit to the second planet, I was brought to the Maia star system, with the same traveling sensation.

"It is very bright here," I heard a female say.

As the energy door opened, the white light was indeed *very* bright. Though not uncomfortable to my inner vision, I couldn't see much through the light. As my eyes adjusted, what I saw astounded me. I was looking at a shining, golden Mayan pyramid similar to those in Tikal, Guatemala. I was extremely surprised to see a Mayan-like pyramid there. I had never heard of a connection between the Mayan culture and the Pleiades.

"I'd like to come back to my body now and close the session because my energy is starting to feel depleted," I said calmly.

Immediately I felt my energy shifting back down through the levels. This went smoothly, and took only about a minute, as I allowed the process to flow. Next, I felt a complete disconnection from the Pleiadian energy, and then a disconnection from the Galactic Council. I was then fully back in my body and felt energetically grounded.

*Wow, that was amazing. What a ride.*

I was filled with gratitude and realized the major significance of what had just happened. First, this appeared to have been an authentic visit to three different Pleiadian worlds – each one having its own unique feeling and qualities. Second, the huge shift in my energy field and consciousness prior to experiencing those worlds was way beyond what I'd experienced in sensing most worlds in higher vibrations in the past. I concluded that the three planets I'd just visited were indeed in another dimension, or perhaps even another universe, given the uniqueness of the energy shift. My experience was so profoundly different, I realized that I might have traveled to a parallel universe that's similar to ours. If that is the case, in that universe, the environment is more benign and the Pleiadians live on planets around their versions of the stars Taygete, Alcyone and Maia. As I indicated earlier, they would not be able to live in our dimension around the stars in the Pleiades we see in our night sky, given the radiation levels. The notion of beings traveling to Earth from another universe is not unheard of, even in the world of astrophysics.

I have since discovered two sources that support the idea that the Mayan culture is connected to the Pleiades. This is especially important, given I saw a Mayan-like pyramid at the star Maia.

First, Hunbatz Men, a Mayan elder, author, historian and spiritual leader, once said, "The Maya, Inca, Cherokee, and other indigenous peoples of the Americas believe that humankind had galactic origins. These peoples all believe that the seeds of human consciousness originated in the Pleiades, which was called Tzek'eb by the Maya."

In addition, I was shocked to see the cover of this elder's book displaying a golden pyramid, similar to what I saw at Maia in my meditation.

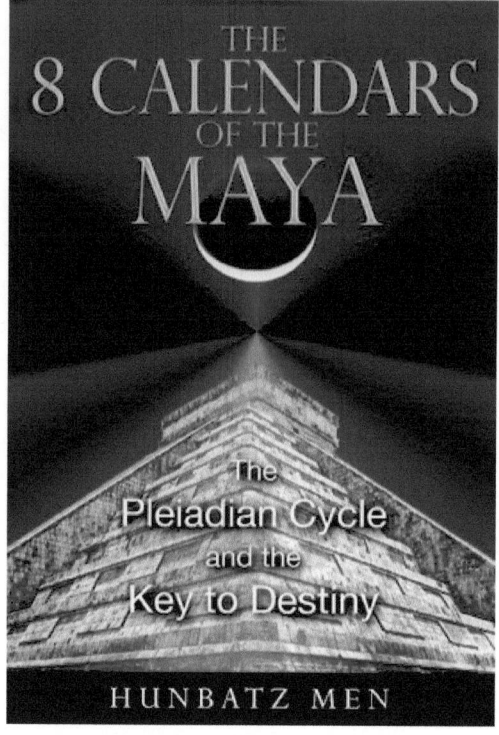

*A golden pyramid on a book about the Maya*
*(Source: Goodreads.com)*

Second, after I described my experience to my sister about traveling to the planets in the Pleiades, she excitedly shared the following with me.

"Some of the things you said are corroborated in the Gaia TV series 'Galactic Messages.' In the Extraterrestrial Races episode, messages are channeled from the Taygetens in the Pleiades through their Earth contact, Gosia Duszak."

Watching the episode, a number of channeled statements were made that beings living around the star Maia in the Pleiades are related to Earth's Maya and Hopi people. I believed the person channeling that information was likely correct, given my experience. I was feeling validated, especially since I had never considered that the star Maia would be related to the Maya or Hopi before the meditation I just shared.

I now feel confident that when my guide Abraham tells me a client's home star system is Alcyone, Taygete or Maia in the Pleiades, he means the client's home planet exists outside our Earthly dimension. Chief Richard's definitive understanding of my Vision Quest interaction with Pleiadians, my numerous experiences with Pleiadians, and my Akashic Record experiences involving the Pleiades have left me no doubt of their existence and interaction in our lives. Of the 37 different star systems the Akashic Records has revealed to me as people's home star systems, the Pleiades is by far the most common. I am confident our place in the Universe is not solely bound to Earth. Fortunately, we don't have to seek out star people to verify this. Our intuition and heartfelt requests to have our curiosity satisfied lead us to the truth. We have a strong ally in the Pleiadians, and this gives me hope for a safe and enlightened future for our planet.

# 15

# NASA'S LUNAR RECONNAISSANCE ORBITER

As the clock ticked down from T-30 minutes, we weren't sure the launch would happen, but stayed abundantly hopeful. I was monitoring the status of my mechanical system on the Lunar Reconnaissance Orbiter (LRO) from the mission operations support room at NASA's Goddard Space Flight Center. The first two launch windows, at 5:12 p.m. and 5:22 p.m., were slammed shut due to stormy weather. But our lunar maiden would not be denied her spacecraft. About five minutes before launch, the folks in the Cape Canaveral launch viewing stands rose from their seats as the Star-Spangled Banner played. This was history in the making. As a nation, our LRO would pave the way for planning where to land humanity next on the unexplored regions of the moon.

When the final launch opportunity came at 5:32 p.m., we got the weather break we needed. With eyes glued to the large screen on the wall showing LRO on the launch pad, my colleagues and I couldn't help but join in the final countdown — 5, 4, 3, 2, 1!

"…And liftoff of the Atlas V rocket with LRO/LCROSS — America's first step to a lasting return to the moon," declared the launch commentator.

Like everyone else in the room, I leaped up from my chair, clapping and cheering — my eyes still fixated on the screen. I felt as if I might jump out of my skin.

*Go-baby-go!* I silently rallied.

The Atlas V rocket with LRO and her companion, the Lunar Crater Observation and Sensing Satellite (LCROSS), roared into the skies over Cape Canaveral, Florida, heading for orbit.

*Atlas V rocket liftoff carrying LRO, Cape Canaveral Air Force Station, Florida (Photo credit: NASA)*

The successful launch of NASA Goddard's LRO on June 18, 2009, marked NASA's long-awaited return to the moon. An unmanned, cutting-edge scientific observatory and the first U.S. mission to the moon in more than 10 years, LRO was the premier spacecraft ushering in a lunar program that will ultimately return humans to the moon. It was simply amazing to be a part of this high-profile mission as the lead mechanical engineer of LRO's complex High Gain Antenna System (HGAS) — the spacecraft's link to Earth for sending back valuable lunar images and scientific data. I had spent four years leading a team of more than a dozen highly dedicated engineers, designers, and technicians as we developed, assembled, and tested this complex, multi-purpose system.

*Atlas V rocket carrying LRO seen with Space Shuttle Endeavour in the background. Both are ready for launch, June 2009.*
*(Photo credit: NASA)*

I will never forget the special moments my colleagues and I enjoyed while supporting the LRO launch and follow-on HGAS deployment that evening from the mission support room at NASA's Goddard Space Flight Center. As one of 20 engineers in the room, my responsibility that day included monitoring my HGAS system status on my computer before and after launch and giving the "go" for HGAS deployment once LRO was in orbit. As with any spacecraft system, if a voltage, electrical resistance, temperature, or other status was reading abnormally high or low, or giving erratic indications, the launch might need to be scrubbed to allow for investigation.

During the last half hour of the launch countdown, the excitement and concern in the room was palpable. As with every spacecraft that a team has poured their life into for years, launch day brings a plethora of emotions. Today we were launching LRO — something we had only dreamed of until now. We were finally putting the spacecraft into service where it belonged — in space.

The LRO HGAS was my most challenging and rewarding NASA project. In many ways, this mission was the highlight of my career at NASA; it was years in the making, the impact it had on the space program was huge, and — most importantly — I had the opportunity to lead a team of extraordinary, highly skilled people in pursuit of this lofty goal. I'm excited to share the highlights and stories of my time as the lead mechanical engineer on this project because this story clearly demonstrates the passion I had and joy I felt working at NASA.

In the years following my Spartan 207 project, which flew in Space Shuttle *Endeavour* in 1996, I worked on numerous design projects, three of which were flight projects. Two of these launched after I joined LRO. I had also graduated from a new and exciting, two-year, hands-on, Systems Engineering Education Development (SEED) training program at Goddard. NASA required this two-year training to be full-time during normal work hours because the workload was so high, and students would be collocating to other branches for hands-on training. Incredibly, we received our usual salaries and retained our positions in our branches, though we did not do any work focused on what our branches were doing over the two-year period.

Katherine, whom I described in earlier chapters, was highly instrumental in developing and managing the SEED program. Going through this program was a huge deal, too, as it opened up many opportunities for me. Systems engineers are a vital resource on NASA teams as they guide design and test decisions for scientific instruments and spacecraft when multiple engineering systems, such as electrical, mechanical or thermal for example, are all stakeholders.

I was eager to be in this full-time program to see if I might like systems engineering enough to leave the Mechanical Engineering Branch. I was at the top of the GS-13 civil service pay scale – it certainly paid well, but going into systems engineering was the typical path for obtaining a technically-oriented GS-14 position. To be a systems engineer I would need to assume greater responsibility, become more highly trained, and work in a more expanded leadership position.

At the end of my two years in the SEED program, I made the surprisingly easy decision to refrain from applying for a systems engineer position. I chose to remain in the Mechanical Engineering Branch where I had been since the Special Payloads Division dissolved. I was happiest there, as I developed deployable mechanical systems. To help clarify what I did at NASA, deployable systems are those that move from a stowed position during launch, to another position once in orbit. An example of a spacecraft deployable system is a motorized telescoping boom, which I incorporated in a preliminary HGAS design for another project prior to working on LRO. The boom concept moved the high gain antenna to a height of eight feet when fully deployed. It moved in the same way as a small, hand-held, segmented telescope would, collapsing down into the largest segment of the telescope for easy storage. A retractable awning is an example of a deployable system used to shade home patios.

I also enjoyed the challenge of engaging in the complex math and physics that went along with developing these systems. My branch head, Jim, was very happy to have me stay in the branch, as he valued me as a branch engineer and would now benefit from the technical and leadership skills I gained from the SEED program.

The Lunar Reconnaissance Orbiter was designed to study the moon in unprecedented detail from about 35 miles above the lunar surface. Its primary mission has been to generate a three-dimensional (3D) map of the entire moon. This high-resolution map will aid NASA in choosing a landing site for manned spacecraft going to the moon's polar regions. The pioneering 3D nature of the images brings out extraordinary detail and depth in lunar features such as craters, volcanic flows, lava tubes and tectonic plate ridges. The moon has no atmosphere to protect astronauts from solar and cosmic radiation, so LRO also investigates the moon's radiation environment. An important third goal of the spacecraft's mission has been to assess resources in the lunar soil, including looking for ice deposits in the coldest craters at the moon's north and south poles.

*Artist's illustration of LRO orbiting the moon 35 miles above the surface (www.science.nasa.gov)*

The moon's surface is, in many ways, a well-preserved record of our solar system's origin story hanging in the night sky, though the moon is now understood to have a dynamic, slowly changing surface.

Late in my NASA career, I was elated to shake hands with Apollo 17 astronaut and Ph.D. geologist, Harrison "Jack" Schmitt who walked on the moon in 1972. Dr. Schmitt had just finished presenting his latest geological assessments of the moon to a large audience at NASA Goddard. I was thrilled that he credited LRO for a number of photographs he used to assess the varied lunar geology where he personally gathered rocks and soil. After his presentation, I hurried over to shake his hand — after all, he was one of only 12 people to have walked on the moon.

"Dr. Schmitt, thank you for your presentation, and it was great to see that LRO's photos helped your geological evaluations. I was the lead mechanical engineer for LRO's High Gain Antenna System."

"Oh! Thank you, Greg, for your contribution to LRO!" Dr. Schmitt said shaking my hand with genuine appreciation.

Smiling at each other with mutual respect, I was elated to be shaking hands with this pioneer of lunar exploration. I didn't want to wash my hand for as long as I could get away with it!

*Apollo 17 astronaut Harrison "Jack" Schmitt and me, NASA Goddard, May 2017*

LRO went to the moon with another spacecraft tagging along: the Lunar Crater Observation and Sensing Satellite, commonly known as LCROSS. LCROSS dragged along with it the spent upper stage of the Atlas V launch vehicle. Four months after launch, LCROSS jettisoned the rocket's empty upper stage into Cabeus, a permanently shadowed crater near the moon's south pole. LCROSS then flew through the debris plume created by the impact to determine its composition. Scientists were hoping to see evidence of ice held in the dust.

A discovery of this magnitude would indicate the possibility of supporting long-term manned missions to the moon and Mars using the resources present.

The upper stage hit the crater at a speed of 5,600 mph, creating a plume extending well beyond two miles. LCROSS flew through the plume, assessing the material using nine scientific instruments. LRO studied the plume from a distance, and both spacecraft confirmed the presence of water in the plume. This finding has the potential to be a huge development!

*LRO at NASA Goddard with me in foreground, August 2008*

In the image above, LRO is shown fully assembled in a large cleanroom at NASA Goddard's integration and test complex. The HGAS is the long vertical structure mounted to the LRO panel over my left shoulder. The solar arrays, responsible for gathering solar energy to power LRO, are located over my right shoulder. The gray blankets and reflective silver areas, along with heaters hidden under the blankets, are designed to regulate LRO's temperature as it orbits the moon.

The High Gain Antenna System was critical for mission success. The vast amounts of scientific data, including lunar photographs, would be sent to Earth using the high-speed capability provided by the high gain antenna. LRO's small s-band antennas were suitable for sending spacecraft status information back to Earth and receiving commands from Earth. This was a relatively small amount of information.

If the HGAS failed to deploy, it would not be able to point its antenna toward Earth to send the huge amounts of science data LRO was gathering. The much slower s-band antennas would need to take on the unintended role of transferring scientific data to Earth, resulting in just a fraction of the data being sent.

Forty-five minutes after LRO left the launch pad, the spacecraft had separated from the rocket, and was racing toward the moon at seven miles per second — the mind-boggling speed required to break away from Earth's gravity. The mission timeline called for solar array deployment shortly after. All of us in the mission operations support room kept our eyes on our computer screens, monitoring the health of our spacecraft systems.

The solar array would be deployed before HGAS to charge LRO's batteries. Like HGAS, deploying the solar arrays was critical for mission success. The amount of power needed to operate the science instruments and all of LRO's systems dictated the need for three, identically sized solar panels. If they did not deploy, only the outer solar array panel would collect energy from the sun and only when it was solar facing. If that happened, LRO would be significantly handicapped.

Every engineer in the room was wearing a headset to communicate with the rest of the team. For solar array deployment, everyone would be polled to verify their system was running nominally before the deployment would be allowed. Mike, the solar array lead engineer, would be polled last. HGAS deployment would follow an identical polling process.

Mike and I were sitting together in the mission operations support room. Two chairs down from us were the engineers monitoring the eight-pound motors and drive units used in our two systems.

Mike was a friendly, highly capable engineer a few years older than me. Since our systems were the only two that would deploy and then move throughout the mission, we valued having each other as we developed our systems. During that time, we compared design and test approaches, combining some of our long-lead-time component procurements, and shared resources when we could. We were readily inclined to discuss our thoughts and needs with each other because management smartly gave us adjacent offices. During this project, I was back in Building 5's W34 suite of offices, where I had been located during my internships and Spartan 207 days.

With my headset on, I listened as the subsystem engineers in the room were polled for their "go" or "no-go" response for solar array deployment.

"Power -"
"Go!"
"Telemetry -"
"Go!"
"Attitude Control -"
"Go!"
"Thermal -"
"Go!"

The polling continued swiftly around the room. If a critical LRO system was having an issue, a "no-go" would be voiced, and deployment polling would pause, and no further actions would be taken until the underlying issue was resolved. The steady stream of "go" responses was exciting to hear in my headset and I momentarily related to the flight controllers I'd heard say "go" in countless nail-biting 1960s and '70s NASA documentaries of Apollo missions destined for the moon.

Mike was the last to be polled, giving a calm "go."

After Mike gave the go-ahead, commands were promptly sent to the spacecraft to power the four release actuators holding the folded, three-panel, solar array closed. To everyone's relief, the solar array deployed fully and follow-on commands to the motors rotated the solar arrays into the sun. Smiles were seen on everyone's face. We had achieved another major milestone.

Immediately following this, mission operations announced that the High Gain Antenna System was going to be polled for deployment. My heart began beating faster, and my temperature rose. Two things had to happen successfully for full HGAS deployment – releasing the latches securing HGAS to LRO, and the follow-on 90-degree rotation of the HGAS into its latched position. With my eyes glued to my monitor as the polling began, HGAS was looking good. Its temperatures, electrical readouts and hinge rotation readouts were all working as expected. Another long string of go's confidently came across everyone's headset. Mike did not need to be polled, and he was settled comfortably back in his chair with the look of a satisfied engineer. I was last to be polled.

"HGAS -"

"Go!" I said firmly.

I felt confident HGAS would deploy successfully.

Within seconds, my computer display clearly showed that the latch and restraint system holding HGAS to the spacecraft had released and HGAS was rotating through its 90-degree sweep. Achieving the full 90 degrees of hinge rotation had been no easy task during my hinge development effort, given the high rotational resistance from the massive, now-unbelievably cold, cable harnesses spooled around the hinge. Standard spacecraft design and test protocols guided me in making sure the system would work.

Ten seconds after HGAS began rotating through its 90-degree path, the eight-foot long HGAS latched securely into place.

The mission operations folks were watching the same HGAS displays that I had on my screen and announced to the team that HGAS had fully deployed. Cheers went up in the room. I laid back in my seat and smiled at Mike. We had come a long way.

Receiving the offer from my branch head to lead the HGAS development and delivery was an honor. It was also an extraordinary opportunity. Guiding my highly-skilled team to project completion under demanding budgetary, schedule, and technical constraints was a transformative journey. We fully embraced the technical challenges, and in the process, gained a deeper appreciation for the layered oversight and high standards demanded across every level of NASA to ensure mission success.

Because I want to shed light on what it takes to successfully complete a major NASA project, the next chapter summarizes the HGAS development and testing, while reflecting on the human side of the mission: the interpersonal dynamics within NASA, and the emotional journey of working alongside a dedicated team of experts through four intense years leading up to launch day.

In addition to the project details, I also open-up about a romantic relationship I had outside of work. I explore the joyful moments, the challenges we faced, and the valuable insights I ultimately gained.

These experiences — both professional and personal — profoundly shaped the person I am today.

# 16

# NASA'S LRO HGAS IN THE MAKING

*I wonder what these folks want to know about the HGAS? I'll bring some drawings, and I imagine the meeting won't last very long.*

I was a year into leading the High Gain Antenna System (HGAS) development and the project was moving smoothly. My designer, Yoon, a very capable, highly experienced mechanical designer with a heavy Korean accent, was halfway through months of generating the system's fabrication drawings. He and I had worked on flight projects in the past and enjoyed working together.

"Yoon, we need to support a one-hour meeting tomorrow in another building. I got a call from branch management requesting we answer questions for some technical managers from outside the branch about our design."

"Oh? I wonder what this is about?" Yoon asked with a curious look.

The air was pregnant with an unspoken sense of concern. We were on a tight schedule, and we didn't want anything to slow us down. We both felt our design was sound, especially the critical launch restraint system, which was based on a test-proven design from another spacecraft. In addition, we had recently passed a high-level design review at Goddard.

Yoon and I took seats opposite each other, halfway down the large conference table, as nine other people shuffled in for the meeting. I put a few HGAS assembly drawings on the table to use in the discussion. Four men and women wearing suits, whom I didn't know, took seats to my left. Among the rest were at least a couple of familiar engineers I had worked with.

*This is a large meeting. I wonder what all this is all about.*

Yoon and I were half holding our breath as we looked at each other, surprised by the large attendance. Unfortunately, we were about to get blindsided with a confrontation that crossed the line of professional inquiry.

The engineer who was apparently the lead technical inquirer, sitting to my left, leaned over the table and pointed at specific areas on the drawings, asking us to alleviate his concerns about our design and deployment test approach. I explained how the system worked. To my surprise, his tone quickly became confrontational and dismissive. My temperature began to rise, but I stayed calm. Out of respect, I gestured to Yoon to answer his questions. Yoon struggled, however, given his nervousness and challenges speaking English. I needed to jump in. I could tell Yoon appreciated my taking the helm, and I didn't want the inquirer to leap to incorrect conclusions.

As I explained finer details in the system, the inquirer dove in deeper, raising his voice, defending his short-sighted view of our design and test approach. The room was dead silent except for our volleys. This was seemingly endless. The inquirer even had the gall to question Yoon's capability as my designer.

I knew the inquirer would be reporting back to his management, which was above the level of my branch, and could cause serious and unnecessary repercussions to our HGAS project. In his arrogance, he could cause the very thing he wanted to avoid – a delay in our schedule to deliver HGAS to the spacecraft. Even worse, his misunderstanding could cause technical misdirection and result in the failure of the project. I'm sure my branch management would not have allowed this meeting to take place if they knew the depth of his misgivings.

Feeling like Yoon and I were on trial, I confidently, respectfully, and assertively explained the necessity and function of each design aspect the lead inquirer questioned. I was effectively on my own to defend Yoon's position as my designer and avoid any negative consequences resulting from this meeting.

Finally, the reviewer became quiet. He and his colleagues talked among themselves for a moment. Fortunately, they came to a positive conclusion, stating they felt comfortable with our design.

On the way back to Building 5, Yoon and I felt like we had just fought off a rogue band of technical managers. We were both a bit shaken by the experience. I didn't hear any more concerns about our HGAS development approach after that meeting.

I shared what happened with my branch managers at our next monthly HGAS status meeting. My branch head was apologetic, not having realized what I would encounter in the meeting. I always had a good rapport with my branch managers, and they had consistently supported my capability and project needs. In my 35 years at NASA, the inquiry meeting was the only time I experienced such unprofessionalism. While it was highly uncharacteristic of how NASA operated, it's not surprising it occurred during the high visibility, considerably complex Lunar Reconnaissance Orbiter (LRO) mission that cost $500 million.

The successful LRO launch and HGAS deployment described in the previous chapter were exciting and fulfilling, and they represented major achievements for me, the LRO team and NASA. Yet, the LRO HGAS development took years of dedicated efforts focused on design, fabrication, assembly, and testing to make this happen. Innumerable companies and product teams were involved every step of the way. The story of how this came to be is important, as it provides insight into the processes and interpersonal dynamics involved in successfully bringing a complex, leading-edge NASA system like the HGAS into being while working under strict budget and schedule constraints. This chapter describes this disciplined developmental process, and it begins with me being chosen to lead the entire HGAS project.

"Greg, I'd like you to develop LRO's HGAS as the lead mechanical engineer," my branch head, Jim, said after asking me to his office. "I asked Alphonso if he felt you had the skills needed for the job, and he said, 'oh yeah' without hesitation."

The HGAS would be used to transmit scientific data, including photographs, to Earth during LRO's upcoming lunar mission. Alphonso had been mentoring me as I developed a conceptual design of my first HGAS for the Global Precipitation Measurement (GPM) advanced scientific weather satellite. Fortunately, there was plenty of time in GPM's schedule for me to learn about previous NASA HGAS designs and to investigate new design approaches.

After less than a year, however, my HGAS conceptual design effort on GPM was put on hold due to spacecraft programmatic uncertainties. I learned a lot during that exciting project, and it would serve me well for the LRO HGAS.

I was given the LRO HGAS project in mid-2005, shortly after my GPM HGAS project. I had been at Goddard for 22 years and developed enough technical and leadership experience to be well-positioned to succeed in developing and delivering the LRO HGAS. This experience came primarily from being the lead mechanical engineer on three previous flight projects.

First was the Super-fluid Helium On-Orbit Transfer (SHOOT) experiment on the STS-57 Space Shuttle mission. For that, I led the development of the mission-unique hardware required to secure the SHOOT experiment to my branch's large truss structure used for Shuttle missions. More enjoyably, I then led all handling operations for that Shuttle payload both at Goddard and at NASA's Kennedy Space Center. The second was Spartan 207, which flew in the Space Shuttle's STS-77 mission – I described that earlier in Chapter 11.

The third flight project was a 3.5-meter-long deployable truss boom for the Deep Space Climate Observatory (DSCOVR), a National Oceanic and Atmospheric Administration space weather and Earth observation satellite. Formerly called Triana, DSCOVR provides early warning capability from a deep-space orbit, as it detects space weather and harmful solar wind activity that could impact Earth.

*DSCOVR mission logo with truss boom shown deployed*

Developing the GPM HGAS was the latest, and final essential work experience I needed to take on the LRO HGAS. It was less complex than the LRO HGAS at the time.

Also significantly aiding my LRO design effort were the many scientific instrument conceptual mechanical designs I created for spacecraft proposals over the years using Computer Aided Design (CAD) software. I enjoyed doing CAD design work, and I had become proficient in it. For one memorable proposal, I created mechanical concepts for three scientific instruments that would fly on a proposed spacecraft through the 60-mile-high salty geysers emanating from Jupiter's moon, Europa.

I smiled at Jim, as Alphonso's highly supportive professional opinion of me was welcome news to both of us. We both recognized Alphonso was a good judge of my skill level due to his success in developing HGAS and solar array systems in the past.

"Greg, here's a drawing of the LRO spacecraft."

LRO had the shape of a tall box, and two sides appeared unused.

"This side is where the deployable solar array needs to go, and this side is where you'll put the HGAS," Jim revealed. "You'll need to design this HGAS so the antenna can see beyond the edge of the deployed solar array, which means HGAS needs to have a long boom. The LRO spacecraft has been in development for a couple of years already, and a clear understanding of the HGAS requirements only recently came to light. You'll need to develop your HGAS preliminary design within six months, which is when the LRO spacecraft preliminary design will be completed. You have some catching up to do."

"Jim, I'm excited to take on this job if Alphonso feels I can handle it."

It was obvious HGAS would be a very complex system, and I would need to hit the ground running.

"Great, Greg. Alphonso thinks you're ready for it, and that's what I needed to hear. It's yours."

I felt like I was about to pull onto the Daytona Speedway in the middle of a race. I recalled the numerous times I'd heard cars speeding around the track during the Daytona 500 race as I walked across campus at Embry-Riddle. The speedway was right next door to the school.

The first, and probably most important, task I needed to complete was identifying and acquiring the key technical personnel to work on this project. Jim and I discussed the various experts I should gather for my HGAS team, such as a designer, structural analyst, thermal engineer, radio frequency engineer for developing the antenna, and many more. I was effectively taking on a GS-14 level systems engineering role as the HGAS lead mechanical engineer, and I was grateful for my participation in the two-year Systems Engineering Education Development (SEED) program I had completed recently. This project did not come with an automatic GS-14 promotion, however, and this was normal.

I would develop the HGAS mechanical designs with an experienced designer leading the way, while the other subsystem engineers and I worked together to make sure everyone's designs were compatible and met the overall HGAS requirements.

My mechanical designer would be tasked with designing nearly all the HGAS parts that would fly, plus designing many non-flight systems to support the HGAS development and testing.

Mike, LRO's solar array lead engineer, was ready to identify a designer to begin developing his system, as well. It just so happened that two experienced designers were readily available for us to choose from – one I knew well, and the other I'd never heard of. Suk Yoon was the designer I knew well, and I chose him, while Mike preferred the other designer. Yoon, as he liked to be called, was a highly skilled designer with whom I had worked on several projects. SHOOT, which flew successfully on the STS-57 Space Shuttle mission, was one of them.

Yoon had been designing complex spaceflight hardware in our building since well before I was hired at Goddard. Although his Korean accent made communicating challenging at times, we were excited to take on another mission together. We got off to a good start with Yoon developing a road map of what he would develop, per the basic requirements I provided.

Yoon and I developed several slightly different preliminary designs for the HGAS, giving us options for the two-axis gimbal that would rotate the antenna, and for the launch latches and restraints that would secure the HGAS to LRO for launch. Performing trade studies on various design options was a common practice that was encouraged. This would lead up to the Preliminary Design Review (PDR) for the HGAS and LRO. I enjoyed this part of the project immensely because we were creating something brand new. It was exciting.

Throughout our many interactions over this four-year HGAS project — from conceptual design to launch — Yoon and I got along great. Patience, mutual respect, and appreciation made this possible. We developed some very complex systems together and worked smoothly as a team throughout design, fabrication, assembly, testing, and spacecraft-level work.

Nearly all the engineers who came onto the LRO HGAS project were assigned by their branch heads. I already knew most of the engineers from working with them in the past, and I was pleased to have such competent teammates. We were an efficient team, and we needed to be, as the months rolled quickly by.

Several elements required my teams' constant attention throughout this project: We needed to fabricate and test the device while meeting critical schedule milestones and staying within budget. This involved identifying and balancing priorities based on long-term and short-term needs. Two of the critical schedule milestones were the Preliminary Design Review (PDR) and Critical Design Review (CDR). We had to successfully pass these reviews while staying within our budget. If we encountered cost overruns or scheduling delays, our project might cause the entire LRO mission to fail in meeting its cost and schedule goals.

My HGAS team and I presented our preliminary design using Power Point presentations — the standard method at the time — at the PDR, and then presented our fabrication-ready design nine months later during the most important LRO project review — the CDR. The design review boards were each staffed with a dozen senior engineers, and the large presentation rooms were filled with LRO team members and NASA technical managers. Every system on LRO was presented by the engineer leading its development. For example, I presented the mechanical aspects of the HGAS, while my Radio Frequency (RF) engineer presented the details about the HGAS antenna he was responsible for delivering to me. Several spacecraft systems engineers also presented how they were optimizing the spacecraft and planning to verify its functional requirements. LRO passed both reviews with high praise, allowing us to continue our work.

I was proud to work with such an outstanding team of dedicated, highly skilled men and women on LRO. My HGAS and the spacecraft were ready to be fabricated with the completion of the CDR. Fabrication was an exciting phase, as we would bring our designs into reality.

After passing the CDR, close to a year was needed to manufacture my specialized flight and non-flight parts. It was a monumental effort, since hundreds of parts were needed. They were mostly made of aluminum, but some used unusual metals and coatings that could take many weeks to deliver.

My parts were mostly manufactured through the shop at the other end of Building 5. A world-class machine shop, it was capable of manufacturing nearly all the mechanical parts in a spacecraft. Nearly a dozen NASA-approved fabrication facilities around the Washington DC beltway were available to produce parts when our shop reached capacity. I enjoyed working with the managers, engineers, and inspectors in the shop. They made themselves available to customers like me to address questions and concerns whenever they could.

I particularly enjoyed going to the area of the shop to pick up parts that were manufactured for me, since that felt like Christmas. On nice days the rollup door was open, letting in sunshine and fresh air. My HGAS parts were being manufactured at the same time as the entire LRO spacecraft, so the two or three people staffing the parts pick-up area were always very busy. Patience was required. Before accepting the parts I ordered, I always checked the manufacturing logs for discrepancies. It was a good day when there were none. Often, though, the parts logs identified mistakes that were caught during inspection. I could sign for the majority of those parts, but sometimes the errors weren't acceptable, and I rejected them, requiring another round of manufacturing. For example, the launch restraints that separate during HGAS deployment required dimensions that are accurate to within the thickness of a human hair to function properly; if what was being delivered was outside the dimensional tolerances, I had to reject it.

My experience leading flight projects in the past told me I needed to hire an engineer as an assistant when I reached the fabrication phase. For this project, management brought Glenn to my attention because he had the experience for the job. He was slightly younger than I was, and was confident, calm, and adapted easily to the tasks I asked him to complete. I made room in my office for Glenn's desk, and we enjoyed working together. Glenn was indispensable, helping me by writing test plans, managing some of the parts manufacturing, supporting tests, and more.

As parts poured in, Yoon and I, plus many technicians from various branches, worked side-by-side to assemble my two separate HGAS's. We first assembled the much simpler HGAS mockup and then put together the flight HGAS. The weeks-long assembly process for each system was complex but went smoothly. I sometimes felt like I was on display during the effort, as the viewing window next to our HGAS assembly area gave curious onlookers in the hallway a closeup of our progress. Even so, I was glad that others could watch the project taking shape. It was rare for assembly activities like this to be on display, and I'm sure it was educational and fascinating for most spectators. We were busy, too. Two or three people were typically working on assembling HGAS at any one time.

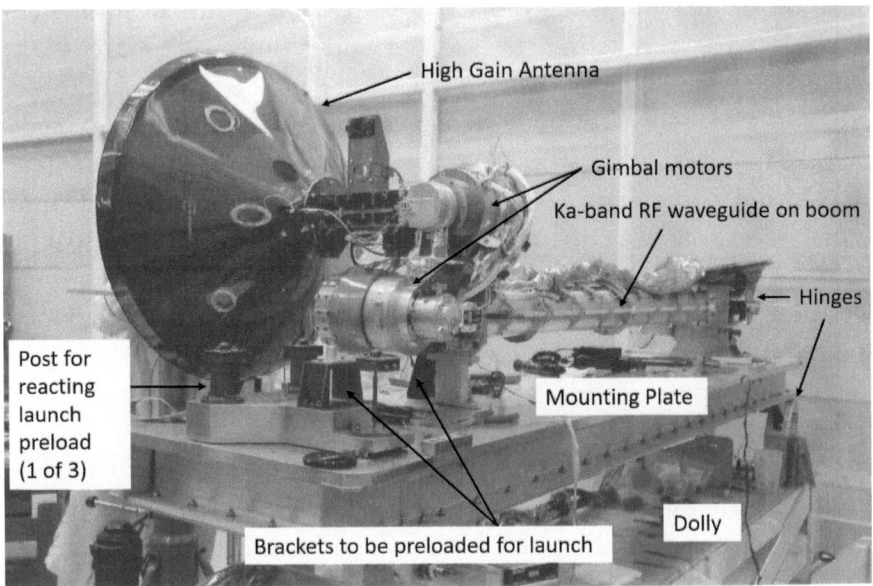

*LRO flight HGAS during assembly*

Dozens of Goddard engineers and technicians had a hand in designing, delivering, and assembling the flight HGAS components. The innovative, 30-inch diameter high-gain antenna was designed and manufactured by a California company. This was the choice of the Radio Frequency (RF) engineer assigned to my team.

The large, fully wired, two-motor gimbal was developed and delivered to me by a team of electro-mechanical engineers upstairs from my office. The gimbal could point the antenna anywhere within a hemisphere. The Electro-Mechanical Branch handled anything requiring motors. I never wanted to get into motor design, so I was happy to give the gimbal development to them.

The hinge design came from a brilliant colleague, Jason, who led the HGAS development for the Solar Dynamics Observatory (SDO) that has been advancing our understanding of the sun since 2010.

Other valuable developments Jason made for his HGAS, which I utilized, were the metals and coatings used for his launch restraints and latches. The metals and coatings were chosen after a different combination of materials caused his HGAS to seize as he ran his system through a test simulating the vacuum and temperature extremes in space. I considered Jason to be an "engineer's engineer," like Alphonso. His ability to design complex systems was a cut above most engineers I worked with.

During my work on LRO, I also began dating a special lady. Hanna (not her real name) and I crossed paths at a well-attended annual St. Patrick's Day party that my Unity church hosted in 2007. The room was large enough for the many friends and family who attended. Good food, music provided by our own church members — including myself as a guitar player — and a great view of the harbor always made these parties enjoyable.

Hanna and I met a couple of years before at a pool party, but the timing wasn't right for us to consider dating. Now we were happy to connect with each other again. I was 46 and Hanna 45. She was a very attractive mother of three happy, healthy young women, and a successful accountant at a local accounting firm. Hanna's oldest was living on her own out of state, while Hanna's younger daughters lived with her, as they were still in high school.

Hanna was an avid reader and enjoyed participating in a book club. She also enjoyed gardening, activities with her children and friends, and spending time outdoors. She had established a healthy balance in life. The father of her children was very attentive to them and lived nearby.

I had recently bought a house on a wooded lot in Crownsville, Maryland, 20 minutes from Hanna, and I enjoyed swimming with the local Masters swim club, playing guitar with friends, practicing Tai Chi, attending the local Unity church, and engaging in metaphysical activities.

Being with Hanna felt natural and enlivening. We quickly fell in love, and we appreciated joining other couples for dinner, walking or hiking locally, watching movies, and occasionally doing activities with her children.

However, all was not well between Hanna and me, for a couple of reasons. The primary reason was our night-and-day views on the world of metaphysics. Hanna felt my metaphysical experiences were mostly based on illusion. For example, I had gone out-of-body many times before meeting Hanna, and told her about the experiences, but she thought I must be mistaken. Because of this disconnect between us, I think I refrained from telling her about two out-of-body experiences I had during the Vision Quests I participated in while we were dating. I felt that telling her would likely have been counterproductive.

I didn't fault Hanna for her views, and I respected her beliefs. She supported my interest in spending time following my metaphysical interests, and I appreciated her for that. One day Hanna and I were talking about plans we wanted to make for the year, and I listed four multi-day, out-of-state events I wanted to attend if time permitted. One was a UFO conference, and another was Vision Quest. The specifics surrounding the other two escape me now, but they both were spiritually or metaphysically based. Hanna listened calmly.

"Greg, I would be okay with this as long as we have one vacation week a year away together somewhere."

Looking back, I realize Hanna was being very considerate. As it turned out, I didn't have the time or dedicated interest to do three of the four events I'd brought up. The one I did manage to attend was Vision Quest. Meanwhile, Hanna and I enjoyed a nice vacation out of state at least once each year. Going to Yellowstone in Colorado, Sante Fe in New Mexico, and taking a trip to see her relatives in the Colorado-Wyoming area bring fond memories.

We did our best to accept each other's opinions and experiences around metaphysics, but we broke up on several occasions for weeks or months at a time, because I was uncomfortable with our differing perspectives. Despite this, I wasn't happy being away from Hanna and we both repeatedly, and excitedly, reunited with the best of intentions to simply enjoy being together.

The other strain on our relationship was my reluctance to discuss the sexual abuse I had experienced as a young teen. The highly inappropriate behavior I was subjected to profoundly affected me and consequently affected my relationship with Hanna. The abuse focused on physical activities I was urged to participate in, but it was much more than that. The abuse was also emotional, and this had a much more profound effect on me, given I was not mature enough to process the experiences as an adult would. The mistreatment came from outside the family by older people who should have known better. It wasn't until I sought therapy after college that I began to unravel the resulting confusion I developed around intimacy and sexuality.

The level of intimacy Hanna and I experienced — mentally, emotionally, physically, and spiritually — could have gone much deeper had I been willing to overcome my fears about discussing the abuse I experienced as a young teen, and its effects. I also realize I was not nearly attentive enough to Hanna's daughters because of my reluctance to get closer to Hanna. In retrospect, I'm confident Hanna would have been very receptive to discussing what I was embarrassed about and ashamed to bring up.

Hanna patiently waited for my long hours on LRO to end, as she looked forward to having more time together after the mission. Even though we tried to make our relationship work after LRO was finished, we would discover it wasn't enough.

Meanwhile, there were other hurdles I had to overcome at NASA, as my HGAS project moved forward. When my HGAS mockup was fully assembled, I had the task of verifying it would deploy and re-stow properly. This was an essential test and felt like a moment of truth. A successful deployment test would complete an important milestone on my schedule and would be reported all the way up to NASA Goddard's Center Director at his next LRO status briefing.

It was January 2008, two and a half years after Yoon and I began formulating our designs. Yoon, Glenn and a couple of other mechanical technicians and I were all excited, and a bit nervous, as we set up the elaborate test system for the first time. The HGAS mockup accurately represented the mass and center of gravity of the flight HGAS, as well as its critical hardware. The mockup was destined for use on the LRO spacecraft test mockup after this test, where it would stay.

*Deployment test preparations for the HGAS Mockup, January 2008*

The photo above shows us preparing the HGAS mockup for deployment. I am holding the HGAS mockup while Glenn is to my right and Yoon is in front of me looking at the HGAS.

With a room full of interested onlookers — including my branch head and my HGAS mentor, Alphonso — I pushed the button on a power box to send a precise electrical pulse to the two latches, expecting HGAS to deploy. Nothing happened.

*Why didn't the latches release? This is likely a wiring issue.*

Keeping calm and wanting to resolve the issue quickly before people started leaving the room in disappointment, I began looking over the electrical connections. Fortunately, Alphonso calmly came over to me with an observation.

"Greg, this light needs to be on for it to work," he said quietly, knowing it was a simple oversight. Boy, did I feel foolish. Alphonso flipped on the box's power switch, illuminating a green light.

Still feeling foolish, I turned to my colleagues in the room and said, "Okay, sorry, we're ready now!"

Pushing the pulse button, the two latches released with the expected loud thud and our HGAS slowly and steadily rotated downward. The system completed its 90-degree travel in about 15 seconds and then audibly latched to a stop at the spring-driven hinge. Everyone applauded with excited clapping and smiles. We had reached a milestone, and I was happy to have so many of my colleagues witness the success. I was proud to share this achievement, and I knew everyone enjoyed witnessing it. I liked watching other people's tests, too. They were inspiring and educational.

I only needed to perform one full deployment test like this on the HGAS mockup. My flight HGAS would require this test twice – once after we finished assembling it, and once after enduring the rigors of a thermal-vacuum test.

*Preparing the Flight HGAS for a deployment test*

In the photo above, I am wearing a white garment that prevents particles from my clothing and body from getting into the air. The HGAS needed to be kept very clean from that point on, as did the spacecraft. LRO's camera lenses would produce poor quality images with just a thin, unseen layer of debris.

I performed my first flight HGAS deployment test in the cleanroom shown in the photo above. HGAS deployed successfully and was a huge milestone for the LRO project and NASA management.

The thermal-vacuum test, which came next, would verify the HGAS's ability to operate in the harsh environment of space. This test would cycle the HGAS through temperature extremes of plus and minus 250 degrees Fahrenheit while in a vacuum.

Most critical to this test was deploying the HGAS in extreme cold, as its thermal control system kept key areas of HGAS warm. Would the special metals and dry lubricants used in the latch release mechanisms work as designed, or would the system seize closed? For this deployment test, HGAS would only be allowed to rotate out a few inches due to the short metal restraining cable we attached to it.

The electrical pulse for releasing the latches was sent from outside the thermal chamber. A light inside the chamber had been turned on for this deployment test and an observer looking through a small window on the chamber excitedly announced when HGAS deployed. The deployment was such a relief, and I could breathe easily.

After this success, we opened the chamber door, lowered HGAS into its fully deployed position, and supported it with a specially designed stand. From that point on, we would spend a week simulating HGAS's life orbiting the moon. The main test events would be demonstrating the antenna's ability to transmit data, and the gimbal's ability to cycle through its full range of motion. During the motion, heaters simulating the Sun would blast one side of the gimbal while the other side experienced the cold of space. During all of this, the HGAS thermal control system needed to keep HGAS within specific temperature limits to pass the test.

The tests went well, with only minor issues surfacing. The successful completion of this test, coupled with a follow-on full rotation HGAS deployment test back in the cleanroom to verify the hinge had not been damaged during the test, was the largest milestone for HGAS. It was now qualified for flight.

Installing the HGAS on the LRO spacecraft in mid-2008 was a highlight for everyone involved with LRO. The spacecraft was being assembled in a large cleanroom with immense viewing windows, and LRO was a big deal for many space enthusiasts. Celebrities and congressmen were occasionally seen admiring LRO through the cleanroom windows as engineers and technicians assembled and tested the spacecraft. George Takei (Helmsman Sulu from the original *Star Trek* TV series of the 60s and 70s), Nichelle Nichols (Bridge communications officer Uhura from the original *Star Trek* series), and Morgan Freeman were three actors I was excited to unexpectedly see in the vicinity of the LRO cleanroom.

As I accompanied the HGAS to facilitate its integration to the spacecraft, I was smiling, having come to this point after three-plus years in the making. I was also a bit nervous.

*Just breathe. You're ready to handle this installation. Yoon will be there with a slew of other mechanical technicians to assist us. Plus, I'm delivering HGAS on time, so people will be excited to see me and HGAS.*

I knew the people who would be involved in this installation in the LRO cleanroom, and I was looking forward to seeing them.

When I entered the cleanroom in my cleanroom garment, HGAS had been rolled inside and a dozen people were milling about, preparing for the integration. Electrical cable harnesses, a fiber optic cable, an S-band antenna coax cable, heaters, and the RF waveguide all needed to tie into the spacecraft at the HGAS hinge area. We also had latches and restraints to install on LRO. All this would take hours.

Gordon, an engineer I knew on the LRO project, approached me and said he would be leading the overhead crane operation to lift HGAS off the dolly and over to LRO.

"Gordon, I'm carrying a lot of stress," I said. "If I come across as being difficult, or impatient, I apologize up front for it now."

I felt a layer of stress drop off me just saying that.

"Okay, Greg," he quickly acknowledged, and began telling me how he wanted to lift HGAS.

Gordon's approach for lifting HGAS was different from what I had put in my test plan, but I refrained from micromanaging the effort. He was in charge of the lift, and his approach would not jeopardize HGAS. I stepped back and watched as HGAS rotated to a vertical position using the overhead crane.

Once the HGAS was positioned where I needed it at LRO, Yoon and I performed the mechanical installation and stowing process in a little over 90 minutes. Other people got busy connecting HGAS's vital systems to LRO. It was all coming together well.

The day would be over once we performed a "pop-and-catch" deployment test and then restowed the HGAS. The "catch" aspect would be accomplished using the eight-inch-long restraining cable I'd used in the thermal vacuum test. Since this would be the first time the electrical signal to pop HGAS's two latches would come from the spacecraft, everyone was especially excited. I was more than happy to sit back and let the spacecraft engineers run the deployment test.

Commanded from the adjacent room, the two electrically redundant latches securing the HGAS to LRO let out a pop and HGAS was instantly driven out by the spring torque in the hinge. Yoon and I smiled at each other while everyone inside the room, and those observing from the window, clapped and cheered. A long-awaited milestone had been reached. After I restowed the boom with Yoon, we were congratulated by many. I was tired but very happy.

The HGAS was the final major subsystem to be integrated onto the spacecraft, marking the transition into six months of rigorous, spacecraft-level testing. This critical phase was designed to ensure that all onboard systems functioned cohesively across every stage of the mission.

During this period, the HGAS underwent an extensive series of evaluations to verify its performance and compatibility with the spacecraft. One key test included antenna functionality while the entire spacecraft endured simulations of the vacuum of space coupled with the extreme temperatures expected during its lengthy mission.

Another screening involved a thorough Electromagnetic Interference (EMI) test to verify LRO's electronics would not be adversely affected by electromagnetic radiation.

The HGAS passed all tests without issue. The LRO spacecraft required only minor adjustments, underscoring the success of the design and testing process.

The HGAS and LRO completed post-transportation checkouts, tests, and final launch preparations smoothly at Cape Canaveral Air Force Station in Florida, where LRO would be launching in June 2009.

I received my GS-14 promotion during the latter half of my HGAS project. As the lead mechanical engineer for LRO's HGAS, I was doing GS-14-level work, and my branch managers encouraged me to apply for the promotion though the Human Resources branch. The application process was long and labor intensive, but worth it in the end.

My personal life wasn't as successful. Hanna and I broke up a couple of years after LRO launched. Although we loved each other, I was too uncomfortable with our divergent views of metaphysics. I realized having mutual core values and goals was very important. Since then, I've also realized that being willing to open up on all levels to the partner I love is essential for personal growth and creating a healthy, happy, loving relationship.

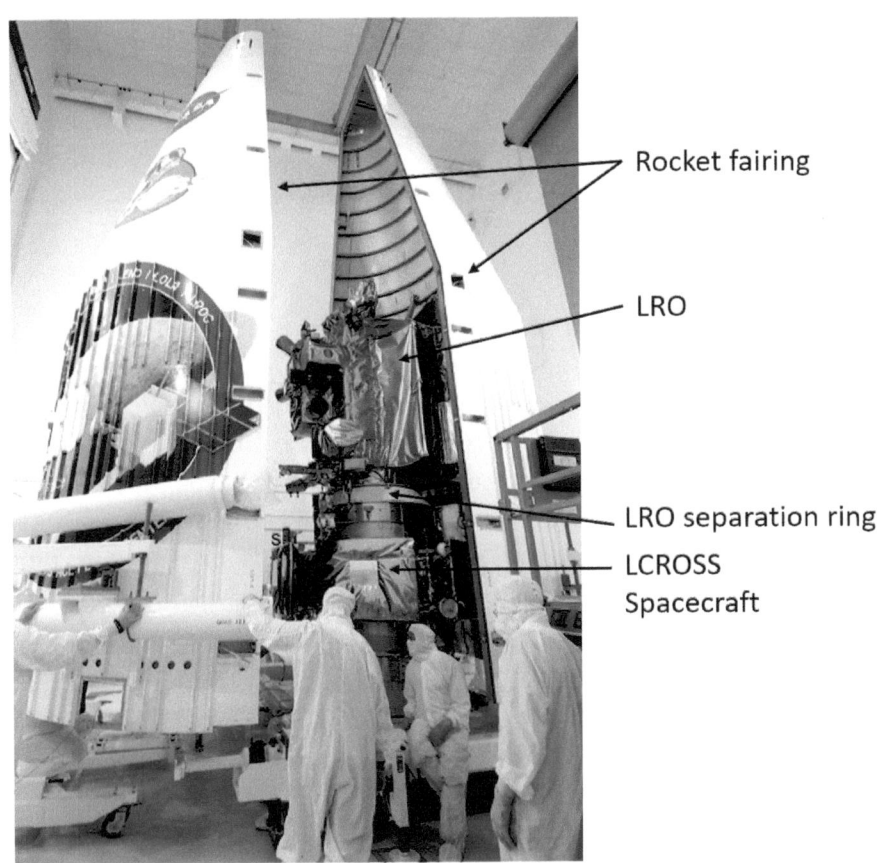

*LRO mounted on top of LCROSS during spacecraft encapsulation process at Cape Canaveral Air Force Station, Florida. (Photo credit: NASA)*

# 17

## HEALING AND PAST LIVES

"Greg, I want you to go back to the life when you were a fisherman, and you died at sea."

Anxiety began welling up inside me, challenging my deeply relaxed, peaceful state. A scene of a boat sailing under gray skies appeared in my mind's eye. It was a wooden boat, maybe 30-feet long. Seeing about eight men in the boat, worsening weather began unfolding. Dark clouds and swelling seas were joined by driving rain, and a foreboding feeling took hold of me. Tears began welling up in my eyes as I lay on the floor. My breathing deepened, becoming somewhat erratic.

"Jane, I see a boat of men in loose-fitting cloths struggling in a storm," I reported in a soft, distressed voice.

"Greg, you will observe the boat from now on with emotional detachment."

My breathing calmed as I watched the boat being tossed about on the dark, stormy sea. At one point, my mind's eye zoomed in on a sailor and I saw the broken mast, or some other piece of timber, crash down on his left arm. He let out a scream. The dull ache that had been plaguing the ulnar nerve in my left arm for the past 12 months began to throb.

While quietly under hypnosis, I continued revealing to Jane what I was seeing and experiencing. I had no doubt that the injured fisherman was me in a past life.

It was the summer of 2000, and I was in a weekend class during the third and final month of basic hypnosis training. James Rayme, a highly regarded teacher in the field, wanted the eight of us to pair up and spend a couple of hours taking each other through a hypnosis session with goals of our choice.

My hypnosis partner, whom I'll call Jane, had me lie comfortably on the padded floor for my session. I was excited to see if we could neutralize the elusive condition that had been irritating the ulnar nerve in my left arm for so long. Before the session, I had reason to believe that the sailor's demise was the cause of the pain.

We were alone in a quiet, private room and Jane brought me into a thoroughly relaxed state in body and mind within a couple of minutes using the deep relaxation technique we had learned.

While hypnotically experiencing the scene as an injured sailor, we had the perfect opportunity to attempt to neutralize the traumatic influence the sailor's damaged arm was having on my ulnar nerve in my current life. Remaining under hypnosis, I was eager to spend the rest of my session focusing on doing this. The fact that I likely <u>died</u> in the storm as the fisherman didn't seem as important as healing my arm from the impact of the fallen beam. My healing involved visualizing the beam no longer being on the sailor's arm and imagining his arm and my physical arm returning to full health. We also addressed the mix of emotions I was feeling while under hypnosis, knowing these emotions were a significant energetic component of the trauma that carried into this life. I felt anxiety and a mix of sadness and anger – all from the gruesome arm injury combined with the knowing I was going to drown in the storm. Addressing each emotion brought me to a peaceful resolution.

I'm happy to say that after a full year of doctor visits, two electrical conductivity tests at my left elbow, MRIs of my arm and neck, energy healings from myself and several people — which included intuitive verifications that I did experience the death I visualized – this hypnosis session finally brought an end to my nerve pain. When I left the hypnosis training that day, my nerve pain was still present, but it was reduced. To my deep gratification, I noticed the pain go to zero over the two weeks that followed, and it never returned. I was finally healed.

# HEALING AND PAST LIVES

This experience demonstrated to me that not only can I heal an illness by identifying and addressing the root trauma and emotions that caused it, but I could do so even if they originated in a past life. I'm excited to share two other stories that demonstrate the power of healing through investigating past lives. The first one involved me in 2019.

I walked into the procedure room wearing a patient gown that opened in the back.

"Please lie on the table Mr. Martins, and we'll give you a couple of shots to numb the area," the young doctor said as he prepared his tray.

I climbed onto the cushioned table, face down, thinking this was going to hurt like hell. I was nervous but surrendered to the moment. I was about to get two steroidal epidurals to alleviate nearly-excruciating pain in my thoracic spine — the middle section of my spine.

I was told the injections would coat my irritated nerves to help reduce the pain and swelling caused by acute inflammation. The least I could expect was temporary pain relief. Optimistically, I could experience relief for many months or even permanently. I was hoping for the best.

A nurse approached me and opened the back of my gown. Wiping my spine with alcohol pads, she confidently said, "These numbing shots will feel like pin pricks."

*I hope she's right.*

I recalled the painful experience I'd had years before when a Chinese acupuncturist unexpectedly inserted a needle a half inch deep into my ankle. I didn't want to feel that again. Two pinpricks later, I lay amazed at how the nurse's shots could be so painless.

With my head rotated to the right, I looked up at the large television screen hanging from the ceiling. I knew this would display a real-time X-ray of my spine for the doctor to use as he guided his needle ever closer to my spine. I remembered a time years ago when I watched a high-resolution, real-time, video display of my skeletal foot wiggling around as I moved it in front of an X-ray device. It was fascinating and funny to see.

I rotated my head to my left. I didn't want to watch the needle going in my back. I was tough in many ways, but this wasn't one of them.

"Here we go Mr. Martins. Please lie still."

I didn't dare move. I felt a light, sustained, sting.

*He must be inserting the needle. I can't believe this doesn't hurt!*

I was truly amazed. In a few moments another light sting let me know he was on his second shot. Thankfully, this didn't hurt either.

The epidurals took about 10 minutes to administer. I was grateful for such an easy, painless procedure, and my smile reflected it. Moving gently as I got up, I thanked the two appreciatively, and they shared equally happy smiles.

"These injections could take up to 14 days to take effect, Mr. Martins," the doctor revealed.

"Ugh," I uttered quietly, dropping my head. I didn't want to hear that. Turning my head to the doctor I replied, "I hope it doesn't take that long."

They gave me verbal discharge instructions and handed me the instructions in writing. I left hopeful but was still in a lot of pain.

This pain began a month earlier in May 2019. I was finishing up my computer-aided designs at NASA for a scientific instrument proposal. At that time, I was enjoying the ease of the project – I had retired from NASA 14 months earlier and was working part-time as a contractor for ATA Aerospace, helping the team I worked with when I retired. I had enjoyed a year of occasional design work, and settled into a relaxed, stress-free life.

Unfortunately, I also began experiencing pain in the thoracic area of my spine at the bottom of my rib cage. I went to see an orthopedic doctor and an X-ray he took during the visit didn't reveal anything peculiar. Looking at MRI images with a report a few days later, however, the young doctor was perplexed, saying he couldn't understand how such extensive inflammation could occur in my spine without an injury. I assured him I hadn't done anything to my knowledge to irritate the area.

The MRI indicated significant inflammation in the "facets" of thoracic vertebrae T9 through T11. Facets are the protuberances on either side of vertebrae that limit their rotation. Additionally, I had moderate to severe inflammation in the small central openings of these vertebrae where the spine exists. All this had been causing me significant pain.

During the month between the MRI and the epidurals, I received a painful cortisone shot in my back, followed by a 10-day course of oral steroids, all intended to bring me relief.

I counted the days after the epidural, deeply hoping it would kick in. On the 14th day the intense pain finally disappeared. I was both elated and dumbfounded that the medicine took the full two weeks to kick in. I felt like a new man. I was <u>finally</u> pain free.

In a month or two, the pain began to resurface, though at a much lower intensity. This is when I began to wonder if a past life might be the source of this unusual inflammation. My orthopedic doctor was very clear that he had no explanation for the cause, and I didn't want the pain to keep lingering.

I was in for an enlightening surprise when I sat down in front of my Native American altar to ask my Oversoul and Abraham, my reader of the Akashic Records, if my thoracic spine symptoms were due to a past-life injury. Seated quietly on a padded cushion, I relaxed my body and mind, raising my vibration by clearing my chakras and centering in my heart.

I asked my question with emotional detachment, and I began seeing scenes from the American Civil War in my mind's eye — an encampment, a Confederate flag, a glimpse of a battle scene. Within 10 minutes, the discomfort in my spine slowly increased to an almost intolerable level. My sitting posture was good, so I eliminated that possibility as the cause of the pain. During this experience, I saw a sword and got the distinct sense that it had been thrust into my back as a Union soldier in the Civil War.

I had never liked studying the Civil War, having some unknown resistance to it that went well beyond a simple lack of curiosity. Now I knew why.

I hurriedly asked my spirit helpers if they would please do a healing on me to alleviate the pain I was in. I felt energy begin moving in my energy field. I sat patiently as they worked on me. I was astounded when my inner sight, as if viewing from my physical eyes, watched a Civil War soldier get up from my seated position and walk out of my body and away to my left. He wore a clean, well-kept uniform, the pants having a stripe down the side.

*Who was that?!* I marveled. My energy felt slightly lighter. I will never forget that amazing vision. After 10 to 20 minutes of energy work from my spirit helpers, my pain lowered to a level similar to when I started the session.

I had been given an undeniable insight into the source of my pain, and I was excited to think that I might be able to eliminate the inflammation and pain by addressing this past-life trauma. After all, I had successfully healed my ulnar neuropathy by addressing the past life that apparently caused it.

Over the next week, I did energy healing work on my back while alone. This partly entailed imagining the sword wound healed and disconnecting myself from the Civil War. I also ran divine white light energy into and out of the area to accelerate the healing. All this helped but wasn't completing the healing.

At this point, I had returned to gently swimming laps for exercise at the local pool, but I avoided twisting and arching backwards. I was glad to be getting aerobic exercise again, but I had to keep it gentle.

I decided to reach out to a shaman, both to verify that my condition was indeed caused by a Civil War sword wound, and to help me heal it for good.

*Where does one find a local, modern-day, shaman? On the internet, I presume! After all, they likely advertise to stay in business.*

A shaman is a person who is skilled in working with the subtle energies of a person's energy field and consciousness, and with the energies of spirit animals, nature, and other dimensions. A shaman would help me heal using their unique insights and energetic influence.

Walking along the aging concrete sidewalk after parking under an old oak tree, I felt a bit odd going to a shaman's "office" in a small business park. My mind was battling with the stereotypical image of what a shaman's world looked like. The string of offices in front of me were adjacent to a well-established townhouse community. Walking around back, the quiet, comforting presence of the woods just ten feet behind the buildings made me feel more at peace. The shaman's lair was just past a psychologist's office.

Entering her waiting room, I felt calm, peaceful energy. Nature pictures, thriving plants, and a couple of comfortable-looking wicker chairs made me feel I'd chosen well. A woman slightly older than I soon entered the room with a satisfied client who left with a smile.

"Hi, you must be Greg," Paige asked with a smile.

"Yes, Hi. Nice to meet you," I replied as I stood up. Paige appeared relaxed and pleasant. This was the demeanor I wanted in a shaman — I knew she would be a clear intuitive.

In the therapy room, a chair and tall plant took up the right corner, and a massage table with blankets and a pillow sat under the window to the left. A thin, decorative, window shade allowed natural light to gently bathe the room. As Paige changed the pillowcase, she began asking me questions about my visit.

Lying on the table, I experienced an hour-long session while in a relaxed, somewhat meditative state, as Paige and I energetically addressed my back pain. Paige was sitting in the chair across from me, and we both asked our higher consciousnesses and spirit guides to bring us into the energies of the pain so we could see what I needed to do emotionally, physically, and mentally to neutralize it. Paige sensed that my Civil War story was correct, and she saw details of the experience that went well beyond my limited awareness of it.

"Greg, I see you at a house in the Civil War time frame. It belongs to your parents or one of your siblings. There's an argument. You are a Union soldier, and your two brothers are Confederate soldiers. You're leaving the house and one of your brothers thrusts his sword into your back."

I imagined this unfold in my mind as she described the scene. It seemed completely genuine because my intuition was resonating with it. Throughout the session, Paige and I shared back and forth what we were intuitively seeing and experiencing. Our higher consciousnesses, my subconscious, and our spirit guides were all involved in this unfoldment. Paige felt that the brother who stabbed me regretted doing so shortly after, but that I died two weeks later from a resulting infection. She also revealed that this same brother is someone I know in my current incarnation, though I don't know who.

We spent the rest of the session doing energetic healing of the sword wound as if it were in my energy field as I lay on the table. This made sense because the wound existed in my energy body so strongly that I was experiencing its effects in my physical body as significant inflammation and pain. We also recognized the need to release the emotional trauma from that life to fully neutralize the energy of the stabbing. I forgave my brother and family from that life for any grief or ill will they may have been harboring. I also released the sadness I felt for the tragic loss of life on both sides throughout that war.

I'm happy to say that after a month of repeating the forgiveness work almost daily, and repeatedly imagining the wound healed and gone, my pain completely subsided, and it has not returned in any way. Also, I have not had any problem swimming the four main strokes in the pool during workouts, which involve a great deal of spinal movement. The swimming strokes include backstroke, breaststroke, butterfly, and freestyle, which is sometimes referred to as the "crawl."

I am blessed and grateful for the miraculous healing abilities our bodies possess. Healing often requires a holistic approach, since emotions, thoughts, and beliefs are typically at the root of illness. Since we are multidimensional beings, it also makes sense that the energy, memories, and feelings from our other lives may bleed over into this lifetime.

Recently, I've been excited to hear from an Akashic Record reading client of mine, Susana, who has been experiencing a significant reduction in her lifelong debilitating psoriasis due to our sessions together.

During two separate Akashic Record sessions I initiated with her present, I was shown influences for her ailment stemming from this life and a past life. After we worked through the energies from these influences, Susana experienced noticeable healing. She generously offered her personal testimony below.

*My skin and I: I recall having skin issues as a small child. I remember when my parents and I moved from Buenos Aires, Argentina to Montevideo, Uruguay, my mom would take me to the beach, as the salt water and sun would temporarily help eliminate what my mom called "las manchitas"—an overgrowth of dark skin that looked like brown spots. The ocean water helped exfoliate the skin to a new, healthier look. Unfortunately, this effect was only temporary, as "las manchitas" would come back within days.*

*As I grew older, the brown spots turned into psoriasis patches, and hence my incessant journey for healing began. After moving to the United States as a teen, I visited numerous dermatologists looking for relief. I tried* lots of remedy gels and lotions, but they only helped alleviate the symptoms temporarily. Tanning beds and ultraviolet light treatments would also have a temporary effect. To make matters worse, stressful situations exacerbated the condition.

After years of these treatments to no avail, my embarrassment of being seen with the skin condition, and my frustration with feeling continually robbed of my freedom, I decided to approach healing my condition from a spiritual level. In 2012, I was introduced to Kundalini yoga, a practice that helped me de-stress and unveil layers of karma that no longer served me. In the process, I rediscovered love and honor and how to take care of myself in a much healthier way. I loved Kundalini yoga so much that I decided to become a certified teacher of the practice.

Through yoga I met wonderful healing practitioners, and my library of healers grew exponentially. I was introduced to shamanism, Sat Nam Rasayan, past life regressions, Reiki, Emotional Polarity Technique (EPT), Crystal layouts, the healing sounds of the gong, True Heart Healing/Theta Healing, and much more. I tried them all, and to my delight, they all helped. I realized that I was peeling away layers and layers of "stuck" energy.

Years went by and my hope for healing never died. My intuition told me I could heal this. My drive for freedom from psoriasis was strong. I, like many others, address healing life's traumas unremittingly. I've learned this takes work, but as one of my teachers said, there is a way through every block. I believe in synchronicities and that nothing happens by chance. I also believe everything is orchestrated for our highest good. There are often lessons and opportunities for healing by recognizing what life's synchronicities try to convey. An expression I've heard many times over the years proved to be very applicable to my healing — every sickness starts with an emotion; you clear the emotion and the sickness goes away. I never stopped believing this.

Throughout the illnesses my parents experienced later in life and their subsequent passing, and the illness of my younger son, my skin condition continued to worsen. I decided to move to Florida where the sun and ocean water would help alleviate my condition like it had many times during my childhood.

I never stopped searching for healing options. My inner guidance was telling me that, in time, I would be introduced to a new healer. Now in my 60s, I've often asked my spirit guides and angels to lead me to the person who will help me heal from psoriasis. A few months ago, I saw several healing ads in a local holistic healing magazine. As I scanned through them, I was drawn to just one by a person named Greg Martins. I knew at the time that this was a sign from my guides. I meditated to ensure this was the right person, and there was no question. I needed to contact Greg. After a short phone conversation with him, we set up an Akashic Record reading appointment to look into what experiences from this life, or past lives, could be causing my skin condition. Our first session occurred in May 2024.

During the reading, Greg was shown a number of applicable past lives but was strongly guided to first address my childhood from this life. He saw that my well-intentioned mother had unknowingly repressed the natural emergence of my hopes, dreams and ambitions. Greg spoke of a strong, green vine he saw running from my mom to my solar plexus as a child. He saw me as a young girl, about age six, appearing unmotivated and expressionless with the vine securely anchored to her gut. Greg expressed that my inner child was repressed and needed releasing.

We agreed the vine needed to be removed.

Greg said he was imagining the vine dissipating and dissolving. At the same time, I gently claimed back my power, forgiving my mom, and rekindling the connection to my inner child that I hadn't realized was missing. I began to cry – a lot. I felt a deeper part of me surfacing, and I humbly and gratefully opened fully to it. After that cathartic moment, I felt more deeply empowered and capable. Greg pronounced he saw my inner child excitedly jumping up and down with a big smile while the vine was nowhere in sight. I noticed during the first two weeks following the session that I did indeed feel more empowered. This was highly significant to me.

A few weeks after the session, however, my skin condition worsened as it had never before. I was miserable! The pain and burn of my skin were so intense, I was desperate and in tears.

Greg reached out to me a few weeks after our session to see how I was doing, and I revealed my painful condition. He expressed his disappointment about my skin, and encouragingly shared that he'd heard sometimes illnesses temporarily worsen once a spiritual healing process has begun. This made sense and I was willing to grab onto any hope that I could. I felt a *second Akashic Record session would be helpful. We agreed to address the fires he said he'd seen in my past lives during our first session.*

*Greg and I sat comfortably on couches for our second session. During the session, it was revealed that a medieval fire took my house, and local authorities left me feeling very resentful for causing further heartache and distress in my life. This caused a traumatic imprint in my energy field, and I believed it was being shown to me so I could clear its energy to help my healing. As I forgave those who wronged me in that life, and addressed strong emotions I was experiencing from it, I felt the trauma begin to clear. While I was doing that, Greg said that to aid in my healing he was envisioning energies of that lifetime disconnecting from my body in this life.*

*Shortly after, Greg asserted, "Susana, my mind is showing me a version of you with perfectly clear skin. You are much freer now, energetically. Apparently, you have done the work needed for the healing to manifest," he continued with a confident, excited decree.*

*Greg asked me to continue envisioning myself as having clear skin each day to help it manifest.*

*I never thought that our second Akashic Record healing session would have such an impact on me. After a few weeks, my skin started to clear. Although it has not healed completely yet, I can admire the areas of my skin where the lesions used to be and are now clear and smooth! Is my dream coming to fruition? I believe it is! A lifetime of suffering, embarrassment, frustration and hiding behind my clothes is finally coming to an end. I can see and feel the freedom I've been longing for my entire life. I am grateful.*

Healing can come about in many ways. I've learned that past life causes for illnesses are not as rare as we may think. Whether we explore those past lives in a hypnosis session, during meditation, or through the use of the Akashic Records, the traumas that cause illness can be addressed and neutralized, miraculously restoring us to health.

Using the Akashic Records to guide us to our home in the stars provides another way we can enhance our well-being, sense of wholeness, and intuitive abilities. In the next chapter and accompanying appendix, I will write about people's home star systems and home planets. I will also provide validating experiences from clients, when available. Exploring these details is fascinating and offers us a greater sense of who we are on higher levels of consciousness and what our place is in the Universe.

# 18

# HOME STAR SYSTEMS & HOME PLANETS

Sue responded with a disappointed look.

Trying to be reassuring I replied, "I checked your soul record a couple of times this week, and Sirius A came through clearly as your home star system. I thought sure it was correct."

"Greg, I feel so sad when you say Sirius. I don't know why. I was hoping you'd say the Pleiades, since I've felt so strongly connected to them, and they've always felt like home."

Sue and I were sitting across from each other in wicker chairs at my sister's house on a sunny Florida evening in 2023. I had met Sue once before, months ago, and she had a kind, honest openness about her.

"Okay, Sue, well let's check into your soul record right now to see what this is all about. Why the sadness about Sirius?" We were both perplexed.

"Great, yes," Sue enthusiastically replied with a smile, sitting up straight in her chair, looking at me eagerly.

"Sue, while I'm checking your soul record, see if you can intuitively sense an answer, as well. Call on your angel to help you."

Sue was game and silently proceeded. I telepathically called on Abraham, my reader of the Akashic Records (ARs). I felt his energy quickly emerge to my left — the usual location.

*Abraham, will you please open Sue's soul record?* I silently asked.

In a moment I felt her record open a couple of feet in front of me. This is where I always feel records open. When I felt Sue's energy in it, I was ready to proceed.

*Abraham, would you please clarify why Sue feels such sadness about Sirius, and feels drawn to the Pleiades?*

I quickly sensed something catastrophic had occurred on Sue's home planet at Sirius that caused her and many others to leave and go to the Pleiades. I didn't receive details about the nature of the catastrophe.

Sue and I looked at each other and shared what we received. Sue had also sensed the reason for leaving Sirius was that a catastrophe occurred.

"Greg, this makes so much sense and explains why I feel sad about Sirius."

"Sue, I'm also getting that you relocated specifically to Taygete in the Pleiades as your new home."

Sue looked at me with a smile.

I added, "This isn't the first time I've found a client who left their home star system. In the Pleiades, you must be living in a dimension beyond our physical realm, given the intolerable radiation levels existing there."

We were very appreciative for quickly sensing the reasons for her deep sadness about Sirius and her draw to the Pleiades. This level of validation was profound, but not unusual.

Over the years, I've learned the ARs are a reliable source for determining a wide range of things. They can point to a person's home star system, home planet, their appearance on their home planet, their Oversoul's name, and offer a name for their soul angel. I've found that connecting to my home planet comes with a gentle feeling of home. Connecting to my Oversoul brings me a deep sense of wholeness and increased intuitive ability. I use the terms "home planet" and "home world" interchangeably.

I've had many experiences that validate the home world concept. On one occasion, I experienced an unexpected face-to-face, non-physical visit from a rare type of extraterrestrial. It happened a week after sharing the results of a profound home star system AR reading with a friend, Penny (not her real name), who looks like these beings on her home world.

My experience with the ET came while lying in bed before sleep. Quieting my mind, I began relaxing my body with a couple of deep breaths. I was looking forward to a restful sleep. Suddenly the face of something like a praying mantis appeared in my mind's eye, as if it opened a door to communicate with me.

*Well, hello,* I responded telepathically, keeping calm.

I'd never seen an ET who looked like this, but I'd heard of them. I wasn't surprised at this impromptu visit, however, because I'd recently affirmed Penny is one of them on her home world. This was a Mantis extraterrestrial. I was not afraid, though the ET was startling to look at. Its face was slender, with very large black eyes dwarfing its head. I didn't sense whether it was male or female, but I clearly felt a subtle feeling of love coming from it.

*I'd like to see more of its body.* Within moments I could see from its waist up. *Thank you,* I said, surprised. It was very slender, with colors of tan and black. I didn't see wings.

*Do you know Penny?* I asked. No reply. In a few moments it vanished.

Although I was disappointed that it didn't speak to me, I was elated with the experience. I will always remember the visit and I don't know anyone else connected with these beings.

Several weeks before that encounter, I was at a small party at Penny's house. When I was preparing to leave, the conversation prompted Penny to say that she felt her father on a higher plane has the form of a Mantis ET. I was surprised to hear her refer to him as "father" because that implies the Oversoul concept.

"Penny, I feel a strong intuitive affirmation about him being your Oversoul."

I then explained the Oversoul concept to her.

"His name is Siddah," Penny added, appearing comfortable with the concept.

"Siddah — that resonates too," I acknowledged enthusiastically. "Would you like me to check into your AR to verify it, and see what other information I can gather about your home planet?"

"Sure, that would be nice," Penny replied, though her tone indicated she didn't feel it was necessary. She seemed confident she had already established a relationship with her Oversoul and home world essence.

I went out the door excited about the fascinating opportunity she'd just given me. I'd never come across anyone having the form of a Mantis on their home world.

Armed with Penny's birthdate and full birth name, I sat down alone at my Native American altar and prepared to do the AR reading. It was November 2018, just a week before I saw the Mantis being. I was glad to have time to spend on this reading, having retired from NASA just eight months earlier.

The first thing I did when I called in Abraham was to verify what Penny looks like on her home world. I clearly saw the form of a Mantis. The name Siddha also resonated as correct when I asked if this was her Oversoul's name. Because Penny is an offspring from her Oversoul, they both have the same type of body on their home world.

As a reminder of the Oversoul concept, Penny's aspects of consciousness are her Oversoul's even though Penny is having a life on Earth in a human body with a physical mother and father. The higher part of her soul is her Oversoul. This is why Penny and I both refer to him as her father. Yet Penny will always retain her uniqueness, identity, and free will as Penny. Further, her Oversoul's aspects of consciousness are never separate from God. He is made of God's aspects of consciousness but always has uniqueness and identity as himself. It follows then that Penny's aspects of consciousness are God's and never separate from God. I believe that everything is manifested from God essence, and that nothing is ever separate from God.

During my AR reading for Penny, I also found several other useful pieces of information from the Records to give her. A higher-self name for Penny is Roza, and the name of her soul angel, sometimes referred to as a guardian angel, is Rayula. Her home star system, which is where her home planet is located, is called Gavaton, and her home planet is called Trita. The constellation in which her home star system resides is Virgo. The galaxy in which Penny's home star system resides blew my mind, and I will discuss that shortly.

Since we are one with our Oversoul, we can develop the ability to sense them. To assist in this, it is helpful to clear our energy field and chakras a bit and then raise our vibration by centering in our hearts. If we have a higher-self name to raise our vibration and intuition, we can say the name silently and then ask our angel to connect us to our Oversoul. It's normal to be unsure if we are communicating with our Oversoul when we first attempt it. Asking our soul angel to make the connection is helpful since the angel can make the connection accurately. We don't need to know our soul angel's name to get their attention.

I found that asking my angel to bring me into close connection with my Oversoul worked well when I first started communicating with him, so I recommend this approach.

When Penny wants to feel her connection to her home world, she can ask her Oversoul to connect her to it. Knowing the name of her planet will enhance her connection to it. Penny is the only client I've found from her planet, Trita, but I have found other clients who share the same home planet. I'll provide examples of this later. I will also share some descriptions about planets I've been introduced to in the ARs. I didn't receive any details about Penny's planet, Trita.

Asking Abraham if Penny's star system is in our galaxy, his response was simply "M86." I assumed this was her galaxy's designation, where "M" refers to the French astronomer Charles Messier, born in 1730. He discovered and cataloged 110 astronomical objects.

Abraham then gave me some very interesting information about the galaxy and the Mantises there. Some of the information I didn't understand, and all of it was offered without request. I was first told galaxy M86 is in a super cluster of galaxies. This was followed with details about the galaxy, such as M86 is a giant lenticular-shaped galaxy that is somewhat bell-shaped. Plus, the terms "S0" and "E3" were relevant. At the time, I had no idea that S0 and E3 were galaxy designations.

Additional information rolled into my mind as I remained intuitively receptive — M86 is old, forming early in the Universe, and the Mantises from M86 do a "quantum leap" to get to Earth. Also, these highly evolved beings communicate using telepathy. I don't know specifically what the "quantum leap" mode of travel entails, but the phrase implies scientific advances or psychic capabilities far beyond what we understand or can achieve now.

When I looked on the internet to see what all this meant, I was astounded to find that my intuitive hearing was so accurate and, even more profoundly, that Penny's galaxy, M86, is 24 times farther away from our galaxy than our neighboring Andromeda galaxy. Andromeda is 2.2 million light years from Earth. I've done close to 100 home world readings over the decades, and this is by far the furthest home world I've found. M86 is in the Virgo super cluster of galaxies. How could a species so far away find out about Earth? Perhaps they access the ARs, or a similar database to find populated worlds?

I also discovered that the E3 and S0 designations I was given during the reading define the shape of galaxy M86 as slightly elliptical and lenticular.

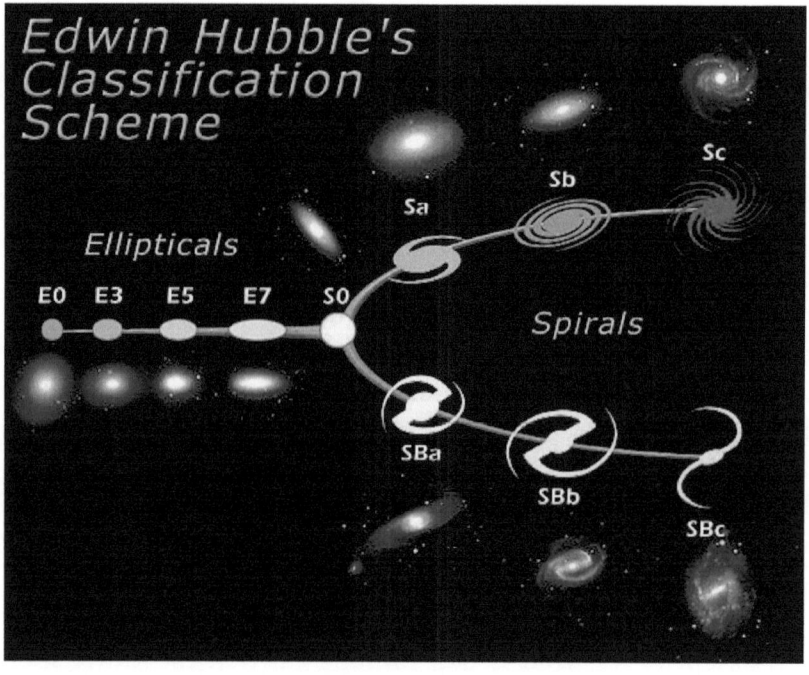

*E3 and S0 galaxy shapes found on a galaxy classification chart (Source: Wikipedia.org)*

The next home star system AR reading was for a friend, Coleen, who was once told her soul essence is from the angelic realm. I was intrigued by this because I was under the impression that angels would not lower their vibration to be in Earthly physical form for an entire lifetime. I'd heard that angels may appear in physical form to assist us in times of need, appearing as a friendly passerby perhaps, but they wouldn't stay long. I asked Coleen if I could look into her soul record for her place of origination – where she first received uniqueness and identity associated with her. Coleen eagerly agreed to the reading.

Coleen is thoughtful, patient, and inquisitive. Metaphysically, she feels connected with angels and the consciousnesses associated with plants. She also has a very grounded life, working in a civilian administrative capacity for the military.

I accessed Coleen's soul record while alone at home. I asked my soul angel, Anthony, to assist in this reading, since after all, he is an expert on angels. I saw that Coleen came into this life with a strong connection to nature spirits and angels. I also saw that she resonates well with animals. Her soul record indicated she worked with nature spirits in past lives, as well. Interestingly, I also sensed that Coleen's higher consciousness particularly resonates with the Christ consciousness. This refers to a state of consciousness that transcends ego, limited thinking and duality, and is connected to the pure light and consciousness of the divine.

I was told that Archangel Ariel helps Coleen work with energies that run between the fairy realm and the material realm. Archangel Ariel is the patron saint of animals and the environment. Ariel's name means 'lion or lioness of God', and as an archangel her role is partly to protect the Earth, its natural resources, ecosystems, and wildlife.

Next, I asked where Coleen originated – is it in the angelic realm or somewhere else? The star Sirius B was clearly given to me. Sensing her AR, I found she lives on a large planet covered in green mist that resonates at a much higher vibration than Earth. On her world, love and wisdom — divine feminine and divine masculine — are blended together. Love and peace are prevalent. I saw Coleen as a slender, almost transparent, humanoid. Since she and her planet are of such high vibration, perhaps we wouldn't see the planet, or her, if we went there in a spaceship. Her planet has an abundance of water, and like other planets I have sensed at Sirius, this one appears to have dolphins. I sensed Coleen has connections with the fairy realm there.

When I shared this information with Coleen, she accepted it appreciatively and said she'd meditate on the idea of being from Sirius B. Later she confidently and happily affirmed it resonated with her as true. I was glad to see that Coleen's origin is a planet, since this maintained my hypothesis that angels likely don't incarnate in human form for an entire lifetime. I am always open to experiencing exceptions to the norm, however.

The extraordinary story of emotional healing that follows involves a woman who is a benevolent reptilian on her home planet.

"I feel unresolved about an experience I had thousands of years ago on Earth as a reptilian ET," Carly disclosed.

I was astonished. Sitting wide-eyed, I listened intently. It was August 2010, and I had just finished having breakfast at a friend's house. My friend's daughter, Nancy (not her real name) was visiting during a college break with her roommate, Carly. Our casual conversation about Sci-Fi led Carly to share her amazing, but troubling, personal story.

"We were not so pleasant to look at," Carly continued. "Our knees bent in the opposite direction to humans. We had tails, too."

As I listened, I told my higher self and spirit guides that if there was something I could share with Carly to help her, I was all ears.

"I'm struggling with that lifetime because I failed in my mission to protect a military leader. I came to Earth as a high-ranking soldier while the leader was under threat of harm from a negative group of the same ET race. The negative ones had the mentality of 'consume and take,' whereas some of the race had evolved to embracing balance and higher values – this is who I belonged with. Tragically, I arrived on Earth too late, and the leader had been killed."

Carly was clearly feeling guilty and sad.

"I believe my reptilian form in that life was of my home world race."

Surprisingly, my gut responded with a high vibration, centered, affirming energy. I shared this with Carly, and she nodded with a smile.

My friends had gotten up from the table by now to do some cleaning up, so just Nancy, her boyfriend, Carly, and I were left at the table.

I enthusiastically shared the dream I'd had just four months earlier about being in a car with my home world people – the Kezians – to bolster her acceptance of her non-human, home world, form. I described what the beings in the car looked like from my dream, stating we were from the Andromeda galaxy. Carly smiled and appeared to be comforted by my story.

"The 'Nasdanja' are what my people are called," Carly revealed. "Cephia is the name of our home planet. We are also from the Andromeda galaxy."

"Carly, my gut is telling me forgiveness is important for you to consider."

"Yes," Carly agreed, with a somewhat defeated look.

I then sensed a non-physical being come in over my right shoulder. As he spoke telepathically, I realized he was a representative from her home race. Carly's far-off stare disappeared as I shared what he said.

"You are very much loved and well respected. Do not feel guilty about it – it was not your fault."

I sensed his kindness and compassion. I did not sense a reptilian form. I was so glad to receive communication from her people to help Carly break through her troubled outlook. It was clear this past-life memory was really bothering her.

"Carly, can you feel the being from your race around me?" I asked, wanting her to connect to his energy.

"I've been seeing little flashes of light around you."

I could see Carly felt comforted by his input and presence.

"Tell them 'Hi' for me," Carly said in a somewhat subdued tone. "Yes, I can feel them now." Carly began looking more empowered. "I've only shared some of this with one other person — ever."

"Carly, I'm seeing a sword pointed down in front of the legs of three reptilian soldiers. There's blood on the bottom ten inches of the sword." A moment later I continued. "I feel the sword needs to be buried."

"Yes, it was bloody," Carly agreed, as if seeing it her mind's eye.

For the next 10 minutes or so, Carly and I buried the sword. Carly forgave herself and the other reptilians, as best she could.

"Until now, I haven't been able to move beyond these feelings of guilt," she said with some relief. "Some of the reptilians have reincarnated in human form on Earth now. I am one of the good ones who reincarnated. I have a very male essence in this life. When I imagine myself as the reptilian in that past life, I feel comforted – like it is my norm. Now I feel some completion with that lifetime." Carly said, nodding her head with a sense of renewed vitality.

I breathed a sigh of relief. We had been given the insight needed to heal her emotional distress, and we both felt the energy of it had been substantially released.

At home later, I checked in with Abraham and verified that her home world is indeed in the Andromeda galaxy and that her form on her home world is reptilian. I also verified that her people are called the "Nasdanja."

I'm grateful to say that I haven't come across anyone who I sensed carried a malevolent, specifically reptilian, nature in this life. Native Americans, however, have shared stories with other authors of their encounters with such people. Still, I have experienced negative reptilians in "spirit form" many times. I sensed their intentions were to disrupt and lower my vibration. I typically got them out of my energy field by silently saying, with conviction, "I command you to the throne of God now in the name of Jesus Christ." I say Jesus Christ because, in my belief, he carries the divine essence of God within him and he will help me. Bringing his energy into the picture is an extremely powerful invocation. The negative reptilians typically left my energy field, as a result. When I feel the need for extra help in sending away reptilians in my energy field, I humbly call on Archangel Michael. When I feel he has connected with me, I say to him, "Archangel Michael, would you please remove all reptilians from my energy field and bring them to the throne of God now, in the name of Jesus Christ, I humbly ask." Archangel means "angel of the highest rank," and Michael's job is to protect and remove dark forces. With that, I always feel Archangel Michael pull any remaining reptilians out of my energy field. I am always grateful to Archangel Michael for his quick, effective service.

To support the idea that reptilians were on Earth in our ancient past, consider the image of the figurine below. Many other figurines similar to this one have been found in modern-day Iraq.

*Statuette of female reptilian breastfeeding a reptilian baby. Found in ancient Mesopotamia, now modern-day Iraq. Dated to approximately 5000 BC. (Source: Pinerest.com)*

The Andromeda galaxy likely contains hundreds of advanced races. According to the Akashic Records (ARs), three friends of mine hail from a planet called "Kya" in the Andromeda galaxy. The records indicate that Kyans know the people on my home world, Kezia, in the same galaxy. The ARs also indicate Kya is a very high-vibration planet with highly evolved beings. Like Sue's planet at Sirius B, love and wisdom — divine feminine and divine masculine — are well blended in Kyan people.

Five years ago, when I shared with a friend in Maryland that the ARs indicated she was from Kya in the Andromeda galaxy, she recalled an experience from her childhood that supported this assessment.

"Greg, when I was about nine, I saw things floating in the air in my bedroom one night and felt an ET connection with it. I had a sense that Andromeda was prevalent."

She was likely connecting with Andromeda that night and perhaps her home world people.

My friend Tasha (not her real name) originates on Kya, as well, according to her soul record. Tasha also shared some experiences with me supporting this idea.

"Greg, I did some healing work on myself last night after we talked about that disturbing dream I had the night before," Tasha said when I picked up the phone. It was very unusual for Tasha to call me, since she's very busy. This was important.

Tasha continued. "Using my mind, I scanned my body and realized I had a lot of energy cords attached to me that weren't healthy. I cut the cords and then removed some suction cup-like energy pads I sensed on my back. I knew those shouldn't be there. Then amazingly, I intuitively saw and felt a fluid-like energy gush out my feet. I thought, 'What was that?!' I guess I had a lot of invasive energy in my body. After that, I was instantly able to breathe better. What a gift! I've had trouble breathing for the past week."

"Tasha, you did amazing work," I replied.

"After I started breathing better, I unexpectedly felt the presence of Kya — and it felt like home!" Tasha proclaimed. "Since you asked me the other day if Kya resonated with me as my home planet, it had been on my mind. While I was sensing Kya, I experienced myself riding an aquatic animal there – a blue sea creature with a long tail."

"Wow, I did see water and a large aquatic creature when I tuned into Kya today," I said, excited about our mutual discovery.

"Greg, when I listened to your phone message this morning, tears came when you said my soul record indicated that some of my soul family from Kya went to the Pleiades at some point. That felt right. As I said the other day, I've felt connected to the Pleiades for decades, and this helps explain at least part of the reason."

Tasha's soul family includes her Oversoul and her other siblings from her Oversoul — they are all part of the same Oversoul.

When I performed Tasha's fascinating home world AR reading, I was unsure if I should tell her that I found she is a male on her home world. After all, she is an attractive, married woman in this life. How would she take it? My Oversoul said I should tell her, so I came forward with what I had learned. Tasha surprisingly said she found it comforting, and that she felt a strong male aspect to herself in this life. I saw Tasha as a tall, slender male on Kya, and sensed that she had one child there, a son. Tasha replied that this felt right, as well.

Tasha, being male on Kya, would have a female partner there, and her son's aspects of consciousness would be part of her own soul essence. On Kya, her son is separate from her in the physical sense, but they are one energetically. Because of this, he is never truly separate from her. This way of being is identical to the Oversoul concept. Tasha's Oversoul is the son's grandfather, so to speak, and the higher part of his soul. I feel that on my home world of Kezia, I have a son as well.

In Tasha's AR reading, I felt she worked with the Kyan council and was active in interplanetary relations. Sharing this with Tasha, she said it resonated with her, and that she'd been told by another intuitive in the past that she travels inter-dimensionally for some form of work. This is entirely possible because the higher consciousness of humans operates on multiple levels of consciousness and in other dimensions.

I also found that Tasha incarnated on Earth at this time to assist the people of Earth in our spiritual evolution. Many of my spiritual friends have expanded on this even further, saying we have incarnated now to help humanity through the coming changes – the awakening of humanity to a new level of consciousness.

From what I sensed during my AR reading for Tasha, Kya appeared to be a busy place – lots of people, looking like we do, with perhaps some minor differences which I didn't notice. I felt Kyans are spacefaring, and I saw buildings made of something akin to smokey quartz crystal. Kyans can manifest matter using intention, so having buildings made of high vibration crystal seems reasonable.

It is important to note that some advanced beings on Earth can also manifest matter through intention. Mahavatar Babaji, a Himalayan yogi, is one such man. He has mastered our physical plane of existence. Sathya Sai Baba was another Indian master. He could manifest matter in the palm of his hand. He passed away in 2011 at 85 years old. Sai Baba's teachings and activities have had a global influence, and many people have witnessed his mystical manifestations.

At Kya, I saw the sky as blue with green and turquoise. Abraham told me that Kyans weave color with music for therapeutic purposes. I found this intriguing, and I guess the Universe did as well, because a friend of mine, Lindsay, shared a relevant story with me the day after Abraham told me this.

"Lindsay, I like the colored lights in your office," I said, appreciating their calming influence. "I'm writing about a planet in Andromeda galaxy named 'Kya' today, and the ARs reveal that people there enjoy combining color and music as a form of therapy and upliftment."

"That's interesting," Lindsay replied. "My sister's dog was named Kya."

"Kya as in K-y-a?" I asked

"Yeah, K-y-a," she replied, in amazement. "Speaking of color and music, one of my spirit helpers unexpectedly said to me the other day that I had been humming in the key of turquoise."

"What exactly does that mean, Lindsay?" I asked.

"Well, I was intrigued as well, so I went on-line and found that turquoise is related to the key of A-minor. Then I listened to what A-minor sounds like, and I realized that was the pitch I'd been humming in. I was floored."

I was amazed as well. The chord of A-minor consists of three notes and has a melancholy tone, which suits a sad song very well. Chris Caton-Greasley, a music researcher, has also compared A-Minor to turquoise, saying "A-Minor is a gentle, soothing key full of sadness. Looking out the window on a rainy day. It's colour is turquoise." Lindsay and I can't explain why the sound of A-minor is associated with the color turquoise, but it is thought-provoking.

The Pleiades star cluster and the Sirius A and B binary star system are the most common home star locations I have found in people's soul records. Sirius A is the brightest star in the night sky, and the fifth closest star to Earth, at only eight light years away. The Pleiades is about 440 light years away and consists of hundreds of young, hot, blue-white stars.

Arcturus, a bright, red giant star, is the next most common place I've found people come from. It is the fourth brightest star in the night sky, at 36 light years from Earth.

For those who are curious about the many home star systems I've discovered, I've provided an appendix with an exciting summary of over two dozen. I've also provided the names and descriptions of some home planets I've found in the ARs, and how clients are related to them.

The home world appearances of clients vary, depending on the star system. I've found that most clients appear as high-vibration humanoids in a dimension higher than our Earthly dimension. Some clients are highly evolved beings having a form like a shaft of sparkling light, which they can shift into a humanoid form when desired. Occasionally I find a client who can shape-shift their energy form to live in water or on land. On rare occasions I find a client having a form that I believe is physical, such that they likely live in the same dimension as the Earth plane. If we went to their planet in a spaceship, we would be able to see them.

The name of a client's home star system, as provided to me from the ARs, may or may not be listed in astronomer's star catalogs. Only a small number of stars are named in catalogs — the rest are simply numbered.

I have not had a client with Earth as their home planet, but my Oversoul indicates they are here. He said the client's Oversoul would either live in our Earth plane as we do, or in a dimension slightly higher. Also, the Oversoul would not necessarily be the physical mother or father of the client.

A core reason why I wrote this book is to present the concepts of the Oversoul, home star systems and home planets, and how they relate to each other. I have experienced significant benefit from connecting to mine, and I believe each of us gains benefit from connecting to ours.

If you are interested in learning more about your origins, perhaps a star system in the appendix will particularly resonate with you. If one or two do, consider intuitively checking with your angel and higher self, and even your Oversoul, to see if one might be your home star system. Your home star system is a particularly good place to tune into, as is your home planet. These should stir a resonance within you, however slight at first. With practice, the connection will feel homey and empowering.

My intuition works best when I put my intellect and ego aside and move into a state of humility and peacefulness. Fortunately, intuition can be developed. Attending intuitive development classes of any kind can be fun and rewarding, since they help us awaken our chakras and intuitive senses, while giving us opportunities to practice and verify our skills. I often went to these classes in Maryland to be around like-minded people and practice, practice, practice.

For those whose intuitive sense of "feeling," also known as clairsentience, is not your strongest sense, let your intuitive senses of "knowing" (claircognizance), "hearing" (clairaudience), and "seeing" (clairvoyance), guide you as well.

An example of clairsentience is feeling the love that is projected toward us from a loving partner. An example of claircognizance is knowing that something is going to happen. My dad recounted to me years ago that something inside him told him to slow down one day as he drove past a row of parked cars in a well-populated neighborhood. He slowed his car and thankfully was able to stop in time to avoid hitting a child who ran into the street after a ball. The sense of "knowing" may or may not be accompanied by intuitive hearing or feeling.

I have found the concepts of having a home star system, home planet, and Oversoul have proven applicable to every client I've read for, using the ARs. We are multidimensional beings, and Earth is apparently not our only playground.

# 19

# WHEN LOVED ONES PASS AWAY

"Have you lost someone recently? Someone who died mysteriously?"

The ladies stopped talking to Flo, a psychic medium, and looked at me, captivated by Flo's unexpected question directed my way. After a moment of thinking, I replied.

"Yes, my nephew Tyler passed when he was a teenager."

After I explained the circumstances of his death, Flo surprised all of us.

"He is here with me Greg, and he's crying from grief, and also relief, that he can finally tell someone it was an accident – he didn't mean to do it!"

My first very personal loss came when I was 33. The names in this story are fictitious. My close friend, Tiffany, tragically lost her teenage son, Tyler, to a self-inflicted shotgun wound. He had just turned 15 and was like a nephew to me. We spent time together every week, visiting a local video arcade and having ice cream, just the two of us. Tyler was a happy boy, and enjoyed time with his younger brother, Mike, his sister Jane, and close family friends. I keep in touch with all of them to this day. Losing Tyler was tough on all of us, and no one knew whether Tyler's mortal wound was intentional or not. Tyler had gone to visit his stepdad in a wooded lot a few states away. What was clear was that he was alone with the rifle when it happened. His dad kept it on an easily accessible rack in the house.

It wasn't until many years later that I learned from Tyler that his death was an accident. He came to Flo and me in spirit form to tell me first-hand. Flo noticed his presence during the social time after a small church service at the pastor's house. This was my first time attending the church and after service someone pointed out to me that a psychic medium was present. She said the medium's name was "Flo" – short for Florence. I was aware a medium is someone who can communicate with people on the other side of the veil. I didn't feel the need to meet Flo, but I did go into the next room where she was in a conversation and sat on the couch to enjoy a small plate of food. This was when Flo surprisingly turned to me and asked if I'd lost someone recently.

After Flo told us that Tyler's death was accidental, we all just stared at her, listening intently. Flo spoke with certainty and a tone of urgency. Then suddenly, I saw Tyler in my mind's eye with great clarity. I saw him wearing a bandana that held his long, flowing blond hair back – just as he had always worn it. When I sensed his energy on my right, I began to weep. It felt like Tyler. I shared this out loud with tears in my eyes. Feeling Tyler's grief, I silently gave him a huge dose of love and appreciation. I sat in awe of both the intensity of my connection with Tyler, and the validation I was feeling from him about Flo's revelation. While my experience with Flo was the first time my beliefs had been validated in such a dramatic way, my journey in this area had begun many years before that.

As I get older, my appreciation for family and friends increases. Losing loved ones has left spaces in my heart that can never be filled. The hard reality hits that I won't be able to visit them, hug them, grow with them, and create more happy memories together. Fortunately, my feeling of loss has been eased by my metaphysical experiences and core beliefs. These extraordinary journeys and awarenesses have shaped my understanding of death and life beyond the veil. My hope is that this chapter will brighten the lives of those who are struggling with the loss of a loved one.

My mom's side of the family was strongly rooted in Catholicism. The concept of reincarnation and communication beyond the grave was not high on their list. Mom had three siblings, and they all became deeply involved in the church. Marie Anne became a nun as a lifelong vocation. Her brother, Joe, became a priest but resigned his position after many years to marry and start a family. Mom's other sister, Helen, also became a nun, but eventually left to get married. I still enjoy visiting Aunt Marie Anne, and I miss Uncle Joe, whom I visited occasionally until his passing nine years ago.

Mom became a nurse and a traditional housewife and mother. We attended St. Mary's Catholic Church every Sunday, and I went to catechism classes as a child to learn about the Catholic faith. These activities did not enliven my spirit, but I appreciated the opportunity to learn and experience what the church had to offer. I received the sacraments of Baptism, Holy Communion, and Confirmation.

As a child, I recall Mom's sister Marie Anne wearing her traditional black Catholic nun attire, known as a "habit." I also vividly recall seeing some of Dad's widowed, Catholic, Portuguese aunts wearing black when Dad took us to Fall River, Massachusetts for family visits. Some of his aunts wore black or dark clothes beyond the traditional span of one year after becoming widowed. They were always happy to see the young Martins clan, pinching our cheeks and pulling us close.

My curiosity about Bible stories drew me to pay attention in catechism classes. Unfortunately, as I got older, several lingering, continually unanswered questions gave me concern about Catholicism. First, as a teenager I felt reincarnation was likely how souls progressed – it just seemed logical. I came to this conclusion from reading books like Dr. Raymond Moody's international best seller, *Life After Life*. The book is filled with discussions he had with those who had near-death experiences. The book, *Edgar Cayce on Reincarnation* also presented compelling evidence for the reality of rebirth, as revealed using 2,500 of his Akashic Record readings.

Mom and my five siblings were open to the concept of reincarnation, but my dad wasn't interested. My older sister, AnneMarie, even introduced me to Elisabeth Haich's book, *Initiation*, which told of the author's lucid memories of a past life in which she was initiated into the mystical teachings of ancient Egypt's priesthood.

The end result was that I had no shortage of resources to help me formulate my views on reincarnation and life after death.

While the Bible doesn't mention reincarnation, I remember sitting in a church pew looking at the beautiful stained-glass windows, believing that reincarnation was likely valid.

My second concern was that paying penance for what were considered sins by repeating prayers like the *Hail Mary* and *Our Father* seemed hollow and unimpactful. "Sinning" included impure thoughts and actions, and I was told I needed to ask God's forgiveness to stay in his good graces. Although I didn't understand the power of sincere prayer at that age, I felt that sinning included many very normal thoughts and behaviors that shouldn't be considered "unacceptable."

Third, and perhaps most importantly, I innately knew God was in nature and everywhere, so I didn't believe I needed to go through a priest in a confessional to connect with God. However, being young, I didn't appreciate the benefits of having a spiritual man listen to me when I felt the need to confess, or share, something troubling me.

During my early teen years, Mom found the church to be minimally inspiring, so she and Dad went to Sunday services infrequently. I received the sacrament of Confirmation at around age 15, purely at Mom's request, since she felt it was her duty to get me to that point. With respect and appreciation for what I'd learned at the church over the years, and with Mom and Dad's blessings, I chose to stop going to church sometime later. I've never regretted my choice, even though I greatly appreciate what I learned about Christianity. I have always held Jesus and Mother Mary close to my heart because of their power to heal, guide, and protect me when I pray to them, or call on them.

My first experience with death was my maternal grandfather Pepe's passing. As a boy, I was at a loss for words, seeing his lifeless body in the open casket. I recall needing to step up on the kneeling bench to see fully into the casket. While I was sad he had passed on, the funeral home viewings, Catholic mass, and burial were reverent and honoring, comforting me with the sense he was probably taken care of wherever he had gone after death.

I loved my mom's parents, who we called Meme and Pepe, given they were French Canadian. They were always good to me and my siblings. Every summer, they took each of us, one at a time, for a week of fun at their old house an hour away. My grandparents raised my mom and her three siblings in the small, single-floor, three-bedroom house. A large potbelly stove heated the house during the cold, Massachusetts winters. I have fond memories of going to Lincoln Park in Dartmouth for amusement park rides, going bowling with my grandfather, visiting a breakfast restaurant after church, and more. I even liked the powdered milk my grandma served me. AnneMarie hated it.

I don't recall how old I was, but I was amazed when Mom told me Meme received a surprise visit from Pepe's spirit not long after he passed away. Mom said Pepe appeared at the foot of Meme's bed one night. He smiled at her so she would know he was okay and happy. With that Meme said to him, "Don't you come back!" Mom said her mother was not happy with the meager quality of life he provided her throughout their marriage.

As the years progressed, more of my parents' relatives passed away from natural causes. I felt confident they were going to a good place in their spirit bodies because they were caring people.

My first recollection of seeing a spirit came in 1978, when I was 17. I saw our house cat's energy body strut down the hall and up the stairs during a break in one of the weekly metaphysical training classes we had at our house. Our cat, Sufi, was asleep on the floor. I wrote about this earlier in the book, and it was a profoundly clear sighting.

After my experience with the medium Flo and my nephew Tyler at the church, I felt blessed and excited that I could bring closure to Tyler and his family about his death. Over the weeks that followed, I told Tyler's mom, his sister and brother, and close friends who loved him as family. Sharing sensitively with each person while we were alone, they accepted my experience with differing reactions. Most expressed relief, agreeing that they couldn't imagine he committed suicide. One person simply offered a thank-you with a pained smile.

My view of reincarnation was broadened in a very unexpected way when Tyler's sister, Dana, had her first daughter, Jane. When I met the infant Jane for the first time, I was pleasantly surprised to subtly feel Tyler's consciousness within her. I shared this with Tyler's mom, Tiffany, and she nodded in agreement, saying she had also felt Tyler in Jane's energy. I was both elated and awed. Tyler was here in our lives again, though in an intangible and mysterious way. I was so happy to sense him, wondering if someday Jane would have a memory of being Tyler in some way. Alternatively, I wondered if Tyler's consciousness was inseparably blended with Jane's so that she would never have an awareness of Tyler?

History is dotted with examples of people remembering what appeared to be one of their past lives. In the 1930's, a young Indian girl, Shanti Devi, recalled in great detail that she was the reincarnation of an Indian women from a nearby village who died several years before, shortly after childbirth. The Tibetan Buddhist's Dalai Lamas are said to be from the same soul, reincarnating after death and being recognized from their knowledge of personal details of the past Dalai Lama.

As Jane grew, she was particularly drawn to me. I relished the infrequent visits to her house during special occasions. We felt very comfortable with each other – like we were old friends. I often felt sad about not spending more time with her. Dana and Jane lived at least two hours from my house and my work at NASA kept me very busy. Today, Jane and I haven't connected in 15 years or more. Our focuses have simply been elsewhere.

My next great personal loss was my mother's passing from cancer in 2011, the day after my 50th birthday. While Mom lay in hospice, I was, however, blessed with another truly unique and eye-opening glimpse into life on the other side of the veil.

Mom's hospice was the best place I can imagine for end-of-life care. My oldest two siblings had found this magical oasis for Mom. Her personal ground-floor room was lined with windows and had a door leading out into a wooded landscape, allowing the serene energy of Carmel, California to ease her through her transition. The hospice staff was very caring, and we played soft music for Mom on a CD player.

My older sister AnneMarie, my brother Matt, and I stayed together in a very accommodating rental house in town where we enjoyed reuniting as a family with my other siblings living in the area. Mom's imminent passing was hard to accept for my younger sister, Siouxzi, and older brother John. Siouxzi's anxiety partly came from her feeling that Mom would simply cease to exist after passing. The rest of us believed Mom would live on in another dimension.

Mom actually welcomed her impending transition. She was only 76 but felt she had lived a good, long life. She was ready for freedom from over a year of intense treatment and the pain associated with her uterine cancer. She looked forward to the adventure she wholeheartedly believed awaited her after passing. Mom was so ready to move on that she told her doctor she felt she could pass within the allotted time her insurance would pay for hospice housing. I still get a chuckle out of that.

My siblings and I were blessed with having many weeks of one-on-one quality time with Mom during the year preceding her entry into hospice. Staying at her Florida townhouse, we took her to cancer treatments, cooked for her, and relished personal time together. The year was a God-send for so many reasons. As one small example, I have fond memories of taking Mom to "Steak and Shake" for a burger and a shake after her radiation treatments. While we ate, we typically talked about her favorite subject – metaphysics. The apple doesn't fall far from the tree.

During the last few days before Mom's passing, she lay peacefully in what appeared to be a deep sleep. She was unresponsive at that point. It was during that time that I was gifted with a profound experience of sensing the other side of the veil. Matt, AnneMarie, and I were walking to the car in the hospice parking lot after spending time at Mom's bedside, and I became aware of a dome of energy centered over us that loomed about 100 feet in the air and even further out to our sides. The sky was blue, and the weather couldn't have been more perfect.

I told my siblings what I was perceiving, and we stopped when we reached the car. I continued to share as the experience evolved. While looking up toward the invisible canopy, I sensed a gathering of adults there in another dimension. In my mind's eye I saw a long table with a tablecloth, and children running around playing with each other. Then I was silently told what they were doing — they were preparing a celebration for Mom's arrival! I was amazed. This appeared to be a gathering like we would have on Earth. My personal out-of-body experiences from the past showed me their dimension likely looks and feels as real as ours.

I made no intellectual judgments about what I was witnessing but took the experience at face value. I was given a very clear intuitive insight and was grateful that I had been emotionally centered and clear enough to receive it.

Mom passed away a few nights later. The three of us sat quietly with Mom's body the day after her passing, praying for her, and quietly processing our feelings.

"I see a few spirits in my mind's eye," AnneMarie said. "They are looking at me."

Matt and I looked at AnneMarie with our full attention. We were all hoping she would receive something about Mom.

"Where's Mom?" AnneMarie silently asked the spirits. AnneMarie's eyes widened. "Oh my God, they just moved apart, and I see Mom. She's got a huge smile on her face! She just said, 'I made it!'"

We all smiled, looking at each other. We had to give Mom credit – she did it. Clearly Mom was well and in good hands. "Good job, Mom!" was our reply. A very special day indeed.

*Mom and my brother John at our home in Holliston, Massachusetts, 1981*

Mary Thunder, my Native American guide, teacher, and friend, will always hold a special place in my heart. Thunder, as she was typically called, passed away in 2017. A year after passing, I sensed her connect with me, and we had a short conversation. I was unpacking after returning from a Lakota Native American sweat lodge ceremony held at Jon and Kate's — my friends who held the ceremony each month on Maryland's Eastern Shore. I felt clear, centered, and happy. I took off my T-shirt and tossed it on the bed. The T-shirt had special meaning because it was one that Mary Thunder had created to support her personal-growth workshop, called "Mary Thunder's Path of Maximum Service." This workshop was designed to empower participants to align their lives with their heart and soul callings. I was with Thunder and a group of friends when the name of the workshop was formulated. We called it "POMS" for short, discarding "PMS" with a good laugh.

*Mary Thunder and me. I am wearing a "Path of Maximum Service" T-shirt, at her house in Texas in the early 1990s. The Buddhist Monks in the background were visiting.*

As I looked at the T-shirt on my bed, I put my hand on it and gave heartfelt thanks to Thunder for the many ways she touched my life, and the lives of so many. As I stood quietly, being in the moment, I sensed Thunder subtly connect with me. She thanked me as a son, and said she was doing well where she was and had loved ones with her. Thunder had called me "Son" publicly on a few occasions, given we both felt that type of closeness.

Thunder continued speaking to me, requesting I teach by example. She said she'd like to have Grandpa Wallace Black Elk help me with my ET connection work. Grandpa Wallace, Thunder's adopted father in the Lakota spiritual way, had passed away 13 years earlier, in 2004. I was grateful and excited to hear Thunder's suggestion. Grandpa often talked to me about ETs on his own accord when he was alive. I missed Grandpa, as he was kind and made everyone feel like they mattered.

I silently said to Thunder that I helped her son Richard years ago at a Vision Quest by intuitively receiving information for him about his childhood ET experiences. Thunder asked me to take care of Richard out of concern a mother has for her children. Thunder told me there was much more to come for me with the ET connections I'd been cultivating to help people. The feeling of connection with Thunder was very real, yet subtle. To sense her words, I needed to let go of thinking, or "trying" to hear her. By remaining relaxed with a quiet mind, I was able to receive her messages. I felt confident they were her words, not creations of my own mind.

Five years ago, in 2020, I experienced the strongest connection I've ever felt from Mom since she's been on the other side. This was a clear, long-lasting conversation, which, like my other encounters from the other side, occurred without my initiation. Since Mom's passing in 2011, I've experienced her in my energy field just a handful of times — and those connections were subtle and lasted only a few minutes, at most. Perhaps the experience I'm sharing now was stronger because my sister AnneMarie was also with me, though she was on the telephone from California. AnneMarie and I had been excitedly talking for more than an hour about our metaphysical work, the advancements we'd made, and the future work we were excited to do, when I felt Mom connect with me. I sensed her on my upper right and clearly saw her face in my mind's eye.

"AnneMarie, Mom just came in," I said over the phone, containing my excitement.

"Really? Oh my God, what is she saying?"

"I'm getting that she sensed our conversation and came in because she wants to help us. Let me see if she will connect to you too," I added with hope.

*Mom, will you connect with AnneMarie too, on the phone?* I asked telepathically. With that, I felt Mom's energy go to AnneMarie while she stayed connected to me. I remembered this technique worked years ago when my soul sister, Laura, and I were talking on the phone and our Oversoul, Sumara, came to me. In that experience, we enjoyed a little family reunion over the phone.

"Wow, I feel Mom," AnneMarie declared.

"Great," I delighted, while carefully maintaining my connection with Mom.

For the next 25 minutes we talked with each other verbally, and with Mom telepathically. AnneMarie said she could feel and see Mom and sense her messages as well. This was an inspiring and exciting conversation for all three of us. It felt so real and engaging. I sensed Mom was as excited and giddy as we were. She relayed that she was happy and continuing to study mystical topics. Mom even referenced the Seth books written by trance channeler and author Jane Roberts. Mom loved those books while I was growing up.

Mom offered to help AnneMarie and I progress with our work. We were both excited to know Mom would be close at hand for us, and not away in some higher dimension forever.

AnneMarie was embarking on a particularly complex metaphysical profession. Having retired from decades of work as a highly successful international music booking agent, AnneMarie was training to become a facilitator of multi-hour Quantum Healing Hypnosis Technique (QHHT) sessions, created by Dolores Cannon. QHHT is a proven method of hypnosis for healing, past-life regression, and studying reincarnation.

During the conversation, Mom said she was proud of us for responding to our higher callings and being in service to the people. The last part of our conversation included the unique experience in which Mom energetically infused her energy and love into an Egyptian Ankh necklace AnneMarie was holding, and a fluorite crystal I held. I didn't particularly feel the energy infusion, but I trusted that Mom had connected with my crystal. With that, Mom said, "Dream big," and we began saying our good-byes. I felt Mom's energy pull back, and then she was gone. Feeling Mom's personal energy again was very special indeed. This was a wonderful experience, the likes of which I have not encountered since.

My brother John passed away in April, 2024. Once again, I was blessed with contact from him in a very special, corroborated way. Only 67 years old, he passed from kidney failure mainly due to the harsh effects of medications he was on while in an Intensive Care Unit (ICU) at a Veterans Affairs (VA) hospital in San Francisco, California. John was being treated for strong, unexplainable seizures. Fortunately, my other siblings and I were able to visit with him here in Sarasota, Florida six months before he passed – John was feeling fine at that time. Seeing John and my brother Mike was a pleasure. Several years had passed since our last visit together as a family in California. Visiting our 91-year-old father and stepmom on Florida's east coast was also on Mike and John's agenda.

When John visited, he was in about a year of abstinence after years of excessive alcohol consumption. Living in San Francisco, John had also recently chosen retirement from his job as a biomedical engineering technician. He had been repairing and maintaining hospital equipment in San Francisco for decades.

John and I talked over the phone a few times each year to keep in touch. Unfortunately, his alcoholism sometimes led him to bring up emotionally charged, non-personal topics, which I didn't want to entertain. We eventually stayed away from certain subjects.

In many ways, John was extremely smart his entire life. He even scored close to a Mensa-level of intelligence as a teenager. Mensa is the largest high-IQ society in the world. It is a non-profit organization open to people who score at the 98th percentile or higher on a standardized IQ or other intelligence test. John was not only smart, he was generous, chivalrous, and ambitious. During his visit, I was excited to listen to where his newly found, sober excitement for life might steer him.

John and Mike were only a couple of years apart in age and enjoyed getting together often. Mike lived a half hour north of the Golden Gate Bridge, which joined San Francisco to Marin County and the northern side of San Francisco Bay. One of the hobbies and income generators they shared was trading in the stock market from the comfort of their home offices.

John went a bit too far one day in his health care, and I believe that contributed highly to his body experiencing repeated seizures, resulting in a stroke and the end of his life soon after. His body had slowly been recovering from the long-term effects of alcoholism, but he chose to take on highly invasive dental surgery before his body was deemed fully ready for it. He had all his teeth replaced with upper and lower dentures, including implants to secure them…all within a one-week period. Apparently, this radical surgery is legal and somehow allows for appropriate gum and bone healing.

Within about a month of the dental work, John needed hospitalization at the local VA hospital. The doctors were unable to determine the cause of his seizures, but my siblings and I felt the extreme dental surgery was too much for his body to handle. Within weeks, John's doctors said he would need kidney dialysis to survive. His kidneys were shutting down due to toxicity from his medications. Mike knew that John would not want to be kept alive by machines, including kidney dialysis. Since John was unconscious and had no spouse or children, we as a family needed to decide what to do next for him. There was no sign that he was getting better.

I needed to ask John's spirit what he wanted to do – hang on and receive kidney dialysis or join the spirit world for good. Lying quietly on my bed, I first asked my Oversoul and angel to bring in John's Oversoul and angel. They could connect me with John's spirit, and they could help answer my question – they knew what was best for him. I asked them to connect me with John. Within a few seconds, I sensed John.

While maintaining emotional detachment, and staying centered in my higher consciousness, I asked him my question. I sensed that he wanted to leave his body behind and move on, but he was apprehensive about letting go. He wondered if he would be at peace and happy if he moved on. I told him about the condition of his body and that Mom would continue to be there for him if we allowed his body to pass away. I had occasionally sensed Mom's presence with John in the past several weeks. In addition to receiving this input from John, I intuitively felt that his passing would be in harmony with his soul's path. This intuitive input may have been provided by John's Oversoul and angel.

I learned the next day that Mike and AnneMarie both sensed the same guidance when they prayerfully made their own personal intuitive inquiries.

My siblings, Dad, my stepmom Joanie, and I met face-to-face virtually, using "Zoom" over the computer to discuss what to do next for John. Mike repeated the doctors' warning that John would pass away within 24 hours if he were not put on kidney dialysis. After discussing John's condition, with heavy hearts we decided to ask his doctors to stop his medications and allow John to pass peacefully.

Mike offered to read John any phone text messages we wanted John to hear before his passing – our opportunity to say good-bye while he could hopefully still hear us. I wanted to give John a heartfelt message about how much I loved him and offer what I felt would be helpful guidance for his passing, since he had expressed concern about what that would be like. Mike felt John would likely hear the messages because, although he had been consistently unconscious lately, he occasionally responded to Mike's voice with slight hand or finger movements.

My message to John was from my heart:

*Hey buddy. Sad that your body is not doing well. I'm writing because we don't know if you will be conscious much longer. I love you and understand that you don't want to live like this. We have been sending you love and light and want to do what we feel is best for you and what you would want. Mike has been an amazing advocate and caregiver and has been in touch with us and Dad and Joanie throughout your hospital stays. Many doctors have been treating you and doing tests, but the prognosis is not good. If you want to go through the door to the other side, leaving your body for good, I understand completely. I will miss you, but I want you to be happy. On the other side you will have amazing freedoms and opportunities. It was great seeing you in October. I'm glad we had that time together. Maybe your angel and God will give you a miracle healing. That would be great. I feel like your spirit wants to go, given the condition of your body. I love you, bro, and I hope for a miracle. I put you in God's hands. If you do leave your body for good, call in your angel and ask to be taken to the light. Don't take detours. Jesus will show up and protect you in a heartbeat if you call him with sincerity in a time of need. Jesus says he is Divine Mercy. I hope you're not in pain. We want you to be comfortable. Love you lots, John. Always here for you. Greg.*

Mike also read an encouraging and endearing message to John from AnneMarie.

John passed away peacefully that night, Saturday, April 13, 2024.

The next day, AnneMarie and I eagerly attended our usual weekly one-hour Sunday service here in Sarasota which Natalie-Anne, a gifted psychic medium, facilitates. Natalie was born and raised in Edinburgh, Scotland and comes from a family of gifted mediums and healers. The Sunday services open with an inspiring reading from a spiritual, but non-religious, book that differs week-to-week. The mediumship part of the service comes after Natalie calls in angels, Jesus, spirit guides, and more, to protect and facilitate the highest good for all in attendance. Natalie typically gives five or six five-minute-long mediumship channelings to people in the audience to help them with whatever their loved ones in spirit feel is helpful to share. There are typically 40 to 50 people present.

This is when we hoped to hear from John. Was he okay? Natalie felt John come through strongly as she began to open as a medium during the service. Natalie shared what she sensed in front of the audience while addressing my sister and me:

"I have your brother John here. He's laughing about his stubborn personality now – that when he decided on something, that's the way it is. He said, 'It was actually easier this time to let go.' He's pointing at the two of you (Natalie was pointing at AnneMarie and me), and he said, 'Because of you.' He's saying that you gave him the thumbs-up that it was okay to let go. He also said there's no way he could have stayed in that body. He said, 'It was crumbling. There's no way this time.' He's pretty funny, too. He just said, 'No pun intended – I wouldn't be seen dead in that body!' (The room broke out in laughter.) He did not want to be seen and known in that body because that wasn't who he was. He said he understands self-affliction now.

He's done his life review, and he now understands what self-affliction (referring to his years of alcoholism) can do to the physical body. 'But I have no regrets,' he said. He's saying he's not allowed to sit in regret. He did learn very quickly – he's saying, 'Okay it's done and now we're going to step up.' He said he has a lot of work to do. He's saying thank you, and he says, 'my apologies.'" Natalie replied to John, "No need to apologize."

Mom then came through to Natalie. "That's my boy," was Mom's proud message.

When John referred to his *life review*, he was referring to what many near-death experiencers, and those from beyond the veil, have reported: they see a review of their recent life, and are able to make assessments about it.

I was elated with John's message. The experience was way beyond my expectations. Not only was John okay, but he was now highly functional and ambitious. Thank you, Natalie, for sharing your amazing talent with us!

This channeling was clearly authentic. Natalie didn't know anything about John before the channeling, other than that he was on death's door for several days. What John said was in lockstep with what I know about him. Many other people who've received messages from their loved ones during Natalie's Sunday services have told me she was spot on.

I'm elated that our letters to John helped him let go of apprehension about passing over. Scientific studies indicate that the sense of hearing is the last sense to fail when a person's body is shutting down. Michael told me and AnneMarie that when he read our letters to John, he noticed John's body reacted ever so slightly — a twitch of the hand, and slight change in his breathing.

My personal experiences with loved ones beyond the grave have expanded my understanding of life and soul evolution. I see that we live on after dropping our bodies, and our loved ones on the other side are often still available to us. I don't fear death in the least, and I feel that what I don't accomplish in this lifetime, I can perhaps revisit on the other side of the veil, or in a future life. I feel a great sense of peace knowing death is a transition, rather than an end.

# CONCLUSION

I've presented many concepts in this book that have amazing implications, and I want to highlight those I consider most important.

My experience with the concept of the Oversoul has always intuitively rung true for me, whether I'm connecting to my Oversoul or inquiring about a client's home star system and Oversoul using the Akashic Records. In the 1990s, during the meditations I used to intuitively explore whether one of my spirit guides was truly my Oversoul, I consistently felt deeply connected to his loving, high-vibrational presence. These responses affirmed that he was indeed my Oversoul. My mentor, Leah, had been right when she had identified him as my Oversoul previously.

Later, when I felt ready to intuitively verify whether Kezia in the Andromeda Galaxy was my home planet, I asked my Oversoul, White Buffalo, for his opinion. His response was immediate — he connected me directly to Kezia, allowing me to feel the connection for myself. I was amazed. A thread of energy extended out from my solar plexus to a place that felt like home — familiar, safe, and gently empowering. When I inquired if the planet was indeed Kezia, I received an unmistakable, affirming resonance. Over the years, my experiences with Kezia have only deepened, as they became stronger and more detailed.

This connection with my Oversoul and home world has profoundly shifted my understanding of my place in the Universe, revealing a vast, interconnected existence beyond this lifetime on Earth.

Much like my experience with White Buffalo, many of my clients have reported significant benefits from cultivating a relationship with their own Oversoul. Typically, they describe sensing a deep, affirming, intuitive connection. They often receive guidance and love from their Oversoul, along with energetic downloads that enhance their intuition and sense of wholeness.

The Akashic Records are a boundless resource for insight into extraterrestrial connections, general knowledge, and sources of traumas that impact our health in this life. Traumas — whether from childhood or past lives — can cast long shadows, but by identifying and clearing the emotional and mental effects the traumas have on us, the resulting symptoms often vanish, restoring balance and harmony in our lives.

Intuition deepens our conscious connection with our inner selves and the world around us. Fortunately, intuition can be developed with practice. Closely tied to our intuitive senses are our chakras, which serve as pathways between our energy bodies and our physical body. By opening and balancing our chakras, we unlock a range of benefits — enhanced intuition, the ability to feel the energies of nature, and the capacity to channel divine healing energy for ourselves and others. Even more remarkably, our chakras are portals through which we can awaken to the highest levels of human consciousness. I credit my own ability to journey out-of-body to the clarity of my chakras and energy field during those times.

We are multidimensional beings, operating on multiple levels of consciousness day and night. Our dreams offer access to our subconscious mind, our higher consciousness, and alternate dimensions of reality. By paying attention to our dreams on a regular basis, they evolve in complexity and clarity, becoming valuable guides on our life's path. Learning to interpret the symbolism of our dreams can provide profound insight, while being a lot of fun.

Using the Akashic Records, I've found that most people live on their home planet in a dimension beyond the Earthly plane. Some people's home star systems are so close to Earth, we can see their twinkling lights at night, as if they are beckoning us home. While many of the home star systems I've discovered lie within our own Milky Way galaxy, some lie in other galaxies, and at least one exists in a different Universe.

For those who would like to learn more about the subjects I've raised in my book, here are some particularly useful resources:

Visit https://gypsyet.com to learn about Leah Stansell, a highly gifted intuitive, and my dear friend and mentor regarding the Akashic Records, home-worlds, and the concept of the Oversoul. Links to Leah's video presentations, and information about her phone consultations, classes and seminars can also be found on GypsyET.

*Gypsy ET*, a book channeled by Krista Ja Bar Ahmen (aka Leah Stansell), contains many wise and timeless teachings, and is available on Amazon under Krista Ja Bar Ahmen. Other than *Gypsy ET* and my book, I'm not aware of other books discussing the concept of the Oversoul as I've presented.

To further explore Lakota Native American spiritual ways and traditional ceremonies offered by Mary Thunder's family, and sanctioned by her Lakota spiritual elders, visit https://www.bluestarchurch.org. You can also contact me about getting involved in ceremonies. I'd be glad to help.

*Thunder's Grace – Walking the Road of Visions with my Lakota Grandmother,* by Mary Elizabeth Thunder, offers a very personal look into Mary Thunder's life and spiritual journey. This inspiring book is available through Amazon and other book sellers.

*Life After Life,* by Dr. Raymond A. Moody Jr, M.D., is a bestseller providing evidence that there is life after physical death, as Moody recounts the testimonies of those who have been to the "other side" and back.

*Edgar Cayce on Reincarnation,* by Noel Langley under the editorship of Hugh Lynn Cayce, presents aspects of 2,500 of the Cayce readings in support of the concept of reincarnation.

*The Dream Game,* by Ann Faraday, Ph.D., is a book I found very helpful in learning to work with my dreams.

*How to Interpret Your Dreams: Practical Techniques Based on the Edgar Cayce Readings* by Mark A. Thurston, Ph.D., is another book I found helpful in working with my dreams.

*Hands of Light: A Guide to Healing Through the Human Energy Field,* by Barbara Brennan, is an excellent source for learning about the human energy field and energy healing techniques.

Enjoy exploring these resources. They have helped to bring me great awareness and happiness along my spiritual journey.

# CONCLUSION

To bring everyone up to date on my activities, I retired from NASA Goddard Space Flight Center in 2018 after 35 years of service. Retiring was a bittersweet farewell to a dream job that allowed me to work on some extraordinary projects with exceptionally talented and dedicated teams of people.

In 2020, I moved to Sarasota, Florida, seeking a warmer climate and new opportunities to serve others as an intuitive. Outside of my spiritual work, I still enjoy playing guitar, swimming, and spending quality time with family and friends.

I feel immense gratitude, looking back on all the magical experiences I've had. Recently, I experienced a very special moment of shared gratitude with Spirit in early 2023 while standing in the parking lot of my Sarasota home one night. Gazing up at the Orion constellation, the Pleiades, and Sirius, I reflected on the extraterrestrial life there. *Star beings are there*, I thought with an assured smile. I'd experienced them. *They are in higher dimensions than our physical world, but they are there.* I gazed at stars in the constellation of Orion — red Betelgeuse in the upper left, blue Rigel in the lower right, and Mintaka in Orion's belt. I thought about the star Sigma Orionis and the planet Sestine in Orion's belt area. *They all have planets with intelligent humanoid life, based on my experience*, I affirmed. Looking at two other favorites next to Orion — the Pleiades open-star cluster to the right and the bright star system of Sirius to the left — I thought about the many home worlds I'd found there in my intuitive readings.

As I relished the discoveries I'd made, entranced by the night's starry canopy, I thought back to when I used to look up at the stars on my porch as a kid, wondering from the deepest part of my soul what life must be out there. Now, looking up at those same stars in the southern sky, I had found answers. I realized my childhood dreams had come true. I also acknowledged that my other deep-spirited dream of working for NASA had come true. I breathed deeply into gratitude.

About that time in the parking lot, I felt multiple spirits come in on both sides of me, and we celebrated the moment together. They applauded the work I'd done to become aware of the star people and spread my awareness to others. I melted inside, as I opened myself to feel their clear, tender message. We were gathered there together, in the quiet suburban parking lot, gently appreciating each other and the vast active realms among the stars.

I share this story so that it may inspire you to explore your place in the stars, and follow your dreams, for the Universe will surely support you.

I wish you well in all your endeavors, and I hope this book has made a difference in your life.

I would be happy to hear your thoughts and questions. I gladly welcome interviews and invitations to speak publicly. Here are various ways you can reach me:

    Website:              www.GregMartins.com
    Email:                StarJourneyHome@GregMartins.com
    Mailing Address:  Star Journey Home LLC
                             242 S Washington Blvd # 324
                             Sarasota, FL 34236

# APPENDIX: HOME STAR SYSTEMS & HOME PLANETS

Listed below are most of the home star systems and planets I've found when doing Akashic Record readings for clients. A person's home star system is where their home planet is located — their planet orbits the star, like Earth orbits the sun.

I've also described many home planets and the beings living on them. It's exciting to discover what these planets are like, and to help with this I've included many short, interesting AR readings.

Keep in mind that people originating in the Pleiades, and many other star systems, must reside in a higher dimension than the Earthly plane, given the inhospitable nature of their home stars. Also, many people are likely from a higher dimension simply because of the high-vibration nature of their form on their home world.

High-vibration beings existing in a dimension higher than our Earthly dimension would not be visible to us, and they would not be bound by the physical laws of our dimension.

I mentioned the concept of a parallel universe when I discussed my experiences with Pleiadians and their worlds. Abraham told me one of my clients actually *is* from a parallel universe — the Dal Universe. I share this amazing, validating story at the end of the appendix.

The star systems below are generally listed in the order of how often they've appeared in my home world AR readings, with the first being the most frequent. The Pleiades, Sirius, and Arcturus top the list.

To begin with, I've listed the home star systems I've discovered in our Milky Way — the galaxy in which we live. The Milky Way has a spiral shape like our neighboring Andromeda galaxy.

# APPENDIX: HOME STAR SYSTEMS & HOME PLANETS

## Home Star Systems in our Milky Way Galaxy

### Star named "Taygete" in the Pleiades star cluster

Taygete is in the constellation Taurus the Bull. I sensed a planet there called Vema, which is largely an aquatic world. My client from Vema connected strongly with a dolphin there during our in-person AR reading. She felt the dolphin was highly intelligent. The dolphin told us they go to other worlds to help. Perhaps they exist on Earth to elevate its vibration and help humans in subtle ways.

Another client, Laurie, from Taygete came from a planet I sensed having the name Cumi. I found that intelligent life left there for another planet, called Agea, orbiting the star Centrone. I didn't investigate why beings left Cumi, but I felt Agea was still in the constellation Taurus the Bull, though not within the Pleiades star cluster. Interestingly, I felt the Cumi people work closely with the Pleiadian council. Laurie's home world appearance is similar to us on Earth with slight differences. They have a jaw that is slightly larger than ours, and fingers and ear lobes that are longer than ours. These beings are at a consciousness level centered in love on a global level. I also saw Lauri's people wearing colorful clothing like Guatemalans wear.

Taylor, a client from Taygete, also has a strong connection with the Sirius star system. I've found that clients sometimes have a strong connection to a star system other than their home. Personally, I have a very strong affiliation with the Pleiades even though my home star system is in Andromeda.

While I've only described a few, I have found many other clients from Taygete with similar experiences.

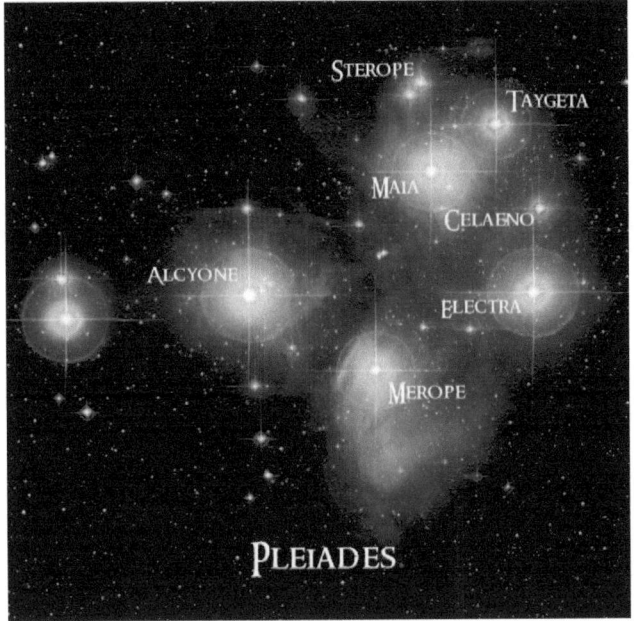

*Pleiades star cluster (Source: Popastro.com)*

## Star named "Alcyone" in the Pleiades star cluster

A client from Alcyone said she is now often able to connect with her beautiful home world, seeing it largely covered in water with a sky of purple tint and shimmering iridescence. Her people live in a dimension higher than the Earth plane and are centered in love and wisdom. In her dimension, a shimmering, iridescent sky sounds plausible because in an earlier chapter I wrote of being awestruck watching trees and plants radiate shimmering, rich colors, during my OBE. I was tapping into a higher dimension.

My client and I both sensed dolphins on her world, and we felt she also works with a high-level council there.

I saw her as a Nordic-looking female on her home planet, with fair skin. On her home world she is tall and slender with long, wavy blonde hair. There, she and others have a consciousness in which love and wisdom are well braided together. I felt this client assists in relations between Alcyone and those in the star system of Taygete in the Pleiades.

Another planet I found at Alcyone is called Hona, and intriguingly, it is the home for two clients. Finding two clients having the same home planet is uncommon in my readings. I did their readings four months apart and did not remember the planet name of Hona during the second reading, adding to the validity of my intuitive hearing. Both readings revealed Hona has water and dolphins.

As with Taygete, I've found many other clients from Alcyone.

## Star named "Maia" in the Pleiades star cluster

Sam (not his real name) is a unique AR client for two reasons. One is that I discovered he is at the Oversoul-level, as opposed to being an offspring from an Oversoul. I shared details about this amazing revelation in my chapter about the Oversoul. He is the only client I have read for with this exclusive attribute.

His other unique attribute is that he is connected to Mayan beings in several star systems. First, Sam has had a long personal relationship with the Maya in Guatemala. Second, the ARs showed me he is from Maia in the Pleaides, and I was shown a Mayan temple on Maia during a meditation. Third, the ARs also showed me Sam's strong pull to the Mintaka star system in the Orion constellation is due to Maya being there. I investigated the AR of Mintaka at Sam's request. Having never looked into Mintaka before, I was very surprised to sense the Maya there.

The ARs indicate Sam's home planet orbiting Maia is called Shriva. He is a male there, and with his female partner he has at least one offspring that comes directly from his soul essence.

## Star named "Ceeton" in the Pleiades star cluster

The name Ceeton is not in our star charts but may be there under a numerical designation. I learned about this star in an AR reading from 1998 when I was fairly new at doing readings. The planet I saw orbiting this star is larger than Earth with a thick atmosphere of swirling clouds.

I sensed it was one of several planets in that solar system. The planet's surface was mainly liquid, with a bit of land. The fluid appeared to be sulfur laden. Although I experienced the energy of the planet as somewhat heavy, I was told the planet is at a higher vibration than Earth.

My client felt comfortable hearing about her unique home world form — her beings are somewhat like penguins. They are mostly aquatic, but they can travel on land as well. Greyish in color, I saw them swimming about. I was alone when I performed this AR reading, and I seem to have been given a deep connection to this planet because one of the aquatic beings looked at me. It stood upright when it left the water, and our eyes connected. Its body was slender with arms like flippers, and lower appendages for walking and swimming.

This reading, like so many, made me question my accuracy. Was I making this stuff up? At that time, I routinely asked my mentor, Leah, to look over my readings for accuracy. Her reader of the records gave this a very high accuracy rating. Perhaps the penguin-like beings can shape shift, given they have a higher vibration than we do on Earth.

## Stars Sirius A and Sirius B

Sirius A is a bright white star — twice as large as our sun and 24 times brighter. Sirius B is a small white dwarf. These orbit each other in the constellation Canis Major. Sirius A is the brightest star in the northern hemisphere and is found to the left of the Orion constellation.

In a practice reading I did alone for a friend, Nicole, back in 1997, I found she is from a planet named "Ahkman" orbiting Sirius A. There she is tall, very slender, with a large head, somewhat like that of the Greys. There she is at a vibration much higher than Earth's. The planet, like most at this level of vibration, might not exist in our dimension. If this is the case, her star's influence would still exist in her higher dimension, but with somewhat different characteristics than what we can measure with our Earthly physical telescopes.

During the AR reading, I also found that Nicole has a strong connection to the Pleiades — as an ambassador of sorts, between Sirius and the Pleiades.

# APPENDIX: HOME STAR SYSTEMS & HOME PLANETS

In addition, I sensed that Nicole had a life in Egypt where she was aware of her spiritual connection to Sirius.

One of several planets I found at Sirius B is called Darius. This is a large, green, misty planet with lots of water, and I found it has dolphins and whales. I'm not surprised to see dolphins and whales here because during my Vision Quests, three years in a row, I was shown a dolphin and a whale with a star scene behind them. It appears they are not found only on Earth.

My friend, Coleen, whom I wrote about earlier as having strong connections to the angelic realm, is from Darius. Her form there is an ethereal, slender humanoid, while Darius is at a very high vibration.

I have found many other clients are from Sirius A and B.

*Sirius and Orion (Source: Pinterest.com)*

When I connect with Sirius in meditation without the ARs involved, I typically see slender, tan-colored beings with conical heads. I never notice any particular clothing.

## Star named Arcturus

I've also found Arcturus to be a common home star system. Arcturus is a red giant star located 36 light years away in the constellation Boötes. The Arcturian beings I've seen in my mind's eye look very human except for skin color – some are tan colored, and some are deep blue. Beings there have a high vibration and high level of conscious awakening.

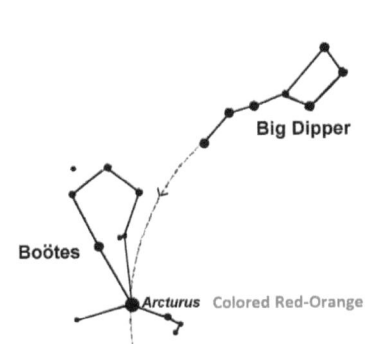

*Location of Arturus.*

*Appearance of light-skinned Arcturians (Source: Groupofforty.com)*

A friend of mine called me one morning in 2020 and asked if I could answer some long-standing ET-related questions she had. I was parked in an IHOP parking lot and was about to go in for breakfast. I wasn't starving, and the coffee could wait, so I decided to dive into the energies of the ET world with Carole for a short while.

# APPENDIX: HOME STAR SYSTEMS & HOME PLANETS

Carole said she'd been told a number of times over the years that the Arcturians wanted to channel through her, and she asked me if I could confirm this. I agreed to check for her. Connecting with my spirit gang while listening to Carole talk about it on my cell phone, I sensed an Arcturian male, in spirit form, appear on my left. In my mind's eye, he looked to be in his mid-thirties in Earth-years. His skin was a rich, deep blue with colored ornamental dots and sequin-like items arranged in artistic swirls on his face and arms. He said he wanted to work with Carole!

We were excited at this quick and profound verification. I sensed he was not part of Carole's soul family but was assigned to work with her. I could tell he was happy to connect with her, and I asked Carole if she could sense him through the phone. To our excitement, Carole said she could! Choked up with appreciation, Carole responded, "I've been wanting to make an Arcturian-connection like this for a long time!"

I asked both my Akashic Record reader, Abraham, and the Arcturian, for a name Carole could use to contact him. I picked up on a name that sounded like "Trumble." Maybe I needed coffee at that point, because I felt the name was close, but likely not his precise name. I asked Carole how the name resonated with her, and she enthusiastically replied that she felt like it fit. Using the name, Carole could call on him directly in the future.

Knowing they were both eager to deepen their connection, I offered them time to open to each other while I energetically pulled back a bit, as I sat in the car and watched the light traffic on the road in front of me. I felt them connecting over the next minute, or so. Carol was ecstatic for this new relationship. I felt humble, grateful, and amazed with our experience.

Carole then asked me if she was Pleiadian on her home world, since she'd been told she likely was. I strongly sensed, however, that she was Arcturian. I asked Abraham what her Pleiadian connection entailed, and I clearly felt she held a role like an ambassador from Arcturus to the Pleiades. Carole said that made perfect sense and intuitively felt right to her, as well.

## Star named Aldebaran

Aldebaran is a bright, red giant star in the constellation Taurus the Bull, between the Pleaides and the Orion constellation.

Jen is a client I found to be from this star system, which has a planet with greenery and water. I found she can live both on land and in the water in her home world form. She is of very high vibration there and works closely with the energies of the planet. I saw large crystals, which can be interpreted as a high source of energy. Throughout our phone consultation, Jen affirmed that my information resonated with her intuition. We often saw very similar images in our discussions. Jen further confirmed her home star system by letting me know an intuitive in the past sensed her home world was in the same general area of the sky as Aldebaran.

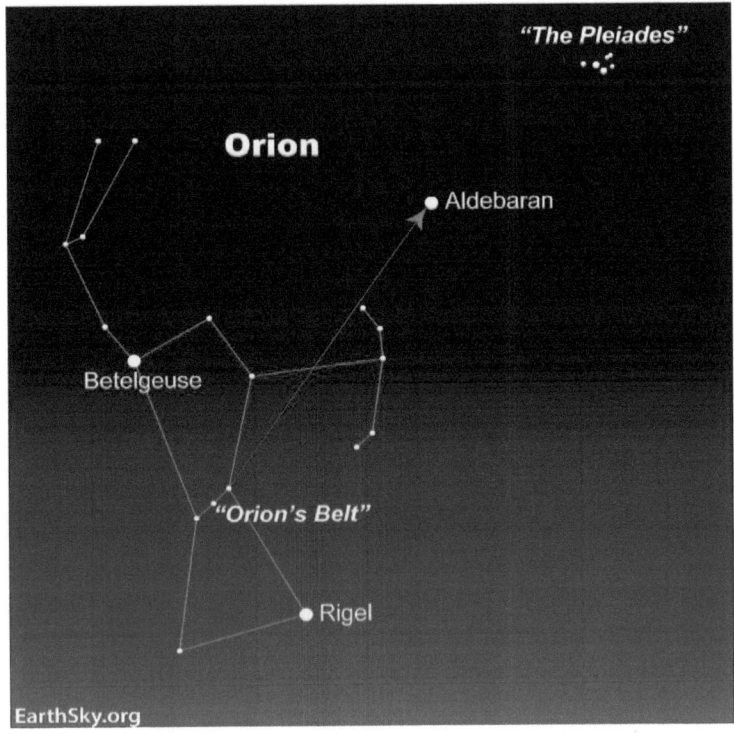

*Orion, the Pleiades and Aldebaran (Source:Earthsky.org)*

# APPENDIX: HOME STAR SYSTEMS & HOME PLANETS

## Star named Agenon

Pronounced A-jen-non, with the "A" accented and sounding like the "a" in "at." The name Agenon is not listed in astronomers' star maps. I found it to be in the constellation Taurus the Bull. To my gratification, I have found three people whose soul records indicate they are from Agenon. Finding multiple people from a star system that is not in astronomers' star maps confirms for me that the star really exists and is not an error on my part.

Two of the people from Agenon are female humanoids with high vibration energy bodies on their home worlds. They resonate strongly with the Divine source. One has a home planet called Elcore, which I didn't receive details about. Surprisingly, I found they are both involved in the Grey's hybridization program in this life. One of the clients, Beverly, was aware of her on-going connection with the Greys and felt, as I did, that her relationship with them is benevolent. Abert, a Grey ET who came into my energy field during our in-person reading, relayed that he was subconsciously mentoring Beverly regarding the hybridization program, and guiding her in a spiritual sense, as well. I also received that the female side of Beverly's family here on Earth had been involved in the hybridization program for hundreds of years.

At one point, I asked Abert to move into Beverly's energy field so she could feel him, and a moment later she reported feeling a nice vibration in her third-eye chakra. This was Beverly's intuition confirming his presence.

## Star named Spica

Spica, also known as Alpha Virginis, is the brightest object in the constellation Virgo. Blue-white in color, it is one of the 20 brightest stars in the night sky. One of my clients from Spica has a home planet called Sojur, according to her soul record.

I found that on her home planet, love and wisdom are well established. I saw her there as a very intelligent and service-oriented female humanoid, approximately four feet tall. I was told her name is Rela (pronounced Ray-la) on her home world. I suggested to her this would be an excellent higher-self name for her to use on Earth because it would connect her to her higher consciousness. Along with this, I received her angel's name as "Ashan." I felt he is male, but nearly androgynous. I also received a name for her Oversoul.

## Star named Betelgeuse in the Orion constellation

Betelgeuse is a red supergiant less than 10 million years old. For comparison, our sun is 4.5 billion years old and is halfway through its life. Betelgeuse is located at the upper left corner of Orion and is noticeably red to the naked eye. If there were a physical planet orbiting this star, it would not have had time to evolve intelligent life as we know it. Therefore, the two clients I found to be from this star, and possibly their planets as well, must have non-physical forms there.

The AR reading I did for a friend's boyfriend indicated his planet at Betelgeuse has water. My friend later said that her boyfriend is drawn to water. While this is marginally compelling, I was floored when my friend said that even before my reading, she felt her boyfriend was from Betelgeuse — now that's confirmation!

I received that her boyfriend is service-oriented at a soul level, and that he has reincarnated on Earth several times. I also sensed that his race has been coming to Earth since ancient times to support humanity's spiritual development.

With an age of less than 10 million years, Betelgeuse has evolved rapidly because of its high mass, and it is expected to end its life with a supernova explosion in around 100,000 years. Scientists say that when Betelgeuse explodes, the colorful display will shine as bright as a half-Moon for more than three months.

## Star named Rigel in the Orion constellation

Several things are fascinating about the impromptu home star system AR reading I gave to a friend, Rita (not her real name), one evening. Rita and I were finishing dinner at her house after I repaired a faucet for her. I'm no plumber, so we were both happy with my accomplishment. While chatting at her kitchen table with music softly playing, Rita said she had been told she had connections to the Pleiades. I wondered if that was where her home star system resided. I silently called in my Oversoul, angel, and Abraham to ask them. I immediately heard "Mica." I felt Mica was either a star or a planet. To see if the internet might say it's a star, I went online using my cell phone. I typed in "star Mica." What appeared were images and details of a *crystal* called "Star Mica." Ironically, Rita said she'd often seen images in her mind of yellowish crystals having flat surfaces – similar to what we saw in the crystal photographs. It seems her higher consciousness may well have been guiding her to look up the crystal she'd been seeing her mind's eye, so she could be introduced to the word "Mica."

*Crystals called "Star Mica"*

Note that a day or two later, I intuitively accepted that Mica is her home planet, and her home star system is Rigel, the blue giant in the Orion constellation.

While Rita and I dove deeper into her AR at the table, I experienced a being enter my consciousness who I felt was her Oversoul. In a few minutes I received a name for her Oversoul. In an attempt to see if Rita could sense her Oversoul as I was, I reached out and held Rita's hand and allowed her Oversoul's energy to flow from me to her. Rita said her arm became tingly, and then the feeling moved into her heart and solar plexus. Shortly after, Rita said her Oversoul's energy felt solid like a mighty tree, and it felt good. I was sure the energy she was sensing was her Oversoul's, as opposed to my personal energy, because I intentionally lowered my energy so it wouldn't be very noticeable. I sensed Rita's Oversoul was grateful to have connected with Rita.

The other remarkable experience during the reading was my sense that she works with beings of extremely high vibration in her higher levels of consciousness and on Mica. I could feel their vibration mainly in my heart chakra, and it was extremely high — perhaps the highest I've ever felt in a reading — like a huge dose of caffeine.

Again, I asked Rita to hold my hand to feel the energy. Gratifyingly, she felt the same very-high vibration in her heart chakra! I shared this experience with my mentor, Leah, later and she said angels are at 9th density, and the beings Rita was working with are at a level of awakening just below the angelic realm. Rita and I were experiencing just a fraction of their energy, I'm sure.

Rigel is a blue supergiant star at the young age of about ten million years old. It is located in the lower right corner of Orion and gives off a distinctive blue color to the unaided eye. Her people must exist in a dimension higher than a physical planet because Rigel's intense radiation would kill life there. A few days after our AR session, Rita shared a compliment with me.

"You are a life saver. Bless you! I always look up at Orion and something resonates with me. I'll look up at Rigel now, too. Thank you!!"

A big smile of appreciation came over my face. I felt excited and grateful that my effort — this heart and soul calling of mine – had proven well worthwhile once again. I felt an "attaboy" approval deep in my gut. I was happy in this line of work.

In addition to Rita's home world connections, her gratitude was referring to intuitive information and guidance I gave her regarding important work she was doing internationally. Further support came when we both excitedly became aware of a group of Native Earthly spirits that had been helping Rita for years. She had sensed them to some degree in the past, but now Rita felt she could benefit from their strong presence more readily.

Rita's reading was particularly experiential for both of us, making it a very validating and insightful, mystical ride — and we thought I was just there to fix her faucet!

# APPENDIX: HOME STAR SYSTEMS & HOME PLANETS

## Star named Bellatrix in the Orion constellation

I found that a friend's home star system is Bellatrix almost immediately upon opening her soul record with Abraham. Initially, I didn't know Bellatrix was in the Orion constellation. When I realized it was, I felt a confirming resonance that this was indeed her home star system. I was happy to hear her say it resonated with her, as well.

Bellatrix is a blue giant star, about eight times more massive than our sun, lying 250 light-years away.

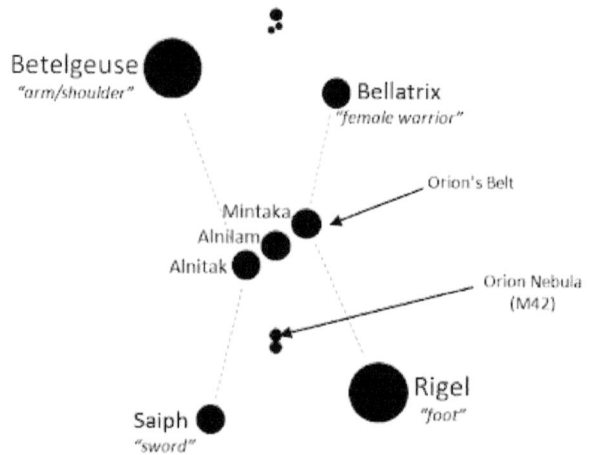

*The Star Bellatrix in Upper Right in the Orion Constellation
(Source: Bushguide101.com)*

## Planet named Sestine by the belt in the Orion constellation

Dragons live there. This is what I discovered in a dinnertime conversation with my friend, Sienna, who I wrote about in the "Akashic Records" chapter. Sienna enthusiastically pulled up a chair at the dining table. We were seated outside in the tented area of a restaurant with her dog by her side. We hadn't visited in a while, so we were happy to reconnect. Large heaters inside the tent blasted hot air every so often.

It was a cool day in November 2022, and other folks were also enjoying lunch at similar folding tables under the tent. Sienna and I were talking about connections to the stars, and she said she'd often felt a connection with the Orion constellation.

When conversations like this start, I inconspicuously center into my higher self, call in my spirit helpers, including Abraham, and hold the intention of being open to receiving information on the topic at hand. After doing that, the word "Sestine" popped into my head. When I shared the name with Sienna, she said it sent a shiver through her. She took this reaction as an intuitive affirmation. I sensed Sestine was either a planet or a star. Next, I sensed that dragons live there in some dimension, and that Sestine is in the vicinity of Orion's belt. I felt a particularly ancient energy in Sestine. Perhaps it was associated with the dragons.

I knew that dragons were an animal spirit helper for Sienna, and I was excited, given this was the first time I'd experienced dragons on a planet. I didn't question this experience, given that dragons have been part of lore for hundreds or thousands of years.

I have another friend who has dragons as spirit helpers. By day, she works in high-level positions for the government and the military, and outside of work she's often helping people as an accomplished shaman. From what people have told me who work with dragons, these amazing mythical creatures have the ability to clear unwanted energy from a person's life, such as restrictive energy that prevents healing and freedom.

I have several animal spirit helpers I call on from time to time, and they each have different abilities, and roles in my life. If I'm feeling energetically or emotionally vulnerable, I can call on my bear spirit helper to protect me. If I want to send part of my consciousness into the astral plane, I call on my bald eagle spirit helper to guide me in and guide me back out, for safety and ease during the travel.

Over the next couple of days after our dinner, I tried to intuitively determine if Sestine was a planet or a star. I eventually realized it was Sienna's home planet.

I told Leah about Sestine, since I thought she'd be intrigued that I'd found a planet with dragons! She asked her keeper of the ARs about it and agreed with my findings. I'm always especially grateful to receive confirmation from Leah and her reader of the ARs, since their input reaffirms my efforts as a reader.

Years later, I was given additional confirmation that Sestine, in Orion's belt area, has dragons in some dimension. I was introduced to an older couple at a gathering who I was told worked with dragons, and the man matter-of-factly told me that he'd known for 40 years that a planet with dragons existed near the middle star in Orion's belt. I was blown away. This was an amazing confirmation — something so obscure as Sestine and her dragons at Orion's belt was now apparently verified. I replied that I'd always seen Sestine to be at the lower right of the middle star in Orion's belt.

## Star named Alpha Centauri

The Alpha Centauri star system is the closest star system to our sun at just four light-years away. This is a three-star system, consisting of Alpha Centauri A and Alpha Centauri B orbiting each other, plus Alpha Centauri C (also called Proxima Centauri) orbiting those two at quite a distance. To date, no planets have been found around these stars that can likely support life. Alpha Centauri is in the constellation Centaurus.

Earlier in this book, I shared my stories of being taken out of body by beings associated with Alpha Centauri on two of my Vision Quests. My friend Pat Smith, who wrote the book *Emergence* about her interactions with these beings, is from Alpha Centauri. I wrote about her earlier as well. Unfortunately, Pat passed away recently, and I have not been able to track down any additional copies of her book.

## Star named Altair

In 2015, a young man in his early twenties asked me for a home world AR reading, and I found, to my surprise, that his home world form is a reptilian humanoid. His AR clearly showed his people as warriors and war-like. I got that his home planet is in our Earthly dimension, so I would think he could go there in a spaceship — once we have the technology to get there — and see his home planet and meet his home world self! Hopefully his home world warrior self would not try to destroy him or his spaceship.

I performed Jeff's reading alone at home in front of my Native American altar and met with him afterward with the intention of having him connect with his home planet and Oversoul and sense his home world form.

Looking into Jeff's AR at home, I saw him as a well-respected military commander on his home planet. I sensed a cobra-like energy in him, and that he'd be comfortable with the feel of dry dirt. The energy felt calm and non-invasive and was a positive aspect of his essence. In ancient Egypt, cobras were associated with initiates and high priests.

I also saw a bright white light in the aura around his head and realized that some of his purpose on Earth is to specifically experience his divine nature. In doing so, his people will experience it at their collective-consciousness level, helping them evolve. Some helpful goals I was given for Jeff included understanding and applying the concept that our thoughts influence the creation of our reality, staying centered and balanced while learning to function independently, and having a positive outlook regarding his home world people.

Not only did I experience his Oversoul as heart-centered and loving, but I experienced a spirit guide of his that was exceptional. He was a highly advanced, gentle, wise, non-reptilian, very human-like officer of some kind. I greatly admired and respected his level of integrity and experience. Jeff was well protected and guided by this man.

I like helping clients energetically connect to their home planet and Oversoul so they can gain confidence in connecting to it on their own later. The activity is fun and validates the information. It also provides a great opportunity for us to correct or refine names in the reading that may feel slightly, or completely, wrong. There are many reasons why names or information in an AR reading may come in somewhat inaccurately. For example, the reader's intuition may be weak during the reading, or the names of various items may somehow have gotten swapped in transmission. Additionally, the reader may misinterpret information, or our spirit helpers may actually help create the distortion to give the reader and client practice in using discernment.

# APPENDIX: HOME STAR SYSTEMS & HOME PLANETS

When I arrived at Jeff's apartment to go over his reading, we went upstairs to where he likes to meditate. The room felt clear and inviting. We started by connecting to our higher selves and then asking for protection and assistance from our spirit helpers. I connected with my Oversoul and angel and asked them to connect me with Jeff's home planet. When I felt the connection to his planet in my solar plexus, I asked that the energy stream be moved over and connected to Jeff. I could feel the energy move into his energy field. Jeff felt the energy almost immediately. His intuitive sense of clairsentience, or feeling, was strong. We both sensed the reptilian warriors on his home planet. Fortunately, Jeff didn't seem distressed about being from a reptilian world. Throughout the session he was calm, receptive, and present.

Unexpectedly, a female spirit next came into my field. I felt she was likely his Oversoul. When I performed Jeff's reading at home alone, I wasn't sure if his Oversoul was male or female, though the name I was given certainly sounded male. However, at Jeff's she seemed distinctly female. She had a kind, mothering disposition. Her appearance was not apparent to me. I asked her to move into Jeff's energy field to my right, so he could connect with her. I immediately felt her energy slowly move over to him. Jeff agreed she felt like a mother figure. Unfortunately, I either didn't ask for her name, or I wasn't able to hear it. The important thing is that Jeff felt her. He could reconnect with her in the future.

Toward the end of our session, while we were steeped in the energy of his home planet, I silently and quickly cleared away some bloody-battle energy that emerged in Jeff's energy field. I didn't mention it to him, since I wanted to stay positively focused.

When I shared with Jeff the higher-self name I received for him, he didn't resonate with it. I probably should have discarded the name from the AR reading, since I hadn't sensed much resonance with it when I received it. Usually, I look for an energy resonance to accompany AR information as a validation technique. When Jeff said he'd always resonated with the name Jonah, I immediately felt the name was perfect for him, as well.

At the end of our two-hour session, Jonah expressed genuine feelings of approval and acceptance of what we'd experienced and discussed. He said he would meditate on it all in the days to follow. We both felt the session was very enlightening.

When I initially sat down with Jonah, I was naturally concerned that he might be uncomfortable hearing his home world form is a reptilian warrior. During the reading, I assured him that he and his soul are just as divine as any being in the Universe. God has us take on different roles for various unknown reasons. Jonah seemed at peace with the idea that at high levels of consciousness on his reptilian home world he understands and resonates with the Divine.

Jonah's home star system, Altair, is only 16 light years from Earth — very close, considering our spiral-shaped galaxy is 100,000 light years across. Altair is in the constellation "Aquila the Eagle" and is twice as large and twice as bright as our sun.

## Stars named Astera and Azeron

These two star names are not found in astronomer's star charts. I found a client from each of these stars. I sensed Astera is in the constellation Pegasus, and Azera is in Cassiopeia. The ARs indicated a planet named Zenra orbits Azeron, and a planet called Portel (accent on the "e") orbits Astera.

## Star named Barnard's Star

The ARs revealed to me that my friend, Lara, is from this star system. I'm happy to say Lara feels a resonance with this star. Being a shaman, she has strong intuitive skills, adding credence to our findings.

The ARs indicate that on her home world, Lara is a tall, slender humanoid male, and has a highly evolved consciousness — balanced in love and wisdom. Her people live in a state of high vibration and awakened consciousness. I saw her Oversoul as being female and up to eight feet tall.

Barnard's Star is a red dwarf – the most common type of star in the Universe. At only six light years from Earth, it is very close to us, like Sirius and Alpha Centauri. Barnard's star is very dim and not visible to the naked eye. Astronomers haven't found absolute proof that a planet orbits the star, but the ARs indicate Lara lives on one there – perhaps it is not in our dimension.

## Star named Deneb

A friend of mine, Pam, came into being at this star system and then left, migrating to a planet called Telera, pronounced Teel-ee-rah, in the Lyra constellation. Leah reviewed my AR reading at my request in 2008, and said her Oversoul brought her into being at Deneb because of its high vibration.

I found that Pam works with the Pleiadian Council, traveling back and forth from Lyra. Pam's people are humanoid and spiritually evolved. They are telepathic and spacefaring.

Deneb is a blue-white super giant star at top of the cross in the Cygnus constellation.

Very recently, I discovered another AR client from Telera. When I did this recent reading, I had forgotten that Telera was Pam's planet, since I found it 16 years ago. I see this as another validating find.

## Star named Galan

I found that this star has a planet with evolved, feline, humanoid beings. Their heads are distinctly cat-like, or lion-like. This sounds absurd, but I'd heard of beings like this throughout the years. I'm excited to have encountered a client who has this appearance on her home world. My first indication of her feline form came while I was accessing her AR with her sitting across from me. Interestingly, retrieving information about her home world was *not* on our agenda.

Amy (not her real name) found my AR reading advertisement in a local holistic magazine, and she wanted to see if her AR could give her life an exciting new direction. She was widowed and had retired from satisfying careers as both a nurse and a PhD psychologist. "What next?" she wanted to know.

Shortly into our reading, a human-like being with a male lion's head appeared in my mind's eye. He was standing quietly, looking at me motionless with a smile. He was wearing clothing and appeared well-groomed. I didn't feel any energy from him. I told Amy what I was seeing and then silently asked Abraham if this was her form on her home planet. I got no answer, so we returned to our prior line of questioning in the reading.

A week after the reading while I was alone, I looked into Amy's soul record and saw her home world form is a bipedal humanoid female feline. Perhaps the male lion is her Oversoul. I didn't check on that, but I received her home star system as "Galan."

## Star named Konez

Here I found highly evolved Grey ETs. This is not the first time I've encountered Greys who were considerate and highly evolved. My friend's soul record indicated her home planet, called Asayo, orbits the star Konez and is located in the Triangulum constellation. I sensed she, and the other Greys there, are highly evolved, and appear somewhat non-physical, having a vibration level well above ours on Earth. I sensed her as a male, having a female Oversoul.

In addition, I found there is a planet in the same star system where the Greys are less evolved and have internal strife as we do on Earth.

The name Konez is not in astronomers' star maps.

## Our Sun, also known as "Sol" (Latin for "sun")

One of my female clients appears to be a very tall, slender female humanoid, carrying a high vibration balance of male and female essence. Her unique feature is not that she resides in a dimension higher than our physical plane, but that she resides on the planet Venus. Yes, Venus! I checked her soul record several times over a few days to make sure I was hearing Abraham correctly.

This is an example of existing on a planet with an environment that is inhospitable to humans. Given that my client exists in a dimension beyond our Earthly plane, she is unaffected by Venus's extreme temperature and atmospheric pressure. On the surface of Venus, the temperature is hot enough to melt lead, and the atmospheric pressure is 75 to 100 times higher than on Earth. Venus is the second planet from our Sun and appears as a bright star in the western sky after the Sun sets.

Before telling my client what I found as her home planet and star system, I wanted to run it by Leah. Would Leah's reader of the AR tell me I was mistaken? When I told Leah, she said, "I don't know, Greg. You may be wrong on this one!" While I was on the phone with her, she checked with her reader of the ARs, and then said in amazement, "Well, you're right! I am surprised, but I am told this is correct."

In my client's AR, I also sensed she is actively involved with working among the energies of Venus's crystalline structure.

## Stars Tibellum, Tyberius, and Tetra

I did not find the names of these stars in astronomers' star maps, but I found a client from each of them. Tetra was a particularly difficult star to sense, which led me to believe, at first, that Tetra may not be an accurate name for my client's home star system. Typically, if I don't feel a resonance with the information I get from the ARs, then I withhold it, knowing it may be partially or completely wrong. I learned later that Tetra's vibration is particularly fine, making it especially challenging to sense. I felt bad for my client, but I reassured her she could likely sense Tetra with some effort.

# HOME PLANETS IN THE ANDROMEDA GALAXY

## Planets Kezia, Anada and Kya

I have had many experiences that validate my belief that I come from the planet Kezia in the Andromeda galaxy. There we have hair-covered bodies. I see the hair as flat, about one-to-two inches long, fairly thick, and brown with shades of black and blond. Our noses are flatter than humans and our mouths smaller. We are telepathic there. I discovered that my friend, Laura, who I wrote about in the "Oversoul" chapter, is also from Kezia.

The Andromeda galaxy, M31, is located 2.2 million light years from Earth.

I found that a client I read for years ago comes from a planet called Anada, which appears to be in the same solar system as Kezia.

I've also found several clients from the planet Kya in the Andromeda Galaxy, which I wrote about in the "Home Planets" chapter.

*Andromeda Galaxy (Source: AstronomyPhotos.com)*

## A HOME WORLD IN ANOTHER GALAXY…FAR, FAR AWAY

### Galaxy M86

My client having the form of a "Mantis" on her home world comes from this galaxy, according to her AR. This galaxy is 53 million light years from Earth, in the Virgo cluster of galaxies. I found that the star in her home star system is called "Gavaton," and her home planet is called "Trita." See chapter 18 for more detail.

# A HOME WORLD IN ANOTHER UNIVERSE

## The Dal Universe

A client of mine, Gerit, about 20 years of age at the time, felt sure he was a "Hathor" ET on his home world. In doing his AR reading while alone at home in 2020, I verified his assertion. When I asked Abraham for Gerit's home star system, he said the Hathors come from the Dal Universe. I was astonished. Theoretical physicists indicate that parallel universes may exist, and there I was finding AR evidence of it.

In Tom Kenyon's *The Hathor Material*, Tom presents information he "channeled," meaning "intuitively received," from the Hathors that supports the parallel universe idea.

*Tom Kenyon's book of channeled material from the Hathors*

A Hathor quote from Tom's book reads, "We originally came from another universe by way of Sirius, which is a portal to your Universe, and from Sirius we eventually proceeded to your solar system and the etheric realms of Venus."

Not only was I excited to see the Hathors say they came from another universe, but I was also excited to read that they went to an etheric realm on Venus. An etheric realm would be a non-physical dimension. I wonder if my client, whose home planet I found to be Venus, has ever felt a connection with the Hathors?

Another aspect of the Hathor's statement extraordinarily aligns with an experience I had during a "star journey" meditation activity in 1990. This refers to the "portal" the Hathors said they used to travel between universes. During my star journey, a woman named Grace and I were lying on the floor and she, our spirit guides, and our intuition were guiding us to various star systems, planets and beings that were helpful for me to connect with at that time in my life. Mary Thunder, who was my guide in Native American ways, suggested I go to her friend, Grace, for a star journey session. Grace specialized in these.

During our hour-and-a-half-long exploration together, I clearly sensed a "portal" in outer space while we were at the Sirius star system. The portal appeared in my mind's eye to be a large, perfectly circular opening, with a span at least several times my height. The blackness of space looked the same on both sides of the opening. I felt that if I went through the portal, I would be on my own, leaving the protection of the galaxy. Grace said she intuitively felt the same. I did not go through it. The portal felt like a passage in and out of our Milky Way galaxy.

The image on the cover of Tom Kenyon's book is an Egyptian carving of a Hathor at the Temple of Hathor at Dendera, Egypt. The temple is one of the best-preserved from ancient Egypt. Many carvings of Hathors are found there.

The value of knowing our home star system and home planet should not be under rated. It is my hope that some of you reading this book will experience connections and benefits that run much deeper than what I have experienced. Perhaps you will have a fully conscious out-of-body experience to your home world. Now that would be

## APPENDIX: HOME STAR SYSTEMS & HOME PLANETS

something! Perhaps you will help as an ambassador of sorts between your people and Earth. For most of us, our experience with our home world and Oversoul will simply bring us the gentle, tangible support that can only come from them.

# ABOUT THE AUTHOR

Greg Martins grew up in Holliston, Massachusetts, a beautiful New England town located 30 miles southwest of Boston. Throughout high school Greg enjoyed playing guitar, jogging, learning karate, and exploring metaphysical topics such as meditation, dreams, out-of-body travel, the human energy field, and the existence of extraterrestrials and Unidentified Flying Objects (UFOs).

Graduating from Holliston High School in 1979 with an aptitude for math and science, Greg enrolled in the Aeronautical Engineering program at Embry-Riddle Aeronautical University in Daytona Beach, Florida. Motivated to work for NASA from age 12, Greg saw his dream materialize when he was accepted into the highly competitive intern program at NASA Goddard Space Flight Center at the start of his senior year of college. Completing two four-month internships in 1983, Greg graduated with a bachelor's degree in Aeronautical Engineering in May, 1984 and began working for NASA Goddard full time.

## ABOUT THE AUTHOR

The first 13 years of Greg's career at NASA focused on the mechanical development of Space Shuttle payloads. Often serving as the lead mechanical engineer, these science-oriented payloads he helped design were flown in Goddard's low-cost, highly successful Spartan, Get-Away-Special, and Hitch Hiker programs.

To further expand his spiritual awareness after college, Greg pursued his affinity for Native American mysticism and began his lifelong involvement in Lakota Native American spirituality and ceremonial ways in 1985.

Inspired by his deep-rooted interest in metaphysics, Greg began working with the Akashic Records in 1993: a non-physical library holding a record of every person and event in history. The Akashic Records are the primary source for Greg's information on clients' extraterrestrial connections, home star systems, Oversouls, and health conditions, as presented in his book.

Mid-career in 2002, Greg was accepted into Goddard's competitive two-year Systems Engineering Education Development (SEED) program, and he graduated the following year. This program immersed students in hands-on projects in engineering disciplines unrelated to their field of expertise. Coupled with training in project leadership, the program provided students with the real-life experience and expertise needed to lead NASA projects as systems engineers.

In the years that followed, Greg applied his systems engineering training within the Mechanical Engineering Branch at NASA Goddard, where he primarily focused on developing deployable mechanical systems for satellites.

Greg's exploration of higher consciousness and other dimensions of reality has provided him with many enlightening experiences and practical tools for healthy living. Greg has created and led workshops in which he teaches participants his many methods for clearing the human energy field, using the mind to move energy. In addition, he has had many fully conscious Out-of-Body Experiences (OBEs), confirming the existence of other dimensions and our consciousness's ability to function while outside the body.

Greg released a Compact Disc (CD) of original music in 2002 called *Live Your Passion* and released another in 2011 called *Star Gazer*. Greg still enjoys playing guitar and performs at local venues.

After 35 years of service, Greg retired from NASA in 2018 and moved to Sarasota, Florida, where he now lives. To share his knowledge and insights with a broader audience, he published his inspiring first book, *Star Journey Home: Connect with your Home Planet and Oversoul* in 2025.

Contact Greg at StarJourneyHome@GregMartins.com, and learn more about his book, music, and current activities at his website:

www.GregMartins.com.

www.ingramcontent.com/pod-product-compliance
Ingram Content Group UK Ltd.
Pitfield, Milton Keynes, MK11 3LW, UK
UKHW041952230426
12048UKWH00008B/292